Palgrave Studies in Workplace Spirituality and Fulfillment

Series Editors
Satinder Dhiman
School of Business
Woodbury University
Burbank, CA, USA

Gary Roberts
Regent University
Virginia Beach, VA, USA

Joanna Crossman
University of South Australia
Adelaide, SA, Australia

Satinder Dhiman
Editor-in-Chief

Gary Roberts and Joanna Crossman
Associate Editors

By way of primary go-to-platform, this Series precisely maps the terrain of the twin fields of *Workplace Spirituality and Fulfillment* in the disciplines of business, psychology, health care, education, and various other allied fields. It reclaims the sacredness of work—work that is mind-enriching, heart-fulfilling, soul-satisfying and financially-rewarding. It fills the gap in scholarship in the allied disciplines of Workplace Spirituality and Flourishing. Using a comprehensive schema, it invites contributions from foremost scholars and practitioners that reflect insightful research, practices, and latest trends on the theme of workplace spirituality and fulfillment. The uniqueness of this *Series* lies in its anchorage in the moral and spiritual dimension of various positive forms of leadership—such as Authentic Leadership, Servant Leadership, Transformational Leadership, and Values-Based Leadership.

We welcome research monographs and multi-authored edited volumes representing myriad thought-positions on topics such as: Past, Present and Future Directions in Workplace Spirituality; Workplace Spirituality and World Wisdom/Spiritual Traditions; Culture Studies and Workplace Spirituality; Spiritual, Social and Emotional intelligence; Nature of Work; Mindfulness at Work; Personal Fulfillment and Workplace Flourishing; Workplace Spirituality and Organizational Performance; Inner Identity, Interconnectedness, Community and Transcendence; Managing Spiritual and Religious Diversity at Work; Spirituality and World Peace Imperative; Sustainability and Spirituality; Spirituality and Creativity; and Applied Workplace Spirituality in Health Care, Education, Faith-based Organizations, et al.

More information about this series at
http://www.palgrave.com/gp/series/15746

James Laub

Leveraging the Power of Servant Leadership

Building High Performing Organizations

palgrave
macmillan

James Laub
Palm Beach Atlantic University
West Palm Beach, FL, USA

Palgrave Studies in Workplace Spirituality and Fulfillment
ISBN 978-3-030-08380-9   ISBN 978-3-319-77143-4   (eBook)
https://doi.org/10.1007/978-3-319-77143-4

Cover credit: PhotoAlto / Alamy Stock Photo

Printed on acid-free paper

This Palgrave Macmillan imprint is published by the registered company Springer Nature Switzerland AG
The registered company address is: Gewerbestrasse 11, 6330 Cham, Switzerland

Praise Page

"Dr. Jim Laub's book *Leveraging the Power of Servant-Leadership* is wise, stunning, and incisive. His contributions to define and help leaders be aware of the grave differences between autocratic, paternalistic, and servant-leadership are among the most radiant research findings in contemporary leadership studies. Dr. Laub's experience and understanding of leadership are vital and immutable, shown in the ancient truth he uncovers: that leadership is not only dangerous and therefore requires uncommon discernment and self-responsibility, but that leadership also evokes in leaders the responsibility to lead with great love and devoted sacrificial service to others and the world."

—Shann Ray Ferch, *Professor of Leadership Studies, Gonzaga University, USA*

"Dr. Laub has given us a magnificent synthesis of leadership stories, studies, metaphors, and history that often reads like a page-turning novel. This book is the place to start for a comprehensive and readable introduction to servant-leadership and leadership studies in general.

While reading Dr. Laub's magisterial volume, I filled my own small notebook with quotes and insights new to me. While deeply rooted in Greenleaf's writings, Leveraging the Power of Servant Leadership goes further to begin answering the questions: "So what?" "What does research say?" "How do I implement and measure the effects of servant leadership?" and finally, "What are the deepest roots of servant leadership in my own experience?"

Bravo to Jim Laub! He has shown that when fine writing joins deep scholarship and infectious passion for the topic, the result is a high gift for readers and learners—a textbook replete with fresh, thoughtful, wisdom-filled pages."
—Don M. Frick, *PhD, Greenleaf Academy, Viterbo University, USA*

"This book provides an excellent introduction to servant leadership, including a rich historical perspective on how servant leadership fits among an array of approaches to leadership. Laub clearly distinguishes servant leadership from other approaches, and does a great job of addressing many of the key criticisms of servant leadership. I highly recommend this book!"
—Robert C. Liden, *Professor of Management, University of Illinois at Chicago, USA*

"Grounded in the seminal work of Robert K. Greenleaf, Jim Laub's book discusses a quarter century of servant leadership research. He expands on existing scholarship and uses his Organizational Leadership Assessment model to explore the fundamental disciplines of servant leadership. Laub presents findings that support the bottom-line benefits to organizations pursuing this approach. And, importantly, he offers a practical how-to guide to leveraging the power of servant leadership tenets and values within organizations and institutions."
—Lea E. Williams, *Adjunct Instructor, ESOL, Guilford Technical Community College, USA*

"In the midst of all worklife turbulence, servant leadership is more timely than ever, and without a doubt, James Laub has written *the* book about servant leadership. It's thorough, it's engaging, it's practical and what's best, it's also theory-driven and research-based. I warmly recommend this book to anyone who wants to develop a servant leader mindset and thus become a good leader."
—Jari Hakanen, *Research Professor, University of Helsinki, Finland*

"Jim Laub's approach to servant leadership is unique and his model is well grounded in research and practice. This book is important and most useful for those interested in learning about successful leadership for creating a healthy work environment."
—Sigrún Gunnarsdóttir, *Associate Professor of Leadership at University of Iceland, Reykjavík, Iceland*

"An invaluable resource to anyone interested in servant leadership. Laub provides a comprehensive summary of the origins of servant leadership as well as

contemporary research findings. Through the use of metaphor and practical examples, he demonstrates how servant leaders can reshape their organizations to become more ethical and effective."
—Craig Johnson, *Emeritus Professor of Leadership Studies,*
George Fox University, USA

"The Servant Leadership community reveres Jim as one of the top thinkers and, for as long as I've known him, he's shown the ability to paint a picture of what Servant Leadership looks like in a compelling manner. This book proves that! If you want to understand Servant Leadership, this book will start your journey by showing you the joy of serving others, the challenges of doing so, and then convincing you it is worthwhile."
—Kathleen Patterson, *Professor and Director of the Doctorate of Strategic*
Leadership Program, Regent University, UK

"Jim Laub's latest book on servant leadership is a 'must read' book, that students as well as practitioners will find invaluable. I love the way the book starts by addressing the 'purpose of leadership.' The unanswered question is 'leadership for what?' This aspect is well addressed. The book draws out the historical development of leadership, situates servant leadership in its proper context, and makes the valuable connection that servant leadership behaviors emanate from a true identity of a servant. Practitioners will find the latter half of the book particularly valuable. These chapters show how a servant leadership mindset is developed, how systems and structures support a servant leadership culture, and various models and tools that will help develop servant led organizations. I highly recommend this book …. well done Jim."
—Dr. Peter Sun, *Associate Professor, University of Waikato, New Zealand*

"Jim Laub is indisputably an expert on servant leadership. His new book goes more than one mile further. By reminding the fundamentals of all leadership and differentiating servant leadership from paternalistic leadership, Jim addresses a fundamental issue. This book offers profound insights that readers will want not only to reflect, but to act on."
—Vincent Giolito, *Lead researcher, Université libre de Bruxelles, Belgium*

"*Leveraging the Power of Servant Leadership* is an indispensable resource and a well-researched tool for any student, practitioner or organization with a compelling resolve to serve and steward healthy, high performing servant led organizations."
—Sally Chew, *Chairman of The Greenleaf Centre*
for Servant Leadership, Singapore

"Jim Laub provides a compelling case for the priority of servant leadership. Laub calls us to see servant leadership not simply as another theory, but rather a mindset that places the good of the led over the self-interest of the leader. In *Leveraging the Power of Servant Leadership*, Laub presents research-based insights for leaders. Take time to discover servant leadership's capacity to positively transform teams and organizations in this important and timely resource."
—Justin A. Irving, *Interim Co-Vice President and Dean, Bethel University, USA*

"A high performing organization is successfully built from its roots in order to ensure the foundation is solid for growth. The OLA instrument has proven to be a great tool for tracking the organization's health in areas that are critical for it to reach the type of cruising altitude that supports sustainability. What is delightful about this book is learning from an author who lives servant leadership that is a precursor of high performance."
—Dale Dan, *President, Kaieteur Falls University, Guyana*

"Jim Laub is a servant leadership pioneer, bridging academic rigor with practical relevance. His model is both comprehensive and easy to understand. This book will sharpen your thinking on servant leadership, provide a deeper understanding where it comes from and how it relates to other leadership theories; it will help introduce servant leadership in your organizational practice."
—Dirk van Dierendonck, *Professor in Human Resource Management, Erasmus University, The Netherlands*

"The structure of this book is excellent and takes the reader from theory to practice to understand and apply servant leadership in organizations to ultimately transform a company into a servant organization. It also provides valuable insights to understand how to measure a servant organization or the progress to become a servant organization. I can highly recommend this book to any leader, organization, practitioner, or individual wanting to make a long-lasting positive impact in the world."
—Charl Coetzer, *CEO of Wisdomy, South Africa*

For Barbara, Wanda, Joy, and Jenny
four servants who lead by example
faithfully following the One who modeled it first and best

Foreword

The servant-leader is servant first. It begins with the natural feeling that one wants to serve. Then conscious choice brings one to aspire to lead. The best test is: do those served grow as persons: do they, while being served, become healthier, wiser, freer, more autonomous, more likely themselves to become servants? And, what is the effect on the least privileged in society; will they benefit, or, at least, not be further deprived? "The Servant as Leader," Robert K. Greenleaf, 1970

It is an honor to have been asked to write the Foreword to Jim Laub's superb book—*Leveraging the Power of Servant Leadership: Building High Performing Organizations*. I believe that it is an important work that deftly applies a well-researched and scholarly understanding of servant-leadership in a way that can be helpfully used in any organization.

I was first introduced to Robert K. Greenleaf's writings on servant-leadership back in 1982. The idea began to take root within my heart and mind at that time. Over the years I have devoted my life and career to working intensively to raise public awareness and practices of servant-leadership worldwide. A good bit of my life's work has involved the editing or co-authoring of some 30 books on servant-leadership.

From 1990 to 2007, I led the Robert K. Greenleaf Center for Servant-Leadership. During those years, I edited or co-edited five volumes of writings by Robert Greenleaf: *On Becoming a Servant-Leader* (1996),

Seeker and Servant (1996), *The Power of Servant-Leadership* (1998), *Servant Leadership: 25th Anniversary Edition* (2002), and *The Servant-Leader Within* (2003). During those same years, I also edited and co-authored a series of four servant-leadership anthologies, including *Reflections on Leadership* (1995), *Insights on Leadership* (1998), *Focus on Leadership* (2002), and *Practicing Servant-Leadership* (2004).

I have long believed that it is essential to become grounded in Robert Greenleaf's original writings, as well as to explore new thoughts and applications that continue to emerge from those who have been inspired by Greenleaf. Robert Greenleaf's writings provide a strong foundation from which many branches have continued to grow and emerge over the past half century. *Leveraging the Power of Servant Leadership* is a significant new publication.

The words servant and leader are usually thought of as being opposites. In deliberately bringing those words together in a meaningful way, Robert Greenleaf gave birth to the paradoxical term "servant-leadership." In the years since then, many of today's most creative thinkers are writing and speaking about servant-leadership as an emerging leadership paradigm for the twenty-first century. The list is long and includes James Autry, Peter Block, John Carver, Stephen Covey, Max DePree, Shann Ferch, Don Frick, John Horsman, Joseph Jaworski, Jim Kouzes, Larraine Matusak, Peter Northouse, Parker Palmer, Peter Senge, Peter Vaill, Margaret Wheatley, and Danah Zohar, to name just some of today's cutting-edge leadership authors and advocates of servant-leadership. With *Leveraging the Power of Servant Leadership*, we add Jim Laub to this growing list of notable authors on servant-leadership.

It is helpful to understand that servant-leadership starts within each one of us, and that it is first and foremost a personal philosophy and commitment that we can choose to practice in any environment. If we understand Greenleaf's best test as the fundamental understanding of servant-leadership, then it becomes clear that the choice to seek to practice servant-leadership is ours to make, and no one else's. Our personally embracing servant-leadership does not require the approval of our supervisor, or our organization's chief executive. We don't need anyone's permission to personally do our best to act as a servant-leader. It is our choice.

Robert Greenleaf's writings have influenced several generations of people. Part of Greenleaf's great contribution to the world was the simple act of bringing together the words "servant" and "leader" in an innovative hyphenated word, "servant-leader." In providing us with a name for something that many of us intuitively understand, Greenleaf helped to link together many who might otherwise have felt even more isolated in their beliefs and in their workplaces.

Leading others can be quite meaningful. Serving others is better yet. However, both serving and leading others—at least for me—is the best. It offers opportunities for wholeness, for making a difference in the world, and for helping to fulfill Bob Greenleaf's powerful work around the servant-as-leader idea.

It should be noted that Greenleaf titled his essay, "The Servant as Leader," and not "The Leader as Servant." While encouraging leaders to act as servants was a remarkable idea, asking servants to act as leaders was (and remains) a truly radical idea! It is also an idea that goes against our expectations of contemporary culture. It is this fact that makes servant-leadership such a unique and potent philosophy.

Some organizations have concluded that servant-leadership is the right thing to do and have subsequently embraced it. Starbucks, Southwest Airlines, The Men's Wearhouse, TDIndustries, and other companies are notable for their spirit of servant-leadership. This has certainly been a critical way in which servant-leadership has grown and advanced over the past 50 years.

In 1992, I conducted research into Robert Greenleaf's servant-leadership writings. Through that analysis of his writings, I extracted a set of ten characteristics of servant-leadership. These were characteristics that Greenleaf most frequently mentioned in his essays and books. They include Listening, Empathy, Healing, Awareness, Persuasion, Conceptualization, Foresight, Stewardship, Commitment to the Growth of People, and Building Community. These ten characteristics are by no means exhaustive. Still, my analysis showed these to be the ones that Greenleaf mentioned most often in his writings, and which led me to codify them into a list and to begin to write about them. Like Robert Greenleaf, I am convinced that it is possible to become an increasingly authentic servant-leader through personal development of these and other characteristics.

Which leads me to back to Jim Laub, whom I have known since the 1990s, and to his wonderful book.

Twenty years ago, Laub shared with me some of his thinking about servant-leadership, and he invited me to be part of a Delphi research study. Those of us who were involved in this process engaged in a three-phase approach in Laub's effort to identify what a servant-leader looks like in practice. The results of this research led him to create the Organizational Leadership Assessment (OLA) instrument, which many organizations have used in their efforts to develop a shared understanding of the meaning of servant-leadership and how to grow as a servant-led institution.

As Jim writes,

> This model is the first model of servant leadership developed through a research-based approach providing an operational and measureable set of constructs to describe what servant leadership looks like in practice. The six central disciplines of servant leadership are described along with three descriptors for each discipline. The OLA model of servant leadership provides a framework for understanding the unique mindset that a servant leader possesses and how this mindset is lived out through the servant leader's behavior.

According to the OLA servant-leadership model, servant-leaders Value People, Develop People, Build Community, Display Authenticity, Provide Leadership, and Share Leadership. This approach results in people who understand what it means to genuinely care for others, and organizations that operate successfully through building goodwill and commitment from its constituent groups.

Laub also emphasizes the fact that servant leadership is "an understanding and practice (a mindset) of leadership that focuses on the well-being of the followers above the self-interest of the leader." His insights into the idea of servant leadership as a mindset is another groundbreaking aspect of this work.

Robert Greenleaf wrote, "This is my thesis: caring for persons, the more able and the less able serving each other, is the rock upon which a good society is built." Laub has a deep understanding of this, and he provides a pathway for how our institutions can be transformed into places of "joy, empowerment and purpose."

Jim Laub concluded long ago that servant-leadership needed to be clearly defined, and that a well-researched model should be created. *Leveraging the Power of Servant Leadership* is a wonderful distillation of his valuable work over the past 20 years. Most importantly, it offers a methodology for understanding and implementing servant-leadership, an approach that has been helpful to many people and organizations. Now, with the publication of this book, Laub's work reaches a much larger audience. May it have a prominent influence for many years to come.

Gonzaga University, Spokane, WA, USA   Larry C. Spears
The Spears Center Indianapolis, IN, USA
2018

Preface

Servant leadership is a mindset that creates a new way of viewing leadership, the leader, and the led. Robert Greenleaf popularized the term back in the 1970's but its history goes back into the distant millennia of leadership practice. This age-old concept presents itself to us today as an alternative to the standard and limited practices of Machiavellian leadership and benevolent paternalistic leadership. Authoritarian leadership has promised much but has failed to deliver. Gallup's far-reaching 2017 study of worker engagement tells us that only 15% of workers worldwide report as engaged in their work. Instead of being engaged, passionate, and creative, most workers are merely showing up and doing the basic tasks necessary to keep their jobs. The effect of this is low productivity, an unsatisfied and poorly used workforce, and frustrated, despairing leaders. We can do better and that is what this book addresses.

This book accepts the basic assumption that every person has the capacity and the responsibility to lead. With this assumption in mind, the book presents a definition and model of leadership that captures this challenge and helps to clear up many of the confusion points related to leadership studies today. It presents the role of servant leadership within the context of the leadership story throughout history and its relationship to current leadership thinking while providing a research-based approach to understanding this powerful mindset of leading.

The following six assumptions are woven throughout this book and will be explained and developed under a consistent theme of moving the world forward through servant leadership.

1. The purpose of leadership is to move the world.
2. Every person has the capacity and the responsibility to lead.
3. Leadership can and should be clearly defined.
4. Leadership matters and our mindset of leadership matters most of all.
5. Leadership is most effectively exercised out of a servant mindset with a view toward putting the good of those led over the leader's self-interest.
6. Power is available to each person and must be leveraged for high performance leadership to occur.

This book differs from most books on servant leadership in that it presents a research-based, academic view of the subject that is appropriate for the college classroom as well as the serious student of leadership within organizations today. The book presents a comprehensive model of servant leadership while contrasting it to other mindsets of autocratic and paternalistic leadership. This is a model of servant leadership that can be taught to individuals and groups and can also be assessed within organizations.

The book was written in an effort to bridge the gap between the academic, scholarly work of the university and the practical realities of leadership in organizations, communities, and the society at large. It is research-based and true to the tradition of leadership studies while offering a non-traditional approach to the understanding and practice of leadership. This book seeks to present an academic approach joined to a clear, understandable, and readable challenge for students to go beyond merely knowing about leadership toward its effective practice.

Who This Book Is For

- For students of leadership who desire to establish a solid base of leadership definition and theory within a historical context related to current leadership thinking.
- For teachers of leadership who desire to integrate an academic approach to servant leadership connected to the entire discipline of leadership studies.

- For organizational leaders and other leadership practitioners who desire a consistent framework for understanding and practicing leadership in practical day-to-day experience.

How This Book May Be Used

- For current leadership courses focused on servant leadership, this book may be used as a primary text presenting a comprehensive, research-based approach to understanding and practicing servant leadership and its relationship to more traditional approaches to leadership.
- For current leadership courses that desire to include an academic approach to servant leadership, this book may be used as a supplementary text in addition to the leadership theory-oriented texts normally used in such leadership courses.
- For leadership development trainers within organizations who desire a connecting text between a scholarly approach and a practical application of servant leadership to the organizational setting.
- For leaders who desire to understand what leadership is at its core and what their own mindset of leadership may be and how this mindset is affecting their leadership practice and the resulting health of their organizations.
- For all leaders who desire a better way to lead to develop and empower leaders throughout their organization to maximize the potential of all workers to create high performance and exceptional results.

You will find throughout this book a challenge to think differently about yourself as a leader; to see your central role as serving the needs of your followers first and viewing them as adult partners. This requires a new mindset, a new way of thinking about leadership. This book is your introduction to creating this new mindset and beginning a practice of leadership that brings out the best in others and creates the optimal conditions for organizational success.

West Palm Beach, FL   James Laub

Contents

List of Figures

List of Tables

1

The Purpose of Leadership: Leadership That Moves the World

Leadership is dangerous. It can produce amazing good or incredible harm. It is not to be treated lightly. It is a powerful force that should only be handled with the utmost care and deepest thought. Leaders handle power, people, vision, intention, and aspirations flamed by the spark of action. It's a wonder that more destruction doesn't occur. It's also a wonder that more good is not accomplished in the world.

Leadership is a volatile mix of action, vision, mobilization, and change when put together in the right amount, at the right time and in the right degree will explode into a new reality, a new vision of what is possible in the world. We should not restrain it because its power to heal the world is greater than its power to harm. We should not contain it because we so desperately need its momentum, its drive, its incredible inspiring presence, but, we do need to channel this power—this focused and determined energy toward change.

Leadership can be subtle. Sometimes you don't see it operating. It can be very deceptive. Sometimes when you think you see it displayed, it turns out to not be leadership at all, but one of its lesser cousins of aggression or boldness. Leadership is often not loud. It is not always forceful, but it is incredibly persistent. Leadership will have its way with the world.

© The Author(s) 2018   **1**
J. Laub, *Leveraging the Power of Servant Leadership*, Palgrave Studies in Workplace Spirituality and Fulfillment, https://doi.org/10.1007/978-3-319-77143-4_1

Leaders will prevail and the result of this persistent action is a world change that no one will be able to ignore.

Leaders create reality. They possess clarity of vision and insight with the will and courage to pursue a new future. The good ones do so while connecting meaningfully to the past and working effectively in the present. The best ones bring an inner life of consciousness, awareness, thought, and spirit that anchors them as they walk into the uncertainty of an unknown future.

Leaders have always been fascinating to us. We are drawn to both their power and their celebrity while being aware of the need to keep a safe distance. Burns (1978) recognized this tension when he observed that

> We search eagerly for leadership yet seek to cage and tame it. We recoil from power yet we are bewitched or titillated by it. We devour books on power—power in the office, power in the bedroom, power in the corridors. Connoisseurs of power purport to teach about it—what it is, how to get it, how to use it, how to 'gain total control' over 'everything around you.' … Why this preoccupation, this near-obsession, with power? In part because we in this century cannot escape the horror of it. (p. 9)

The Power and Horror of Leadership

The power and horror of leadership are with us today. The world recoils at the devastation in the Middle East setting loose a worldwide immigration crisis and brutal killing, recalling for many the dark days of 1994 when in a period of 100 days, over 800,000 people from the Tutsi tribe in the African country of Rwanda were butchered by the ruling Hutus. After the slaughter, the questions began: Why didn't more people act to stop the killing? Why had so many participated in or ignored such awesome brutality? One person who decided to act was Paul Rusesabagina who ran the Hotel des Mille Collines in Rwanda. Paul used his hotel, influence, and simple willingness to act to save 1200 Rwandans who otherwise would have certainly been slaughtered.

The first thing that Paul did was to communicate to the world what was happening as his country spun out of control. "We sent many faxes to Bill Clinton himself at the White House" (as cited in Gourevitch, 1998, p. 132). Paul would stay up until four in the morning, "sending faxes, calling, ringing the whole world" (p. 132). His faxes and calls went mostly unanswered. Paul often was able to save lives simply by refusing to comply. When the authorities demanded that he release one of his hotel guests to them, he stood his ground, "They wanted to take him out, but I refused" (p. 133); when asked why his refusal was heeded, he answered "I don't know … I don't know how it was, but I refused so many things" (p. 133). Some asked why Paul acted as he did, but more began to ask why others did not act in the same way. Paul's response was, "that's a mystery … everybody could have done it" (p. 135). Though individual acts of positive leadership were documented, the harsh reality remains; the world as a whole failed to act—failed to exhibit the necessary leadership to stop the killing. Many claimed that this was not their responsibility, or that it was not their place to act, but are these not leadership questions? Are we not dealing with leadership when we ask whether we are responsible to act in a given situation? We may not be able to agree on the answers, but we must agree on the need for positive leadership at such times.

The Irish philosopher Edmund Burke in a 1795 letter to William Smith suggested that "the only thing necessary for the triumph of evil is for good men to do nothing." In what ways does leadership address these issues? In what way is leadership my personal responsibility and response to the concerns that trouble the world? Perhaps leadership is about good men doing something; about women rising above self-interest to pursue the benefit of the other; about people who just can't stand to sit back any longer as the world around them desperately calls for movement and change.

The Power and Beauty of Leadership

We find the power and beauty of leadership displayed in our world as well. Mother Teresa lifts the head of a dying man and speaks words of comfort and hope into his ear. Nelson Mandela walks free after 27 years in prison, becomes the first black president of South Africa and then leads a bloodless revolution through democratic vote while extending a hand of reconciliation to his former oppressors. Mahatma Gandhi, a stooped old man in his 60s, personally leads a 240-mile march to the sea to protest the British occupation of his country and their monopoly over the salt trade resulting in, India, a nation of over 1 billion people, standing free. Yes, it seems that both the horror and the beauty of leadership action play out on the world stage and the actors continue to pursue their dreams of domination or self-sacrifice.

But what about you and me? Most of us are not world leaders living in such dramatic times. We are not called to lead nations. We don't have the personal power or opportunity to make such a far-reaching impact on the world. Perhaps then the issue is not about having an impact on *the* world, but on *our* world. Is leadership something that pertains to me? Is leading a responsibility that I can choose to pursue or not? If I choose to lead, what kind of leader will I be? The answer to these and other questions is what this book is all about.

Yes, leadership is dangerous. Much too dangerous to leave it unexamined, untested, and untried. Leadership is, in fact, a call and a choice for us all.

Archimedes and the Metaphor of the Lever

Give me a lever long enough and a place to stand, and I will move the world.
Archimedes, 230 BC

Archimedes, the brilliant mathematician and scientist, was born in 287 BC in Syracuse, Sicily. He spent his life developing mathematical solutions toward challenges like the development of the calculus and the determination of circular area and the surface area and volume of a sphere. He was an eccentric who would often lose himself in the development of his theorems while drawing with his finger in the dirt or in a special writing box of sand he often carried with him. His intense focus sometimes led to neglecting personal needs, prompting friends to rescue him from his musings and force him to bathe and eat.

Archimedes moved beyond theory to apply his mathematical principles to the problems of his time. This included the creation of innovative weapons of war. When Syracuse was attacked by Rome, Marcellus, the Roman general, surrounded the city bringing his army to the city gates while using his entire naval fleet to block the harbor. Archimedes created huge cranes that were actually able to lift the Roman ships out of the water and either smash them by dropping them or swing them over the wall into the waiting hands of the Syracuse army (Hirshfeld, 2009). It must have been difficult for Marcellus to realize that he was being defeated by the wiles of a mathematical genius rather than the might of a hardened military leader. This was power of a different sort. He must have felt that a conjurer was creating dark arts to defeat his army. Plutarch in his work *Marcellus* describes this reaction:

> Such terror had seized upon the Romans, that, if they did but see a little rope or a piece of wood from the wall, instantly crying out, that there it was again, Archimedes was about to let fly some engine at them, they turned their backs and fled. (as cited in Hirshfeld, 2009, p. 86)

Another example of Archimedes' ability to solve problems came at the request of the King of Syracuse. It seems that King Hiero's ship had been built but could not be launched. It sat firmly and stubbornly on dry land just a short distance from the water. All the men of Syracuse attempted, through brute force, to move the ship with no success. The ship simply was immovable. Archimedes created an elaborate system of levers and pulleys, put the entire crew onto the ship, and then handed the end of the pulley rope to the King. With a pull of the rope, the King was able to move the huge ship, with its crew, into the sea. King Hiero who had been a skeptic of these complicated machines of Archimedes made a proclamation that Archimedes was to be believed in everything from that day forward. From this real-life experience of practical applied mathematics comes the most famous quote attributed to Archimedes; "Give me a lever long enough and a place to stand, and I will move the world."

Archimedes was certainly thinking of the physical applications that his new machine would address and certainly did not have leadership on his mind. However, with this statement he has provided us a powerful metaphor to analyze and develop a concept of leadership that can, in fact, move the world. We make use of the metaphor of the lever to present a new framework for understanding the discipline and effective practice of leveraged leadership.

Work and Leadership: The Limits of Force

Work involves movement and force represented by the formula $W = F \times D$ (work equals force times the distance of movement). Consider the energy that it would take for you to move your office desk across the floor. The success of your work would be measured by your ability to get the desk moved across the room.

Leadership is often seen in this same way and can be represented by the formula $L = F \times D$ (leadership equals force times distance of movement of followers). This presents a leader-focused view of leadership placing the leader as the central actor upon the followers (those to be moved). The mediating variable is force. This can be physical force, emotional force, or social force, but is ultimately a coercive energy used to get someone to do what the leader wants done. One thinks of Atlas lifting the world up on his powerful shoulders. The problem with this view of leadership should be clear. On a pragmatic level, sometimes a leader cannot exert enough force or the right kind of force to create the desired movement. More importantly, the leader's use of force will often create resistance to the movement they are trying to create. All of the men of Syracuse could not build up enough human power to overcome the weight and inertia of the large ship. Marcellus could not muster the force of his army and navy to overcome the special, seemingly magical machines of Archimedes. We need more than a model of leadership based on the level of force that one leader can exert. Belief in this model of work ($W = F \times D$) applied to leadership has led people to call for ever-stronger leaders, leaders with the personal characteristics to move others to where they need to go. It is time to propose a better way to do leadership. It is time to move beyond brute force toward a different kind of power that truly changes people and empowers them to voluntarily join in the leadership process of moving the world. The metaphor of the lever calls for a different way of viewing the role of the leader, the role of the led, and the overall purpose of leadership. Atlas and his brute strength must give way to Archimedes and his lever.

Unfolding the Metaphor of the Lever

The lever allows for the effect of power to be maximized while the need for direct force is minimized. More movement can be accomplished with less force due to the dynamics at work within the lever. Yes, force is exerted, but the power to create movement is magnified. The leader (the one initially exerting power) is just one part of the process. When considering the metaphor of the lever we are able to identify five key elements that help us form a new framework for understanding leadership effectiveness.

> *Give me a lever long enough and a place to stand, and I will move the world.*
> Archimedes, 230 BC

The Object to Be Moved: The Purpose of Leadership

The output of the work of the lever is movement. When leaders act toward a vision to change something in the world they are focused on the real purpose and outcome of leadership. When leaders expend large amounts of energy in promoting themselves, or building up their organization, they are involved in an altogether lesser purpose. True leadership is about change—world change. Leaders acknowledge that the world is not as it should be and something must be done. They move beyond this to the recognition that if anything is to be changed it will be the leaders among us who will act. It is up to us who see this reality, and are willing to address it through leadership, who take up the call of world-moving leadership. The purpose of leadership is to move the world. This movement can be subtle like steering your team toward a more positive way of thinking or it can be as dramatic as a societal leader like Gandhi moving a whole nation toward independence. There is no doubt that our world needs to be moved and changed. What is needed for this is leadership.

The Leader: Applying Power in the Most Effective Way

How is leadership to be understood? What is the role of the leader in moving the world? Should leaders, emulating Atlas, put their strong shoulder to the huge globe and lift with all of their might? There are some leaders who seem to have been created in this mold and see this as their responsibility and their right. They are challenged to move the world and they will do it on the strength of their leadership power and charismatic gifts. Yes, it seems that throughout history there are significant individuals who seem to have the qualities of the gods and, through their individual might, achieve great things. Of course, these powerful *gods* can just as easily use their gifts to abuse as well as benefit. One of the characteristics of the Greek gods was their arbitrary nature. Yes, they will move the world, but you may not want to be standing near them when they do. This book will present a different view of leading that allows for us mere mortals to become leaders to make a difference in the world. In this view, each person has the capacity and the responsibility to lead. None of us can sit back waiting for someone bigger and stronger to save the day. We are each called to seize the opportunity before us to move the world forward in a positive way.

The Fulcrum: Choosing Your Leadership Mindset

The fulcrum of a lever is that small but critical underlying foundation that, based on its position, determines how much force is required to move the object. Where you chose to place the fulcrum determines if the object is moved and how much effort must be expended to do so. In this leadership metaphor the fulcrum represents the *mindset* that we bring to leadership. What paradigm shapes my leadership understanding and practice? This book presents three distinct underlying mindsets that will direct our leadership understanding. For the most part, leaders are not conscious of the mindset they are operating under and this lack of awareness results in failing to realize the true impact they have on others. This issue of the underlying mindset of leadership has been largely ignored in the leadership literature with the result that we are left to conclude that leadership is not much more than implementing select theories or simply living out individual traits of leadership. The specific fulcrum positions we will be addressing are the autocratic, paternalistic (parental), and servant mindsets of leadership. We lead for ourselves over others, as parents over children, or as partners, putting the good of those led over our own self-interest. These very different mindsets have to do with the leader's view of self, the leader's view of the led, and the leader's view of the purpose and outcome of leadership. As the fulcrum serves to support the lever and must be positioned optimally, our paradigm will determine how we practice the various theories and approaches to leadership. It will determine *how* we lead.

The Lever: Utilizing Leadership Theories and Approaches

What leadership theories inform my practice of leadership? Interest in leadership goes back to the beginning of human experience. People have always been concerned with issues of power, rule, change, and authority. People have always looked for leaders to move them from where they are to a better place.

The study of leadership as a discipline has followed a parallel course with the study of its partner, management, throughout the last century. Beginning in the twentieth century, the study of leadership as distinct from management began its own trajectory and the field of leadership studies was born. Almost all leadership textbooks present leadership theory as it has progressed through the past century. Some of these approaches are management theories under a different title, while others attempt to identify the uniqueness of leadership and how it can best be identified and practiced. Leadership theories properly assessed will create multiple viewpoints on processes and techniques to enhance our leadership practice. When viewing leadership theories and approaches it is recommended that we draw benefit from each of them and then determine which helps us most in dealing with the day-to-day realities of our individual leadership practice.

As the lever requires the right placement of the fulcrum to work optimally, our leadership theory lever needs to be based on a clear understanding of our underlying leadership mindset. Only in this way will our leadership efforts result in true world change.

A Place to Stand: The Practice of Leadership

Where will my leadership be exercised? What skills will I need to develop? In order for the lever to work effectively it must not only have all critical parts in the right place, but there must also be a firm place for the leader to stand. From this part of our metaphor we can draw two key learning points: where the leader can best exercise leadership and what internal foundations and values the leader possesses to perform the external work of leading others.

First, it is essential that the leader have the right opportunity to lead within an organization or group that shares the goal of moving the world in a particular direction. Organizations serve as vehicles for leadership vision; they should not become the purpose and outcome of our leadership. Organizations allow the working out of the leadership process between the leader and the led so that the shared vision can be realized. Certainly, the leader will spend time on developing the organization like a race car driver will work to create the optimal performing race car. However, the driver should always remain clear that the purpose is not to have the most admired car on the track, but rather the one that gives him the best chance to win the race. Leaders must always keep the purpose of leading foremost in mind.

Second, it is essential that the leader exert force on the lever from a stable and healthy inner life that provides a firm place to stand. Too many positional leaders operate out of the weak shell of persona and image while the inner resources of character and values are severely lacking. Leadership requires emotional, intellectual, and interpersonal strength that cannot be replaced by outer traits of good communication, physical stature, and personality. Technique should never trump inner commitment, principle, and values. The leadership literature has begun to address this critical area in the past few years. Kouzes and Posner (2017) present the necessity for the leader to be credible before those they lead. Goleman (1998), and others, (Mayer & Salovey, 1995) have promoted the concept of emotional intelligence as a way to describe the internal and relational competencies needed for effective leadership. Authors like Palmer (2000) have challenged us to explore both the shadow and the light that leaders bring to the world.

> A leader is someone with the power to project either shadow or light onto some part of the world and onto the lives of the people who dwell there. A leader shapes the ethos in which others must live, an ethos as light-filled as heaven or as shadowy as hell. A *good* leader is intensely aware of the interplay of inner shadow and light, lest the act of leadership do more harm than good. (p. 78)

All leaders exert power and that power always has an effect projecting either shadow or light. Archimedes has a tool that allows us to use our power more efficiently and effectively without damaging others. Leaders need a firm place to stand in order to use the unique power of the lever to move the world. To make this work we must utilize all five parts of the leadership lever:

1. Moving the world—maintaining a clear purpose for our leadership
2. The leader—applying power in the most effective way
3. The fulcrum—choosing the optimal leadership mindset
4. The lever board—utilizing leadership theories and approaches
5. A place to stand—discovering the right place to stand to practice leadership

As we focus on the true purpose of leadership, choose our mindset wisely, apply the right kind of power in the right way, utilize the best from leadership theories, and practice our leadership from a strong place of inner strength and awareness, we will have the best chance to succeed in our leadership. Leadership is a dynamic process that involves more than merely being in charge and telling other people what to do. With the leadership of the lever we will accomplish more than we ever dared to dream. We will, in fact, move the world.

Six Basic Assumptions About Leadership

The following six assumptions are woven throughout this book and will be explained and developed under a consistent theme of moving the world through leadership:

1. The purpose of leadership is to move the world.
2. Every person has the capacity and the responsibility to lead.
3. Leadership can and should be clearly defined.
4. Leadership matters and our mindset of leadership matters most of all.
5. Leadership is most effectively exercised out of a servant mindset with a view toward putting the good of those led over the leader's self-interest.
6. Power is available to each person and must be leveraged for high performance leadership to occur.

World-Moving Leadership

Leadership is dangerous; sometimes to those led, sometimes to the leader; but it is also dangerous, and should be, to a status quo that allows the world to stay the same with no challenge to the injustice, failed policies, or continued misuse of people. Make no mistake; we envision nothing less than dramatic world change coming from our leadership. The world has seen enough of positional leaders who do not lead. We must move beyond the concept of the leader as savior, as parent, as god. We want leaders that lead. Leaders who through their action, vision, and mobilization of others help us to move toward needed change.

Paul Rusesabagina was asked what made him so strong to successfully resist the killing in Rwanda, but he really did not have an answer. "I wasn't really strong … I wasn't. But maybe I used different means that other people didn't want to use … during the genocide, I didn't know, … I thought so many people did as I did, because I know that if they'd wanted they could have done so" (as cited in Gourevitch, 1998, p. 141). I suspect that the real leaders among us are somewhat baffled by the unwillingness of others to act when that action will make such a needed difference in the world.

When Steve Jobs challenged John Sculley to move from Pepsi to take the CEO position at Apple Computer, he asked, "Do you want to spend the rest of your life selling flavored water, or do you want a chance to change the world?" (as cited in Clawson, 2003, p. 197). It is the hope of this book that you will be challenged to take on the calling and responsibility of leadership. A lever exists that is just right for your personal vision and passion, a lever that will enable you to move the world around you. Leaders, like you, are needed to leverage the right type of power in the right place at the right time that ultimately will make this world a better place. Palmer (2000) puts this in perspective for us when he states,

> Material reality … is not the fundamental factor in the movement of human history. Consciousness is. Awareness is. Thought is. Spirit is. These are not the ephemera of dreams. They are the inner Archimedean points from which oppressed people have gained the leverage to lift immense boulders and release transformative change. (p. 76)

This kind of transformational change needs to be released to create a dangerous force to challenge the deep complacency of our world. Yes, leadership is dangerous. It can cause great harm or amazing good. We dare not ignore this incredible power that is capable of moving the world.

Conclusion

In this opening chapter we have seen both the horror and the beauty of leadership power. We have considered a metaphor, the Archimedes lever, that can help us to see that a new mindset of leadership can leverage our leadership power to greater effect to move the world to a better place. In the next chapter we take a look back. We look at leadership throughout history to discover that the three mindsets of leading—autocratic, paternalistic, and servant—have always been options for how to think about and practice leadership power.

References

Burns, J. M. (1978). *Leadership*. New York: Harper & Row.

Clawson, J. G. (2003). *Level three leadership: Getting below the surface* (2nd ed.). Upper Saddle River, NJ: Prentice Hall.

Goleman, D. (1998). *Working with emotional intelligence*. New York: Bantam.

Gourevitch, P. (1998). *We wish to inform you that tomorrow we will be killed with our families: Stories from Rwanda*. New York: Picador.

Hirshfeld, A. (2009). *Eureka man: The life and legacy of Archimedes*. New York: Walker Publishing Company, Inc.

Kouzes, J. M., & Posner, B. Z. (2017). *The leadership challenge: How to make extraordinary things happen in organizations* (6th ed.). Hoboken, NJ: John Wiley & Sons, Inc.

Mayer, J. D., & Salovey, P. (1995). Emotional intelligence and the construction and regulation of feelings. *Applied & Preventive Psychology, 4*, 197–208.

Palmer, P. J. (2000). *Let your life speak: Listening for the voice of vocation*. San Francisco: Jossey-Bass.

2

The Story of Leadership: The Historical Development of Leadership Thought

This story covers a great amount of world time in a very short space. Our story begins at the dawn of human existence and continues to the current day. We introduce individuals and groups who serve as representatives of different eras of history to help us understand the flow of leadership thinking and experience through the ages. A common approach when considering the history of leadership thought is to only view the distant past as representing one approach to leadership—that of autocratic rule and despotic power over others. However, as we consider key events in history we will see that the mindsets presented in this book—autocratic, paternalistic, and servant—have been options from the beginning of time. We will view ancient literature as well as modern texts to present an overview of leadership thought from the beginning to the present day.

Our story begins, as all good stories should, inside an unresolved conflict. Two very different brothers enter a field together and a terrible argument ensues. Misunderstanding and jealousy move quickly to anger unleashing an uncontrollable rage. Soon, Cain, the elder, stumbles out of the field alone glancing quickly to see if anyone has witnessed the crime. His brother, Abel, lies bloody and dying face down in the rich soil that Cain so recently and faithfully tilled. The simple, pastoral order of life Cain and his family knew is now shattered. The quiet scene of vegetable

© The Author(s) 2018
J. Laub, *Leveraging the Power of Servant Leadership*, Palgrave Studies in Workplace Spirituality and Fulfillment, https://doi.org/10.1007/978-3-319-77143-4_2

gardens and farm animals is split into a cosmic battleground of love versus self-interest, isolation versus human connection.

Adam, the first patriarch of the first family, could not foresee this nor could he stop it. Eve felt the tension mounting between her two boys but she was powerless to intervene. The first family, according to the ancient biblical text, was split apart by the volatile combination of pride, power, resentment, and jealousy. Why? How could such horror happen when there was no model for it? As the story unfolds, it seems that God, for some unspoken reason, had rejected Cain's gift while Abel's gift was approved. Cain could not accept this, for to have his work, the literal fruit of his labor, rejected was to reject him. After all, Cain was the first-born, standing immediately in the line of power. For God to accept Abel's sacrifice, he being the youngest, just did not make sense to the older brother. Cain was the stronger, Abel the weaker, a simple reality with obvious and deadly consequences. Cain's question and retort to God, "am I my brother's keeper?" set the stage for mankind's ongoing challenge—to focus on self or others. Welcome to the first family: the original arena of leadership practice.

History is written around the use and abuse of leadership power. We've heard it over and over; might makes right—to the strong go the spoils. The leadership of the patriarch and then the autocrat has dominated the story of leadership through the ages but not without an occasional glimpse of a stronger more effective model, a model that possesses the seeming magical power of the lever of Archimedes using a lesser and different force to produce a greater and more powerful movement for change.

Leadership in the Family

As we have just seen, leadership began within the family unit. The patriarch, normally the strongest and most dominant of the group, used his physical authority to serve as main protector and provider. The matriarch also wielded influence and power but did so in different ways to influence her family. Children were to obey, listen, and follow. They needed the strong arm of the father and the wisdom of the mother to feel secure within their role in the family unit. Sometimes the leading of the parent was firm and kind, asking much while providing necessary support and guidance. Sometimes the leading was harsh, self-absorbed, and even cruel. The dysfunctions of the parents bore down hard on the children unleashing patterns of future abuse and neglect. As our opening story suggests, leadership did not and could not deal with the intricate dynamics of the human condition and each family, on their own, had to work it as best they could. Each family created and then bore its own consequences. As Tolstoy (1997) famously begins his novel *Anna Karenina* "Happy families are all alike; every unhappy family is unhappy in its own way" (p. 1).

Leadership in Bands and Tribes

The family unit did not remain isolated from others nearby. As families grew, they found resources and security from coming together in extended family bands. An example of this kind of band was the Moriori from the Chatham Islands located 500 miles east of New Zealand. The Moriori were nomadic hunter/gatherers who spent most of their time surviving by collecting and hunting food from the land. Each man, woman, and child had jobs to do that were determined by their tradition and each day required a basic repetition of behavior. Actions were directed by the movement of the sun and various seasonal changes all well beyond their control.

An egalitarian type of leadership that relied on paternalistic authority within each family was used by the Moriori and other similar family bands. There were no formalized positions of leadership nor was leadership conferred due to heredity. It was likely that higher levels of influence were granted to people who stood out from the group due to personality, strength, or intelligence but community decisions were relatively simple and could be handled through discussion, consensus, or the occasional power play from a more powerful family leader.

Through the years, various groups from the original Moriori band broke off and migrated to other islands. Over time one of these groups was called, similarly, the Maori. As the Maori moved from locale to locale they faced different environmental opportunities and challenges leading to a departure from simple hunting/gathering into the sophistication of food production. The domestication of plants and animals and the development of the art of farming was a large step in the development of a more advanced form of community called the tribe.

Tribes developed as a higher order of social organization which began to depend upon the leadership of the Great Man to create a sense of order, security, and direction. The Great Man was just that, bigger and stronger than the rest. Leadership had moved beyond the egalitarian arrangement of the Moriori where decisions were made through a communal structure, relying on the collective wisdom of elders, to a situation where certain leaders obtained more influence over the tribe. As food production became more organized and jobs within the tribe more specialized (the priest or the tool maker, for instance) the need for coordination of these different facets of society was heightened. People no longer spent all of their time hunting and gathering just to survive so some became inventors and explorers to improve the condition of their tribe. In addition to new tools for farming, new weapons were created, stronger and more powerful weapons—and the capability to pursue the conquest of other groups increased. An example of this was the fateful clash of the Moriori band and the Maori tribe in December of 1835.

The Moriori, as mentioned, were hunter/gatherers, egalitarian, and peace-loving. The Maori, now a more advanced society, came with guns, clubs, and axes proclaiming that the Moriori would now be their slaves. This was a bold statement in light of the fact that the Maori were outnumbered two to one by the peace-loving Moriori. The Moriori, who had a tradition of resolving disputes peacefully, responded to the threat by holding a council meeting where it was decided to not fight back but to offer friendship and a sharing of resources.

The Maori did not have this tradition and responded instead with the systematic slaughter of the Moriori men, women, and children. A Maori warrior reported, "We took possession … in accordance with our custom and we caught all the people. Not one escaped. Some ran away from us, these we killed, and others we killed—but what of that? It was in accordance with our custom" (as cited in Diamond, 1999, p. 54).

The Moriori had simple technology, were inexperienced at war, and were lacking in strong leadership and organization, while the Maori invaders had war experience, advanced weapons, and operated under strong centralized leadership. None are surprised by the resulting carnage. Strong, forceful leadership seems to result in the conquest of the weak. This is simply the way of the world, or at least how the world normally operates. The image of Cain and Abel is stamped on the world and the victors record the history.

Today, in the Field Museum in Chicago a huge display, occupying multiple rooms, tells the story of the Maori people. You can walk into one of their religious meeting houses complete with carvings of their gods. You can see evidence of their culture and daily life. You can even visit a current website www.maori.org.nz to learn about Maori culture including an array of carved bone jewelry and a book on selecting Maori names for your baby.

Nothing, however, remains of the peace-loving Moriori. This story of domination and conquest has been repeated over and over through history confirming a belief that strong powerful leadership always wins over a peaceful, collaborative approach. Force and dominance seem to be critical elements to secure a successful society, but, as we will see, this is not the only way leadership was practiced through history.

Leadership in Chiefdoms and Emerging Nations

As society developed, multiple tribes combined into chiefdoms where a centralized authority resided in a single position of the chief. This began the tradition of awarding positional leadership roles to the sons (and occasionally daughters) of the chief and leadership position by heredity finds its way into our leadership story. As nation-states developed in the agrarian era we see the emergence of all-powerful kings who wield complete authority over their subjects.

An ancient, biblical story from I Samuel 8 (New International Version) tells how the leader Samuel and his God reacted when the people of Israel first sought a king and the implications of all-powerful positional leadership was addressed. We find here a story of a people in transition from a collection of tribes to a nation led by a king. It was not an easy transition. It seems that the people were not satisfied with their tribal ways and demanded that Samuel, their current leader, give them a king to rule over them. This upset Samuel greatly who immediately took the request to God. God was also displeased because he saw behind the request the self-ish motivation of the people and the harm this would ultimately bring to them. The people had two main reasons for wanting a king. First, they wanted to be like the other nations who had a king to rule over them. It seems that the desire to be like others is a powerful and ancient motiva-tion that remains strong to this day.

The people also wanted a king who would go out before them and fight their battles for them. Do you see the problem? The people wanted someone to lead so that they did not have to. They desired only to be contented followers who allowed an Atlas-like heroic leader to lift and carry the world on their behalf. I suspect they also wanted to be able to cast blame on the king once he failed in battle or was unsuccessful in leadership. All leaders today can identify with this irksome practice of being praised one day and then attacked the next.

God gave Samuel a message to deliver to the people. He told Samuel, "Now listen to them; but warn them solemnly and let them know what the king who will reign over them will do." God warned that a king

> will take your sons and make them serve with his chariots and horses … some he will assign to be commanders of thousands … and others to plow his ground and reap his harvest, and others still to make weapons of war … He will take your daughters to be perfumers and cooks and bakers. He will take the best of your fields and vineyards … he will take a tenth of your grain and of your vintage … Your men-servants and maidservants and the best of your cattle and donkeys he will take for his own use … and you yourselves will become his slaves. (I Samuel 8:11–17)

As if this was not warning enough, God then delivers the climax, "when that day comes, you will cry out for relief from the king you have chosen, and the Lord will not answer you in that day" (I Samuel 8:18). So there it is. The king, who by positional right has total and unequivocal power over each and every person in the kingdom, *will* abuse that power and ultimately enslave the people until they cry out for relief. The warning is clear.

If you had heard this message would it have caused concern? Would you have paused to reconsider if only for a moment? Instead of rethinking their request, the people refused to listen to Samuel but shouted "No! … we want a king over us, then we will be like all the other nations, with a king to lead us and to go out before us and fight our battles" (I Samuel 8:19–20). After hearing the people's response, God agreed to give them what they demanded—an all-powerful king to rule over them. He replied simply and directly, "listen to them and give them a king" (I Samuel 8:22). One must be careful in demanding something too strongly. You may actually have to live with the very thing you desire the most.

So, the people got their king. Saul was the obvious choice. He stood a head taller than anyone else in the kingdom. He was attractive and imposing, the clear choice for a new leader of the people. There was some concern, however, when on the day of his coronation he did not show up at the agreed-upon time. After a brief hunt they found him hiding in the baggage before bringing him forth to hail him as their new king. Admittedly, this was a bit of an embarrassing start but Saul recovered quickly and was able to begin his reign with some success. He used his strength and imposing physical presence to bully people into action. Once he called the nation to war by chopping up a pair of oxen and sending the bloody parts to each of the twelve tribes, declaring that "this is what will be done to the oxen of anyone who does not follow Saul and Samuel" (I Samuel 11:7). The people got the message loud and clear and promptly showed up for battle as required. Make no mistake, autocratic leadership works, force does create movement even if the movement goes firmly in the wrong direction.

King Saul possessed an external strength not matched by an inner strength of character and commitment. Saul, deep inside, was a broken self-absorbed man who eventually succumbed to the awesome stress of the leadership role. Leadership, for Saul, became a focus on self-protection and the elimination of any sign of resistance from others. He practiced deceit, to others first and then to himself. He rationalized his actions and blamed others for the decisions he was afraid to make. He bent his will to that of the people and abdicated his responsibility to lead. Saul became an autocratic, self-focused leader and ultimately failed as king. In his final years he was paranoid and obsessed with the threat to his kingdom represented by David whom Samuel had already, in secret, anointed to replace Saul as king.

Samuel entered Jesse's home covertly and under pretense. No one could know of his true mission. If Saul were to hear of it, Samuel certainly would be killed. Samuel had been sent to anoint the new king and God told him that this new king would be Jesse's son from the tribe of Judah. Jesse had his boys brought in for review. Samuel looked at the oldest son, Eliab, and thought, certainly this is the one I am to anoint as king. Eliab was the oldest in a culture that placed the highest value on the firstborn son. He was tall and strong with physical traits that others look up to. Samuel moved to anoint Eliab, but God stayed his hand. What's this? This is not the one? God challenged Samuel's leadership values when he told him, "do not consider his appearance or his height ... the Lord does not look at the things man looks at. Man looks at the outward appearance, but the Lord looks at the heart" (I Samuel 16:7). Samuel, now quite confused, looks to Abinadab, the next eldest son. No, he is not to be the one either. He continues on through each of the seven sons and none of them are chosen. Samuel is at a total loss. The king is to be the son of Jesse and yet all of the sons are rejected? There seems to be only one possibility. Jesse, do you have another son? Oh yes, Jesse replies without hesitation: David, *the youngest*, is out tending the sheep. Isn't it incredible that at a time such as this when one of your sons is to be anointed king, you do not call in your youngest son? This gives us a clue as to the powerful cultural bias against the youngest in the family. David was not even considered worthy to be called to the meeting. He is relegated to the low-level task of tending the family sheep.

Samuel asks for David to be summoned. Jesse now is the one confused. This is not going as anticipated. He sends a servant to call David in from the field. When David enters, God says, "rise and anoint him; he is the one" (I Samuel 16:12). David, the youngest ... the least preferred in this tribal culture will be the next king of the nation. Samuel in front of the skeptical watching eyes of Jesse and his sons anoints David the next king of Israel. Later David, from the perspective of his throne, expressed his humble wonder and gratitude to God in one of his poems, stating, "who am I … that you have brought me this far" (I Samuel 7:18)?

David, you see, was a different kind of king. While Saul focused on self, David focused on doing what was right for the people he was called to serve. David possessed a humility unique in the leadership position of an all-powerful king. He knew where he came from, he knew who he was, and he knew that leadership was not a divine right to serve self, but a responsibility to serve others. David, as those who know the larger story, was far from perfect. In critical ways he failed but he ruled with a different mindset. He held the position of king with absolute authority but ruled with the heart and mind of a servant and he stands even today as the greatest king ever to sit on the throne of the nation of Israel.

The Leadership Choice

Rehoboam had a choice to make, a leadership choice. He was the grandson of King David and had just inherited the throne upon the death of his father Solomon. On the first day of his reign Jeroboam with others arrived for an audience with the new king. They came to ask Rehoboam a question that all followers have; what kind of leader will he be? They had reason to be concerned as they reflected back on what it had been like under the powerful, sometimes abusive rule of David's son Solomon. Rehoboam's father had extended the kingdom out to its farthest reaches. His building programs had created a magnificent temple and his own glorious palace. The rule under Solomon had been a huge success as such things are normally measured. Dignitaries traveled large distances to consult this nation builder who was considered to be the wisest man in the entire world. However, there was a hidden aspect to the rule of Solomon that Jeroboam wanted to address. He spoke of the harsh labor and heavy yoke inflicted upon the people by Solomon. This massive kingdom had been built on the backs of the worker, the citizens of the realm. Solomon had fulfilled the warning given earlier by God that the king would take their sons and daughters, would take the first and the best of their crops, and would ultimately enslave them in order to fulfill his self-centered dreams of greatness.

Jeroboam and the people desired to know if Rehoboam would lighten the harshness and heaviness of the work. They wanted to know what kind of leader he would be. The new king felt the tension that all new leaders feel. He knew, instinctively, that this was a turning point and that his answer would have major ramifications for his leadership. So, he asked for three days before providing an answer. Rehoboam first went to the wise old sages of the kingdom, the men who had advised his father Solomon, and he asked them how he should answer this question about his leadership. The sages gave amazing and unexpected advice. It is incredible in light of the fact that they lived in a time of all-powerful kings, a time of conquest and kingdom building, a time when people were valued, or devalued, by their position in society, and the lowest position carried no value. However, within this context they responded, "if today you will be a servant to these people and serve them and give them a favorable answer, they will always be your servants" (I Kings 12:7). Rehoboam was stunned. What kind of advice is this to give a newly installed king? The king should *serve* the people? The king should give a *favorable* answer? It seemed a foolish notion at best and Rehoboam would have none of it. He rejected the advice and consulted the young companions he had grown up with. His contemporaries offered opposing advice. They told Rehoboam to be clear with the people that he was now the king—the King! Say to them, they instructed, "My little finger is thicker than my father's waist. My father laid on you a heavy yoke; I will make it even heavier. My father scourged you with whips; I will scourge you with scorpions" (I Kings 12:11).

Rehoboam is now faced with a choice, a choice as to what kind of leader he will be. This leadership choice will determine if he will be a leader that uses his awesome power *over* people to force them to do what he desires, or if he will be a leader that serves the good of the people over his own self-interest. This is the leadership choice faced by every leader of every age since the beginning of time. Will I be a self-focused leader or an other-focused leader? Will I be an autocratic or a servant leader?

The three-day period came to an end and Rehoboam presented his decision to the people. His choice is obvious and clear. He used the strong words provided by his youthful advisors; as to the heavy yoke, I will make it heavier; as to the harsh labor, I will scourge you with scorpions. At this point of the story, none of us are surprised by the choice Rehoboam has made. In fact, we are somewhat shocked at the advice given by the elders to listen to and serve the people. Throughout time leaders have opted for power over serving since this appears as the only path to expansion, conquest, and ultimate success. However, there is a cost and Rehoboam will pay that cost sooner than anyone realizes.

When the people heard the answer of their new king, and realized that he refused to listen to them, they made a declaration to no longer serve the king. It is important to note that even an all-powerful king cannot force obedience from his people. Followers may choose to comply over a period of time but ultimately decide if they will serve their leader. Rehoboam found this out the hard way. When he sent out the heavy-handed Adoniram, his general in charge of forced labor, the people promptly stoned him to death and Rehoboam himself barely escaped with his life. After that time ten of the twelve tribes of Israel broke off to form the Northern Kingdom with Jeroboam as their king while Rehoboam was left to lead the remaining two tribes.

This leadership choice remains as king after king, leader after leader decides whether to use their power and authority *over* people or to use it to serve the needs of those they lead. The leadership choice is presented to each of us today. We confront it when we first take leadership action, when we first accept a leadership position, and we also make this choice each and every day we lead thereafter. We then endure, and our followers endure, the consequences of our choice.

Leadership in the Nation/States (Agrarian Era)

Plato lived from 427 to around 347 BC in Athens, Greece. In *The Republic* he presents his view that the best leader of the state is the philosopher king. He quotes Socrates, "inasmuch as philosophers only are able to grasp the eternal and unchangeable, and those who wander in the region of the many and variable are not philosophers, I must ask you which of the two classes should be the rulers of our State" (2005, p. 459)? We probably have a pretty good idea who he referring to by "those who wander in the region of the many and variable." He is referring to the regular people, the citizenry, actually, most of us. The common people are not, in Plato's view, born to lead, but to follow. Plato believed that the true philosopher would be characterized by the following traits: They know the very truth of each thing. They love knowledge, truth, wisdom, learning, and all true being. They are temperate, not cowardly, but just and gentle. They have a good memory. They are noble, gracious, just, courageous, and the friend of truth. Socrates declared that to these philosophers only will you entrust the State. The assumption here is that the philosopher may possess or develop these positive traits while the common people may only possess opposite unacceptable traits. Only the former can be trained to be a philosopher, and only the philosopher can be a king.

Plato recommended a lifelong training program for developing philosopher kings. His program begins by teaching realities, through various types of mathematics. He then proceeds to the dialogue stage where the king in training learns philosophy proper. This stage takes the student to about the age of 35. Plato then recommends a practical experience training stage where the student takes on, for about 15 years, a positional leadership office. The student has moved from the real (mathematics) to the metaphysical (philosophy) to the practical (leadership office), and finally to what Plato (2005) calls the *Good* from which the student draws from the source of all light to order both their individual lives and the lives of the group they lead. They should be ready for this, Plato believed, around the age of 50. Plato's view of leadership by the elite, the philosopher king, was really a belief in the rule of aristocracy, the belief that some are born into a leading class and others are not. Of course, even these elite must be developed as philosophers, but they possess, Plato believed, the raw material to be trained. Others do not have what it takes to lead. This distinct separation between the leader and the led seemed as natural to Plato as the cycle of the sun. The fact that we are still debating whether leaders are born or made suggests that we still are fascinated with the topic. The philosopher king is a compelling concept. Plato certainly would have spoken out against the autocratic or despotic ruler due to the lack of virtue implicit in that mindset. The philosopher king is closer to a paternalistic mindset where the mature enlightened father figure provides and protects the children he leads.

During this same general time of history, beginning in the fourth century BC, a collection of writings emerged in China called the *Tao Te Ching* attributed to the authorship of Lao-tzu. In these writings we find again the thread of the servant-oriented leader who places the good of the led over their own self-interest. Consider these select quotes from LaFargue's 1992 translation of Lao-Tzu's *Tao Te Ching*.

> The Wise Man chooses to be last
> And so becomes the first of all;
> Denying self, he too is saved.
> For, does he not fulfillment find
> In being an unselfish man? (p. 59)

> On tiptoe your stance is unsteady;
> Long strides make your progress unsure;
> Show off and you get no attention;
> Your boasting will mean you have failed;
> Asserting yourself brings no credit;
> Be proud and you never will lead. (p. 76)

> It is wisdom to know others;
> It is enlightenment to know one's self.

> The conqueror of men is powerful;
> The master of himself is strong.

> It is wealth to be content;
> It is willful to force one's way on others. (p. 86)

> Nothing is weaker than water,
> But when it attacks something hard
> Or resistant, then nothing withstands it,
> And nothing will alter its way.

> Everyone knows this, that weakness prevails
> Over strength and that gentleness conquers
> The adamant hindrance of men, but that
> Nobody demonstrates how it is so.

Because of this the Wise Man says
That only one who bears the nation's shame
Is fit to be its hallowed lord;
That only one who takes upon himself
The evils of the world may be its king.

This is paradox. (p. 131)

The *Tao Te Ching* presents a paradox of a leader who suffers, who displays strength through weakness, who chooses to be last and through that stands first, who unselfishly serves others and finds that the natural pride accompanying leadership may disqualify one from leading. This is a leadership of paradox, seemingly contradictory truths coming together to reveal a new and stronger truth. When leaders choose against the use of force to lead others, they must choose a different type of power to move the world. The *Tao Te Ching* speaks of this different kind of power; a power the logical mind of the present finds difficult to accept, but a power, like water, that over time, even the hardest stone cannot resist.

Before we move further in our story, let's stop for a moment to review what we have seen so far. We have seen leadership that puts the needs of the leader above all else, an autocratic form of leading. We have seen the abuse and oppression this kind of leadership inevitably brings. We have also seen the desire to have a more virtuous and wise philosopher king who cares for people like a father nurtures his children. One is an all-powerful leadership of coercion and force while the other is an authoritative parental expression of leadership. However, there is a third view, one of the leader as servant to the led. Within this third view leaders use their strength to empower followers while choosing to relate to them as partners. Each of these three mindset threads weaves through the story and history of leadership providing a choice for the leader as to how he or she will choose to lead.

Now as we move forward in the historical calendar from BC to AD, we come across a leader of a different sort. When Jesus was born in Nazareth he came from the class of "those who wander in the region of the many and variable" to use Plato's words. He came from a small insignificant town, from a region geopolitically positioned to draw no one's attention. He worked as a carpenter for many years until he moved into the public arena in the role of an itinerant teacher. His message was one of sedition, if you happened to be a ruler of the day, or one of freedom and love, if you happened to be from his own class. Interestingly enough, though he did not hold a position of authority or amass a great following during his lifetime, he spoke openly and eloquently about leadership. When a group of his followers were arguing about the positions of influence each of them felt they deserved, Jesus stood their view of leadership on its head with this famous statement. "Jesus called them together and said, 'You know that the rulers of the Gentiles lord it over them, and their high officials exercise authority over them. Not so with you. Instead, whoever wants to become great among you must be your servant'" (Matthew 20:25–26).

Not so with you. It is a clear and unequivocal statement. If you choose to lead, according to Jesus, you must serve. A more radical or subversive statement could not be made about leadership within a culture that valued position, prestige, and power. A more dangerous statement could not be made to an oppressed people who longed to be free from the strong arm of the Roman Empire. Jesus was a different kind of leader who used a different kind of power to lead. He refused to be seen as a king though the people wanted to force it on him. He walked away from those who wanted to place him on a leadership pedestal. He taught, he healed, he railed at leaders who used their position to serve themselves at the expense of the people. He avoided the trappings of religion while reaching deeply into the hearts of people. He told his followers, in no uncertain terms, that they are to lead as servants. One would find this mere pious language except that Jesus took this message to his death. He was killed by those he sought to serve.

After the time of Jesus, century after century followed with little indication that his message on leadership was heeded by the world or by his own followers. Whether in government, business, or religion the idea that leaders would voluntarily serve when they have the power to do otherwise was just too hard to accept. The idea of leader as servant is counterintuitive, as are most ideas ultimately found useful, leading to this mindset being largely ignored in centuries to come. Instead, a more prevailing mindset of leadership would be expressed by a politician and political consultant from Florence in the fifteenth century.

Machiavelli was not hesitant about challenging the role of virtue in leadership, nor could he be accused of promoting a servant view of leadership. He served as an advisor to the Medici family, who held power at the time in the city-state of Florence, and his famous work, *The Prince*, provided advice on leadership for political leaders in difficult and threatening times. He was above all else a pragmatist. He separated leadership from the bounds of ethics and virtue and presented it as a set of practical strategies for gaining and maintaining power. His motto could have been—do whatever it takes. Here is a brief collection of quotes from *The Prince* (2005).

> The nature of the people is variable, and whilst it is easy to persuade them, it is difficult to fix them in that persuasion. And thus it is necessary to take such measures that, when they believe no longer, it may be possible to make them believe by force. (p. 39)

> Upon this a question arises: whether it be better to be loved than feared or feared than loved? It may be answered that one should wish to be both, but, because it is difficult to unite them in one person, is much safer to be feared than loved, when, of the two, either must be dispensed with. (p. 88)

> Therefore it is unnecessary for a prince to have all the good qualities I have enumerated, but it is very necessary to appear to have them. And I shall dare to say this also, that to have them and always to observe them is injurious, and that to appear to have them is useful; to appear merciful, faithful, humane, religious, upright, and to be so, but with a mind so framed that should you require not to be so. (p. 92)

> But it is necessary to know well how to disguise this characteristic, and to be a great pretender and dissembler; and men are so simple, and so subject to present necessities, that he who seeks to deceive will always find someone who will allow himself to be deceived. (p. 92)

> A wise prince ought to adopt such a course that his citizens will always in every sort and kind of circumstance have need of the state and of him, and then he will always find them faithful. (p. 58)

This short collection of advice from Machiavelli presents a view of leadership that has been attractive to leaders at every stage of history.

Machiavelli suggests that the leader will lead by use of force. It is better to be feared than loved since it is very unlikely that the leader can be both. It is unnecessary for the leader to actually possess virtues and good qualities; they must only *appear* to possess them. This deception is not difficult to pull off since people as a whole are easy to deceive. Ultimately, the wise leader will create situations where the people need him as their leader and must therefore remain faithful to him. If this brief summary sounds like some old-fashioned advice unworthy of our more enlightened time, consider the best-selling book *The 48 Laws of Power* (Greene, 1998) that brings us advice as offered by "Law 2—*Never Put Too Much Trust In Friends, Learn How To Use Enemies,* ... Law 7—*Get Others To Do The Work For You, But Always Take The Credit* ... Law 11—*Learn to Keep People Dependent on You*" (p. *ix–x).* Yes, Machiavelli is still influencing leaders today and his concept of the strong autocratic or negative paternalistic leader is still a dominant practice in leadership today.

Leadership in the Nation/States (Industrial Era) in the Twentieth Century

As nations entered the Industrial Era, leadership mostly adopted forms of autocratic dictatorship or the paternalistic leadership of elected politicians. Military leaders emphasized a clear hierarchical rule that placed all authority at the top of the pyramid and then dispensed power down through the ranks. At the same time, organizations were emerging as larger and more impersonal institutions. Workers in organizations were often treated like animals as vividly described in Upton Sinclair's 1930s novel, *The Jungle.* In this novel the worker is accurately and graphically portrayed as unvalued and uneducated and therefore expendable and placed in dangerous and abusive situations. It was out of this systematic abuse of the worker that the labor movement began and unions were instituted to create resistance to the ultimate control of oppressive management. Management had such a hold on workers that they controlled every aspect of their lives as workers literally owed their soul to the company store and were treated as mere property. From the temple of Solomon to the pyramids of Egypt to the meatpacking plants of Chicago, the worker has been considered an expendable commodity due to their desperate need for employment to provide for their families with so few work options to consider. Sinclair (2005) shares about the subhuman conditions that workers were subjected to in the Chicago meatpacking plants.

> Here was a population, low-class and mostly foreign, hanging always on the verge of starvation, and dependent for its opportunities of life upon the whim of men every bit as brutal and unscrupulous as the old-time slave drivers; under such circumstances immorality was exactly as inevitable, and as prevalent, as it was under the system of chattel slavery. Things that were quite unspeakable went on there in the packing houses all the time, and were taken for granted by everybody; only they did not show, as in the old slavery times, because there was no difference in color between master and slave. (pp. 122–123)

Leadership has been feared, respected, imitated, and resisted by those who follow. Leaders have great power to heal or to harm. The led have an incredible potential that under an autocratic rule is lost forever and under a paternalistic rule is limited and left undeveloped. The work can be accomplished, of course, but at such a cost and the cost is not just to the abused worker. The organization and the leader are lessened through the process and the ultimate goal of moving the world in a positive direction is severely diminished.

Our story now takes us into the twentieth century, a time when leadership studies developed into a singular discipline struggling to find its voice. The study of management and administration at the turn of the twentieth century came out of a need for greater productivity as organizations grew complex and industry grew larger and more influential. Burns (1978) refers to leadership as "one of the most observed and the least understood phenomena on earth" (p. 2). The observation of leadership was to increase in the decades to come. The 1900s saw leadership subjected to the rigors of research, organizational analysis, and a strong debate over how it should be defined. During the first part of the century leadership took a back seat as the focus of study and writing was on the concept of management. Within this unfolding leadership story, we see that this recent century resulted in an unprecedented advance in the formal study of both management and leadership.

The predominate approach to studying leadership in the first half of the twentieth century was the Trait Approach which held that leaders could be identified by their unique qualities and characteristics which distinguished them from non-leaders. Stogdill (1974) conducted an analysis of 124 studies completed between 1904 and 1947 and then followed up with a second review of 163 studies completed between 1948 and 1970. His conclusion from these trait-focused studies was that there was no common set of traits that could distinguish someone as a leader. Leaders, it seems, come in all shapes, sizes, personalities, and characteristics. Certainly, all leaders possess some level of "intelligence, self-confidence, determination, integrity and sociability" (Northouse, 2016, p. 23) and certain traits are desirable in leaders, but the possession of select traits is not what makes someone a leader.

At the beginning of the 1900s Frederick Taylor (1911) began to study how to use people to accomplish more in tasks of production. This was the first time that the management of work was studied in a scientific way and the development of the field of scientific management began. Taylor searched for ways to break down each task into its component parts to determine how these tasks, and the people who performed them, could be managed more efficiently. Worker productivity was timed and new ways determined to increase productivity for the good of the job at hand. "The goals of management during these times included standardizing human behavior and minimizing variance in human work. It was, in Gareth Morgan's term, the 'machine company'" (Clawson, 2003, p. 13). One can certainly see how this view of workers as machines brings an improvement over viewing them as mere animals. Workers and their tasks were subjected to time and motion studies designed to improve performance and productivity. No one cared what workers felt or thought but only what they could accomplish. Bringing the production machine to optimal efficiency was the goal—to find the best way to do a particular job, to find the best person to do the job, to provide precise training and procedures to do the job better, and to always make the worker and job outcomes more efficient. However, as we know, people are not machines. As Henry Ford spoke about the workers in his plant, he just wanted to hire a pair of hands, but workers kept showing up with bodies and heads attached. People are so much more than machines or tools. This reality was discovered through a scientific management study conducted in the late 1920s at the Hawthorne plant of the Western Electric Company.

The Hawthorne Studies were designed by Elton Mayo and Fritz Roethlisberger to determine the impact of different environmental factors on worker performance (Hughes, Ginnett, & Curphy, 2006). With workers, men and women, lined up in large workrooms, the experimenters increased the lighting in the room and noted that productivity went up. They then decreased the light, and noted that again productivity went up. As other environmental factors were introduced, invariably the productivity of the workers increased. What was going on? The researchers determined, after multiple experiments in different settings, that the effect on increased productivity was not the environmental changes, but a result of the social factors involved. Workers, being the focus of the studies, were paid attention to, offered the opportunity to share opinions, and provided group work activities. Workers responded positively to being treated as human beings, as people with needs beyond physiological or safety considerations. Workers were people with social needs, self-esteem needs, and self-fulfillment needs, needs often neglected in the workplace. Following the Hawthorne Studies, the 1930s, 1940s, and 1950s saw growth in the human relations approach to managing workers. Researchers continued to explore human dynamics related to motivation, group dynamics, and organizational change.

In the late 1940s and the 1950s a series of studies was conducted at the Ohio State and the University of Michigan seeking to identify the behaviors of leaders. These studies led to the development of the Behavioral Approach to leadership which argues that there are two categories of behavior that all leaders must engage in: task behaviors (a concern for results) and relational behaviors (a concern for people). This research focus on leader's behaviors was an attempt to move beyond the limitations of the Trait Approach with its focus on the characteristics of the leader. Under this new approach, leadership was about what leaders do or how they behave. In the early 1960s Blake and Mouton created their Managerial Grid which provided a separate axis for task-oriented behaviors and relational-oriented behaviors, creating a set of different management behaviors resulting from a varied combination of these two behaviors. An interesting side note is that the name of the Managerial Grid was, in later years, changed to the Leadership Grid without altering any aspects of the model. This change of title represents the emergence of leadership and a persistent confusion about the meaning of the terms leadership and management.

In 1960, Douglas McGregor published *The Human Side of Enterprise* which presented two distinct ways that leaders view workers. McGregor's concept of Theory X, Theory Y made a powerful case for identifying the assumptions that managers carry, unknowingly, about their workers. The Theory X part of the approach contained a collection of assumptions that viewed workers as basically lazy, unmotivated, and resistant to take on responsibility. McGregor stated these Theory X assumptions as:

1. The average human being has an inherent dislike of work and will avoid it if he can.
2. Because of this human characteristic of dislike of work, most people must be coerced, controlled, directed, and threatened with punishment to get them to put forth adequate effort toward the achievement of organizational objectives.
3. The average human being prefers to be directed, wishes to avoid responsibility, has relatively little ambition, and wants security above all (p. 33–34).

When these Theory X assumptions drive our leadership behavior (and assumptions *do* drive behavior) then our leadership will become directive, controlling, and coercive. Since our assumptions often go unidentified and therefore unchallenged, McGregor called out these assumptions and proposed a new set of beliefs about workers to lead to a different set of leadership behaviors. He stated the Theory Y assumptions as:

1. The expenditure of physical and mental effort in work is as natural as play or rest.
2. External control and the threat of punishment are not the only means for bringing about effort toward organizational objectives. Man will exercise self-direction and self-control in the service of objectives to which he is committed.
3. Commitment to objectives is a function of the rewards associated with their achievement.
4. The average human being learns, under proper conditions, not only to accept but to seek responsibility.
5. The capacity to exercise a relatively high degree of imagination, ingenuity, and creativity in the solution of organizational problems is widely, not narrowly, distributed in the population.
6. Under the conditions of modern industrial life, the intellectual potentialities of the average human being are only partially utilized (p. 47).

Theory Y provides assumptions that view the worker as capable, motivated, and open to taking on responsibility leading to a different set of leadership behaviors that provide for empowerment, trust, open communication, and shared leadership. A unique power in McGregor's approach is that we as leaders can change the culture of our organizations and the performance level of workers by changing our underlying assumptions or beliefs about our followers. This reinforces the critical place of mindset in leadership.

In the late 1960s, Hersey and Blanchard borrowed the double-axis model from Blake and Mouton and superimposed concepts of management styles related to worker development levels. This new Situational Leadership approach introduced four distinct management styles (directing, coaching, supporting, and delegating) with the proscription that managers should be flexible enough to use any of the four styles to address the unique developmental needs of their workers. The development level of a worker is determined by their competence level for particular tasks along with their commitment level to the tasks and the job. Another interesting side note is that the original title of Situational Management gave way to a new title of Situational Leadership, continuing to confuse the two terms of leadership and management. This Situational Leadership approach, joined with Fred

Fiedler's Contingency Leadership approach and Robert House's Path-Goal Leadership approach, represents a set of contingency theories that looks at leader behaviors (styles) applied contingently based on situational variables such as follower and task characteristics. Leadership theories continued to develop in complexity and though the understanding of various aspects of leadership increased, the practical application of these approaches became more and more difficult to apply in real organizational settings.

In 1970, Robert Greenleaf published his seminal essay *The Servant as Leader* and the term servant leadership entered the modern leadership lexicon. Combining the terms servant and leader created a paradox and provocative tension that is being debated to the current day. Greenleaf believed that

> The servant-leader is servant first … It begins with the natural feeling that one wants to serve, to serve first. Then conscious choice brings one to aspire to lead. That person is sharply different from one who is leader first, perhaps because of the need to assuage an unusual power drive or to acquire material possessions … the leader-first and the servant-first are two extreme types. Between them there are shadings and blends that are part of the infinite variety of human nature. (1977, p. 13)

Servant leaders focus on the followers and promote their well-being and development. Servant leaders understand power to be a force to be used by the leader to grow the followers and through this empowerment to benefit the organization. Greenleaf brought a more philosophical approach to leadership studies, as compared to a scientific approach, but did so in a way that created a new conversation about the role of the leader, the view of the leader toward followers, and the overall purpose of leadership. The closest Greenleaf came to defining his concept, though it is not technically a definition, is his best test for servant leadership.

> The difference manifests itself in the care taken by the servant-first to make sure that other people's highest priority needs are being served. The best test, and difficult to administer, is: Do those served grow as persons? Do they, while being served, become healthier, wiser, freer, more autonomous, more likely themselves to become servants? And, what is the effect on the least privileged in society? Will they benefit or at least not be further deprived? (1977, pp. 13–14)

Later in the 1970s two significant approaches were added to the ongoing story of the development of leadership thought. First, the Leader Member Exchange (LMX) approach introduced a focus on the quality of the relationship between individual leaders and followers suggesting that the higher the quality of that relationship, based on mutual trust, respect, and obligation, the higher the productivity impact of the worker. The theory first posited that low-quality relationships led to out-group workers while higher quality relationships led to in-group workers. In-group workers were highly motivated, performed at higher levels, and were deeply committed to the organization and its goals. Out-group workers, in contrast, were more self-oriented, less motivated, and less committed to the leader and the organization. Later versions of the approach called for leader-making approaches to seek to bring everyone from the out-group into the in-group.

In 1978, James MacGregor Burns presented a Transformational Leadership approach which he describes as occurring "when one or more persons engage with others in such a way that leaders and followers raise one another to higher levels of motivation and morality" (p. 20). In Transformational Leadership, as in Servant Leadership, an ethical dimension is central to the approach. True leadership is moral and ethical and raises up people to achieve beyond normal expectations. Burns presented this approach in contrast to a transactional approach to leadership which views the leader-follower relationship as a mere set of transactions (i.e. pay for work) that ultimately creates benefit for the organization. While transactional leadership results in expected returns, Transformational Leadership unleashes the potential of both leader and follower to realize dynamic change and optimal organizational success. Bass (2014) later conceptualized Transformational Leadership into the four constructs of idealized influence, inspirational motivation, intellectual stimulation, and individualized consideration providing a way to operationalize and ultimately measure the concept. Subsets of the Transformational Leadership approach (Charismatic Leadership, Visionary Leadership) continue to be studied and expanded.

In the 1990s, Ron Heifetz (1994) presented Adaptive Leadership as an approach designed to help both leaders and followers adapt to problems and realities within changing environments. Leaders, within this approach, are expected to prepare their followers to learn adaptive behaviors to deal with complex issues that cannot be solved by a leader's decisions but must be addressed by both leaders and followers to come up with adaptive solutions.

Before leaving the twentieth century we should note that the story of leadership throughout the 1900s brought us leaders like Adolph Hitler and Mahatma Gandhi, Idi Amin and Mother Teresa, the autocratic leadership of Al Dunlap at Sunbeam and the paternalistic leadership of Jack Welch at General Electric. We also experienced the servant leadership of Jack Lowe, Jr., at TD Industries, Herb Kelleher and Colleen Barrett at Southwest Airlines, and Bill Turner at Synovus. The threads of all three leadership mindsets continue to weave through the ongoing leadership story and it is up to each of us to determine which mindset we will choose and which mindset will prevail in the twenty-first century.

Leadership for the Twenty-First Century: Making the Distinctions Clear

Leadership is continuing to develop and clarify its own voice. Leadership is not management or a subset of management. Unfortunately, many of the management texts being used in Management or MBA courses today still present leadership as one of the four aspects of management, along with planning, organizing, and controlling. This four-part model is a modern adaptation of Henri Fayol's well-known typology of management developed at the same time Frederick Taylor was doing his work at the beginning of the twentieth century. Fayol, a French engineer, saw management as "planning, organizing, commanding, coordinating and controlling" (as cited in Robbins & Coulter, 2002, p. 7). Current management writers have simplified the list and removed the offensive "commanding" term and substituted leadership. The positive side of this is that it allows management students to have a brief introduction to leadership theory, but unfortunately it encourages the ongoing confusion as to the real distinction between management and leadership. Leadership and management, leading and managing, are distinct concepts that need to be understood, studied, and taught as distinct.

Rost (1993) spoke to this when he challenged the prevailing "industrial" view of leadership. He states, "Leadership as good management is what the twentieth-century school of leadership is all about. Leadership is good management is the twentieth century's paradigm of leadership" (p. 94). Rost clearly saw the confusion between the terms of leading and managing and recognized that when leadership authors defined leadership they did so within a management mindset. They were often studying positional managers who were the top administrators of organizations. Those that exhibited the positive traits of good communication, positive relational skills, or innovative organizational design were seen as leaders (i.e. good managers) while those without these positive traits were seen as mere managers. This error led to the common practice of leadership writers presenting management in negative terms and leadership in positive terms, a practice that muddies the definitional waters even more. Rost proposed a post-industrial model of leadership for the twenty-first century, a leadership that was clearly distinguished from management, a leadership that focused on creating change, a leadership that required a different set of assumptions for study and practice.

As the voice of leadership continues to speak more clearly it is a voice that speaks of the future more than the past, a voice that is active not passive, a voice that is able to move others into the leadership process, and a voice that creates the change that it envisions. It is critical that we continue to clarify and strengthen this voice. It is not an issue of making our organizations work more smoothly and efficiently (the work of management); the issue is one of creating positive and meaningful world change that gives our organizations a reason for existing at all.

Competing Perspectives: Existing Threads

The key themes of leadership have existed throughout history. The leadership mindset choice of autocratic, paternalistic, or servant has always existed. Leadership began with a paternalistic mindset within the family unit and then fell into an autocratic mindset as leaders gained greater and greater authority and power within complex societies culminating in the position of the all-powerful king. As we have seen, the servant mindset has also existed as a choice and has been modeled at key points in history to reveal the possibility of this different way of leading. These three distinct mindsets of leadership are woven as threads throughout the leadership story and represent distinct ways that leadership can be understood and practiced today.

The traditional view, the one shared in most management and leadership texts, is that leadership before 1900 was consistently authoritative and militaristic. This single-thread view coupled with the idea that leadership thinking has grown ever more enlightened since 1900 perpetuates a false narrative. Leadership education has fallen into the practice of showing leadership thinking through the last century in clear, distinct stages that are shown to represent uniform and separate themes. In this view, leadership understanding moved in and then out of the various stages of thought (Great Man, Trait theory, Group process, Behavior theories, Contingency theories, Transformational/Excellence theories) in a manner that discredited the previous stage to make room for the more enlightened stage to come. If we continue to operate within this traditional view, we will not learn anything from history except to reject it which puts us at the real risk of repeating the parts of history we choose to ignore.

The competing perspectives of the traditional view and the view presented in this text is that the three main leadership paradigms have always existed throughout history and need to be seriously considered, studied further, and presented to students of leadership.

A Cautionary Tale

Our leadership story has taken us from the first family to the state of leadership studies in the twenty-first century. We have seen the horror and abuse of the autocratic view of leadership. We have seen the paternalistic paradigm of the patriarch and the philosopher king that views the led as children who need to be cared for and corrected. We have also seen a servant approach that goes against the grain yet emerges to create powerful societal, community, and organizational change.

Before we conclude our leadership story, let's stop and reflect upon the role that we play in this continuing story. Throughout history some chose to act; they step into the arena of leading to see a personal and then a shared vision realized. Their leading has a powerful effect. It always does. Many lead to bring honor to themselves and we all must admit that this motivation for pursuing leadership is as strong and compelling today as it has been throughout history. This drive to promote self to the exploitation of others must be challenged and legitimate alternatives presented. Before moving on from our story, let's stop and consider the legacy of all-powerful leadership that leads for the good of self and ultimately misses the true purpose of leadership. Here the poet Percy Bysshe Shelley tells us of a great leader from the distant past whose desire for a powerful legacy did not turn out as he had envisioned.

Ozymandias

I met a traveler from an antique land
Who said: Two vast and trunkless legs of stone
Stand in the desert … Near them, on the sand,
Half sunk, a shattered visage lies, whose frown,
And wrinkled lip, and sneer of cold command,
Tell that its sculptor well those passions read
Which yet survive, stamped on these lifeless things,
The hand that mocked them, and the heart that fed:
And on the pedestal these words appear:
"My name is Ozymandias, king of kings:
Look on my works ye mighty and despair!"
Nothing beside remains. Round the decay
Of that colossal wreck, boundless and bare
The lone and level sands stretch far away.
(as cited in Rogers, 1968, p. 340)

Conclusion

Our leadership has the potential to create a legacy that is more than a broken lifeless statue on a faded pedestal. Instead, our leadership can truly serve to move the world in positive and needed ways not as leaders to be remembered, but to commit ourselves to make a lasting and meaningful difference in the world. One thing we see from our leadership story, especially from the last century, is an ongoing confusion around what leadership is and how it is to be defined. It is to this important task of clearly defining leadership that we now move our focus to consider the critical role of definition making and improve our understanding of leadership and clarity of leadership practice.

References

Bass, B. (2014). *Transformational leadership* (3rd ed.). New York, NY: Routledge.

Burns, J. M. (1978). *Leadership*. New York: Harper & Row.

Clawson, J. G. (2003). *Level three leadership: Getting below the surface* (2nd ed.). Upper Saddle River, NJ: Prentice Hall.

Diamond, J. (1999). *Guns, germs and steel: The fates of human societies*. New York: W.W. Norton & Company.

Greene, R. (1998). *The 48 laws of power*. New York, NY: Penguin Books.

Greenleaf, R. K. (1970). *The servant as leader*. Indianapolis: The Robert K. Greenleaf Center.

Greenleaf, R. K. (1977). *Servant leadership: A journey into the nature of legitimate power and greatness*. Mahwah, NJ: Paulist Press.

Hughes, R. L., Ginnett, R. D., & Curphy, G. J. (2006). *Leadership: Enhancing the lessons of experience* (5th ed.). Boston, MA: McGraw Hill.

Heifetz, R. A. (1994). *Leadership without easy answers*. Cambridge, MA: The Belknap Press of Harvard University Press.

LaFargue, M. (1992). *The Tao of the Tao Te Ching: A translation and commentary*. Albany, NY: State University of New York Press.

Machiavelli, N. (2005). *The prince*. San Diego, CA: Icon Group International.

McGregor, D. (1960). *The human side of enterprise*. New York: McGraw-Hill Book Company, Inc.

Northouse, P. G. (2016). *Leadership: Theory and practice* (7th ed.). Thousand Oaks, CA: Sage Publications.

Plato, & Icon Group International, I. (2005). *The republic*. San Diego, CA: Icon Group International, Inc.

Robbins, S. P., & Coulter, M. (2002). *Management* (7th ed.). Upper Saddle River, NJ: Prentice Hall.

Rogers, N. (Ed.). (1968). *Percy Bysshe Shelley selected poetry*. Boston, MA: Houghton Mifflin Company.

Rost, J. C. (1993). *Leadership for the twenty-first century*. London: Praeger.

Sinclair, U. (2005). *The jungle*. San Diego: Icon Group International, Inc.

Stogdill, R. M. (1974). *Handbook of leadership: A survey of theory and research*. New York, NY: Free Press.

Taylor, F. W. (1911). *The principles of scientific management*. New York, NY: Harper & Brothers Publishers.

Tolstoy, L. (1997). *Anna Karenina*. New York: Barnes and Noble Books.

3

Defining Leadership: The Critical Role of Definition Making

An oyster sits at the bottom of the bay and a small bit of sand or a wayward food particle works its way inside its bivalve shell. A distinct and growing irritation begins. The oyster then does something amazing to address this irritating intruder. It begins to secrete a combination of aragonite and conchiolin (forming nacre—the same substance that forms the outer shell) to wrap around the particle protecting the oyster from the discomfort. As this secretion continues to place layer upon layer around the particle a completely new object is formed—a pearl, an item of great beauty and value.

This kind of inspired annoyance can inform our entryway into leading. We see things that irritate us: a pothole in the middle of a road, a dangerous intersection crossed by children on the way to school, a child coming to our classroom hungry each morning, a law passed that discriminates against people who cannot speak up for themselves, a team immobilized without a clear vision to follow. Leaders are not satisfied, comfortable people. They have the will and ability to look beyond a focus on self to view a world in great need and they are willing to confront this need and act toward change.

How many people do this? How many naturally take the irritants of life and use inspired annoyance to produce something beautiful and

© The Author(s) 2018
J. Laub, *Leveraging the Power of Servant Leadership*, Palgrave Studies in Workplace Spirituality and Fulfillment, https://doi.org/10.1007/978-3-319-77143-4_3

valuable through leadership? How many people will respond with positive action to the challenges they face? Did you know that only 1 in 10,000 mollusks will produce a pearl in the wild? Most pearls, since the 1930s, have been grown and harvested through human assistance. To do this, an irritant is placed into the shell of the mollusk (the larger the irritant, the larger the pearl). The mollusk is returned to the water and the pearl then forms over a one- to three-year period. Every mollusk has the ability to produce a pearl, but not all will do so in the natural state. People, of course, are not mollusks but the metaphor may prove helpful. If we are looking for natural leaders to rescue us from the irritants of the world, we may only find them at the dismal rate of 1 to 10,000. Another compelling question might be, can non-natural leaders become leaders with the assistance of others? Yes, this is both possible and necessary. Some leaders seem to be born with a dynamic set of leadership traits that somehow fit their unique time and situation. However, if we wait for a modern-day Atlas to carry the problems of the world for us, we will never address the awesome opportunities and challenges of our world. The age-old leadership question has always been, are leaders born or made? The metaphor of the oyster and pearl may give us a different perspective on the answer. There may be some that are born as uniquely gifted, but these are too few to rely or wait on. We must encourage more people to escape the gray, lifeless world of non-leadership to engage the possibilities of world-moving leadership. However, when we enter into the field of leadership studies we find that it lacks a consistent process for defining what leadership is and how leadership is to be successfully displayed. The purpose of this chapter is to address this lack of clarity and propose a typology to assist us as serious students and practitioners of leadership to become successful definition makers.

Identifying the Problem

What is leadership? Some scholars do not believe that this question can be answered in a definitive way. They feel that the concept itself is, and will continue to remain, vague and undefined. However, it is the strong conviction of this author that it is critical as leadership writers, teachers, scholars, students, and practitioners to clearly define the concepts we use. It is not enough to suggest that leadership can be to each person whatever he or she determines it to be. Certainly we will not be able to come to agreement on leadership definitions that all will use. That is unlikely and unnecessary. However, each of us should do the hard work of defining our concepts and then committing to talk about leadership within this specific definitional framework so that we can be clearly understood. We should explain what we mean when we use various leadership terms, like leader, leadership, follower, or management, and we must then use these terms consistently to avoid undue confusion, and confusion certainly exists within the current discipline of leadership. Anyone who has looked into the ever-growing field of leadership studies is well aware of the confusion and lack of clear understanding on the key terms of our discipline. Yukl (2001) states,

> It is neither feasible nor desirable at this point in the development of the discipline to attempt to resolve the controversies over the appropriate definition of leadership. Like all constructs in social science, the definition of leadership is arbitrary and very subjective. (p. 6)

In contrast to this view, this author contends that we should develop a typology of leadership terms to provide clear guidelines while giving much needed direction for ongoing leadership studies. We should state what leadership is and make clear what leadership is not. We should seek more definitive statements about the terms we use when talking and writing about leadership.

The Importance of Definition Making and Precision

It is critical that we enter into the difficult task of definition making. This is a discipline that requires precision and a focus on clear essentials of the terms we seek to define. Rost (1993) spoke to this challenge when he addressed the overall study and discipline of leadership through his text, *Leadership for the Twenty-First Century*. Rost decried the lack of consistent, usable, and precise definitions of leadership terms by writers, practitioners, and scholars. He challenged the leadership academic world with his belief that "leadership studies as an academic discipline has a culture of definitional permissiveness and relativity … there are almost no arguments about definitions in the literature on leadership. There are almost no critiques of other scholars' definitions" (p. 6). To address this concern, Rost called for a new school of leadership, a group of scholars and practitioners who would intentionally work to challenge, define, and clarify concepts so that the discipline can move forward in a systematic manner.

Why are definitions of leadership and its subsets, like servant leadership, so essential? One reason is that if we don't define our terms clearly we end up with non-definitions posing as definitions. You see this frequently in both the popular and scholarly leadership literature. Maxwell (1998) states that "leadership is influence—nothing more, nothing less" (p. 17). This statement says something important and useful about leadership but is not a complete definition. Influence, to be sure, is involved in leadership, but there is more to leadership than this. Authors may claim that leadership is relationship or leadership is communicating effectively or leadership is vision casting. This kind of thinking, and writing, will not suffice for the kind of scholarly work required for ongoing leadership and servant leadership studies. When we play loose with words it is easy for peripheral issues to become central and central issues to become peripheral, and then leadership becomes whatever one wants it to be. Eventually an incredibly valuable term means anything and everything, and then, it means nothing. As Rost (1993) states, "it is no longer acceptable for leadership scholars to ignore the issue of what leadership is" (p. 17).

If we don't know what leadership is we cannot research it or measure it because we have not determined the essential elements or constructs that form the concept. Again, Rost states, "responsible scholarship requires that one clearly articulate the nature of leadership if one is going to expound on it" (p. 70). How do we know whether leadership is being practiced? How do we identify emerging leaders? These are all practical and essential questions that can be answered through a clear and reasoned defining of leadership terms.

Identifying the Confusion Points: Seven Clarifying Questions

Our attempt to define leadership terms must deal with seven questions to bring clarity to the ongoing confusion in our use of leadership terms. Once we have established definitions we can evaluate them based on how well they help us to address the following clarifying questions.

Clarifying Question #1: What Distinguishes a Leader from a Non-leader? How Can We Identify Emerging Leaders?

This author was asked by a group from a national youth organization to sit in on a discussion concerning a new leadership development program designed for young people. The purpose of the program was to train emerging young leaders. How then, they asked, will they determine who is an emerging leader or who is not? How does one identify an emerging leader? Our definitions of leadership terms must help us identify and evaluate both existing leaders and emerging leaders. To do this we should be clear on what distinguishes a leader from a non-leader. What criteria will we use to determine this? How will we determine when someone is leading or is not leading?

Clarifying Question #2: How Can We Distinguish the Act of Leading from the Role of Positional Leadership?

The positional leader is one who has an appointed or elected authority role within a group or organization. Examples are the CEO, team leader, floor manager or vice president. When we claim that someone is *the* leader, we are conditioned to think first of the person positionally in charge of others: the top leader, the supervisor, the boss. We do the same, of course, with the term manager. The end result of this confusion is that we tend to use the various terms interchangeably and therefore muddy the waters even more. We confuse the positions of leadership with the function of leadership. Think of it this way. We all know of positional leaders who do not lead. There is a distinction therefore between the position of leading and the function or actions of leading. So, we need a definition that provides for this clear distinction. The only way out of this uncertainty is to do the challenging work of saying exactly what we mean by the terms that we use. We must clearly define them.

Clarifying Question #3: What Distinguishes Leadership from Management? Leaders from Managers?

The confusion increases even more when we add the concept of management to the discussion. Is leadership different from management? Most today would say yes, but there is often a lack of clarity in defining the terms to distinguish them from one another. There are several viewpoints taken on this question in the leadership literature today. One viewpoint considers leadership and management as basically the same thing, a position of authority within a group. Another view is that leadership is a subset of management as displayed in most management education texts today. The common typology used to explain management consists of the four-part designation of planning, organizing, leading, and controlling. In other words, leadership is viewed as one way that management is done. This manner of positioning leadership as a subset of management perpetuates confusion around these terms.

Others, often leadership writers, create an inappropriate value judgment that presents leadership in terms of positive qualities like being relational, communicating effectively, and building learning organizations while managers are presented as hierarchical, withdrawn, and authoritative. This is inaccurate and unfortunate. We need to find definitions that do a better job of distinguishing leadership and management (or leading and managing) in ways that do not build up one concept while denigrating the other. We need to honor both functions and understand the valuable contribution that both make to our organizations and our leadership.

Clarifying Question #4: Is the Definition of Leader the Same as That of Leadership?

Obviously the two terms, leader and leadership, are connected, but they are different and this distinction provides valuable insight to our understanding. The leader is only one part of the leadership process. Leaders may initiate the process but they are not all that is involved in leadership. Leadership requires the dynamic response of the followers into a process that goes beyond the leader's initial vision and action. Drawing these distinctions will enable us to see how leaders move into leading and how leadership as a process is created and maintained over time to produce real change.

Clarifying Question #5: What Is the Role of the Followers in Leadership?

Followers are critical to the leadership process. The neglect of followers in many definitions on leadership has resulted in a separate study called followership, an attempt to determine what makes for an effective follower. Unfortunately, in most discussions of leaders and followers there is an unspoken assumption that we are dealing with *positional* leaders and *positional* followers. We automatically assume a hierarchy of position without stating it. Could it be that leading and following are best understood as different functions that join together to create an active process for change, a powerful energy and process we call leadership? We will explore this possibility in our efforts to define our leadership terms.

Clarifying Question #6: What Distinguishes Leadership from Other Human Social Processes?

Is leading the same as envisioning the future? Is it the same as taking courageous action? Is it a synonym for effective communication and relationships? Since leadership writers have sometimes failed to accurately and precisely define leadership terms, we sometimes end up with the conclusion that leadership is nothing more than an expression of positive human processes. No distinction is provided to make clear what leading is and what it is not.

Here are some questions to make us think about this deeper: (1) Are good leaders, good communicators? (2) Are good communicators, leaders? (3) Are leaders always good communicators? Most would answer a quick "yes" to question #1. Good communication is normally seen as essential for good leadership. But what about question #2? If a person happens to have a gift of communicating effectively verbally or in writing will this person then be a leader? No, it takes more than good communication skills to make one a leader and good communication skills may or may not be essential to determining if someone is a leader. Question #3 may cause some good debate, but it should be answered in the negative. Being a leader is about specific essential functions. Good communication will enhance leadership, but it does not help us to define it.

Let's look at this issue from the perspective of the criteria of relationships. If positive leadership assumes the presence of positive relationships, then does the presence of positive relationships assume that leadership is present? The answer must, of course, be no. The point is that leading and leadership need to be distinguished from human processes that may be a part of *describing* positive leadership but are insufficient to *define* what leadership is at its core.

Clarifying Question #7: When Do We Know If Leadership Is Occurring or Not Occurring? How Can We Accurately Measure (Research) the Concept?

Is it possible to define leadership in a precise enough fashion to determine if it is occurring in a particular situation? Can we then go beyond identifying it as present or absent to measure it at a meaningful level? Do our definitions allow us to establish research questions that can be answered objectively? If we begin with an assumption that leadership is something specific and measurable, then we will be able to identify the essential elements necessary to define this phenomenon of leadership.

Criteria for a Good Definition

A good definition of any concept or reality should be measured by the following four criteria and all of these should be addressed for a good, usable definition to be in place. These four criteria are a summary from those offered by Rost (1993).

First, our definition must be *clear and specific*. Too many definitions of leadership are vague statements that do not attempt to focus on what is specific and essential to our understanding of the concept. Some definitions are descriptions of only a part of leadership and do not therefore give us a clear and comprehensive picture of the concept.

Second, our definition must be able to meaningfully *differentiate* between concepts. What is unique to leadership that clearly identifies it as separate from other concepts? For instance, if leadership is different from management then our definition should be able to be used to clearly make this distinction.

Third, our definition must include all of the *essential elements necessary* to fully identify the phenomenon. What is essential to defining the core of what leadership is and what is not essential? What are the central (vs. peripheral) issues that make leadership what it is? Consider the old story of an elephant being described (or defined) by three blind men. One blind man describes the elephant as a long and slender tube that moves through the air. Of course we know that he is only describing the trunk of the elephant since that is where he is standing and that is all that he can "see" with his hands. Another blind man describes the elephant as a large immovable wall. This man stands next to the elephant's huge body and accurately describes the only part of the elephant he has experienced. The third blind man tells us that the elephant is like the trunk of a tree; round, tall and strong. Of course, he is grasping the leg of the elephant and is totally unaware of anything but that single part. Each of the blind men is accurate but only in part. We would not be able to identify the creature they are describing from each one's limited perspective. What is worse, we are likely to conclude that the phenomenon described is something totally different from an elephant. The question needs to be asked, what makes an elephant an elephant? What would be the most concise list of essential elements that when combined together would define this, and only this, creature? This essential list would then define for us an elephant, and nothing else.

Unfortunately, definitions of leadership are more like partial descriptions of a certain part of the whole while other essential ingredients are ignored. Therefore, we need to focus on what the core, essential ingredients of the various leadership terms are within our definitions. That is the task before us in this chapter. Jonathan Ive, Senior Vice President of Industrial Design for Apple, describes this process in relation to Apple products when he states, "you have to deeply understand the essence of a product in order to be able to get rid of the parts that are not essential" (as cited in Zufi, 2013, p. 39). Ive goes on to claim that "it is really important in a product to have a sense of the hierarchy of what's important and what's not important by removing those things that are vying for your attention" (as cited in Zufi, 2013, p. 95). We need to apply this same evaluative process to our definitions of leadership terms and focus clearly on the essence of what each term really means.

Finally, our definition must be *usable* by practitioners as well as by scholars. It must be a definition that allows us to identify emerging leaders while creating specific ways to train these leaders in what leadership is and how they can maximize their leadership understanding and practice. We should be able to use our definitions to create such clarity that research questions can be accurately stated, scholars and practitioners can make decisions about the presence or absence of leadership so that the essential ingredients are clear and measurable.

In summary, a good leadership definition …

1. must be *clear* and *specific*
2. must be able to meaningfully *differentiate* between concepts
3. must include all of the *essential elements*
4. must be *usable* by practitioners as well as by scholars

Scenarios of Leadership: You Be the Judge

To prepare ourselves for this critical process of definition making, let's consider four scenarios (two individual and two organizational) to challenge our thinking. As you complete the reading of each scenario, take some time to think through the reflection questions allowing these brief thought experiments to open your thinking to a deeper and clearer understanding of our need for definitional clarity.

Individual Scenario #1

As an eight-year-old girl from suburban Los Angeles, Tara Church was about to feel her world move. She was a part of a Brownies troop studying the impact of trees on the world's environment. As a part of a planned project Tara, and the other girls in the troop, planted a tree they named Marcy the Marvelous Tree. For Tara, this single act served as the beginning of something larger, a growing vision for change. She envisioned and helped to create an organization called the Tree Musketeers, an organization run by children. The mission of Tree Musketeers was to empower young people to be leaders of environmental and social change in Earth's communities. Tree Musketeers initiated programs resulting in millions of children worldwide getting involved in planting trees and other social initiatives with over 2 million trees planted worldwide. They received multiple regional, national, and presidential awards for their programs of social change. Tara served as Chair of the Tree Musketeers board of directors which was always staffed and run by children until the organization closed its doors in 2017.

Reflection: *Is Tara Church a leader? What criteria of leadership definition do you use to answer this? At what point in the story did Tara become a leader?*

Individual Scenario #2

For three months in 1989 a crowd of approximately 100,000 young people and workers staged a protest against Chinese government corruption and the leadership of Deng Xiaoping. They gathered at Tiananmen Square, which means "heavenly peace," in the capital city of Beijing. The protest captured the attention of millions as calls for political freedom and human rights were raised before a watching world. Tragically, the protest ended in a massacre of hundreds of unarmed civilians at the hands of the People's Liberation Army. Amnesty International claims that 213 people were still imprisoned, or on medical parole, in connection to the protests even 15 years later. One of the most arresting images from that event was of a young man standing resolutely in front of a row of tanks blocking entry into Tiananmen Square. This display of personal courage was seen as inspiring by some and foolish by others but the bold action of this young man stands as an icon of personal courage, risk taking, and commitment to a noble cause.

Reflection: Was this young man a leader? What rationale do you use to provide your answer?

Organizational Scenario #1

Maria is responsible for making sure that her business runs smoothly and efficiently. To improve her skills she recently completed her MBA with a focus on finance and organizational planning. She has been using these skills to help her organization work through a difficult downturn within the industry. She has implemented several programs designed to protect the diminishing resources of the company. These programs have involved, among other necessities, the downsizing of several middle management positions and the streamlining of an overstocked inventory. Maria is also responsible for taking key organizational goals sent down from the main office and turning them into workable and measurable objectives for her workers. She is implementing a strong accountability plan to insure that her division meets the goals and is then evaluated as successful. Maria likes her job and is good at making things work. This is a very difficult time but she knows her company needs the organizing skills she brings to the problems they face. Maria has an important position in the company and if she is successful at her current assignment she certainly will be in line for a higher role.

Reflection: *Is Maria a leader? At what points in this scenario is she displaying leadership?*

Organizational Scenario #2

Greg is the CEO of a medium-size company that specializes in providing organizational solutions through executive coaching and team building. Greg started the company ten years ago and is proud of the way it has grown while seeking to maintain a close-knit family feel. Greg enjoys being CEO, but lately has found it increasingly difficult. Some of the new talented staff he brought on a year ago are beginning to push for change. They seem dissatisfied with the direction the company is going, or more precisely, they are complaining that they are not able to discern what the direction is. They keep asking "what kind of company are we trying to become as we grow? How should decisions be made now that we are a larger, more complex organization? What is our vision for the future?" Greg tells them to be patient and to wait until the future becomes less turbulent and more clear. The organization has always been successful and Greg sees no reason why this will not continue in the future. They have a tested and proven product and a market that seems to need what they provide. Greg recognizes the talent these new people bring to the company but he is deeply concerned with the disloyalty their comments communicate to the rest of the "family." Why do they keep asking about the vision of the company? Vision? Don't they know that they have a good thing going here? He is reminded of one of his favorite quotes, something his dad used to say, *If it ain't broke, don't fix it.* Greg is beginning to think that maybe these new people are not *identifying* the problems, but maybe they *are* the problem. Greg has always been good at fixing problems.

Reflection: *Is Greg a leader? Is Greg leading within the scenario described here? At what points in this scenario is he displaying, or failing to display, leadership?*

Did you have any difficulty in identifying the leaders in these four scenarios? Could you discern when leadership was occurring and when it was not? What definition will you use to decide when leadership does, in fact, exist? Please keep these scenarios and questions in mind as we move now into the challenging task of defining our leadership typology.

A Typology of Leadership Terms

The following definitions of leadership terms are presented as a starting place, a benchmark for future discussions and challenges. These definitions will, and should, be challenged. They are presented as attempts to provide usable and effective answers to the seven clarifying questions presented earlier. Certainly they are not the final word, or the only way to present these concepts. Our desire here is to move the study of leadership forward in a meaningful way while seeking to address the various confusion points around leadership terms.

Defining the Term: Leader

It is important that the definition of the term leader be distinguished from the *position* of leader. We all know of positional leaders who do not lead. It is vital then that we note the difference between leading and simply holding a role, or office, that some would call *the leader*. The following definition accomplishes this purpose. It focuses not on a positional role but on what the leader does, the functions of leading. This definition provides an action approach to leading versus a trait or a positional approach. Terry (1993) states that action is "the human universe within which leadership must exist." He suggests that "leadership has always been considered action, even if that connotation was unexamined and intuitive" (p. 53). The person who *takes the lead* is the one who acts within a given situation. The young man in Tiananmen Square, who stood before the armored tanks of the Red Army and individually stalled their entry into the square, stood up to take courageous action. He took the lead. He entered, through this action, into the realm of leading. The definition proposed here has four key ingredients (essential elements) which must each be present in order for a person to be called a leader, or to say that a person is leading.

Definition of Leader—A leader is a person who sees a vision, takes action toward the vision, and mobilizes others to become partners in pursuing change.

Now, let's consider the four essential elements of this definition:

Vision. Vision is the ability to conceptualize a preferred future. It is the ability and willingness to see what is not readily apparent. It often begins with seeing what is around us in terms of perceived needs. We care about the problems we see and begin to reflect on what we should do about it. This focus on reality then moves into the realm of possibilities. As our competency in vision creation grows we find ourselves better able to look further and deeper into the future to conceive new realities. We, in fact, create the future in our mind's eye.

Action. Action is personal power applied to doing what needs to be done to move toward the vision, the preferred reality. If we stay with our visions alone, we can be easily dismissed as mere dreamers. However, leaders act toward their vision of the future. They take on the personal responsibility and risk of moving into the future and bringing it into the present through courageous action. Leaders have a bias for action. They know that initiative is the entry point into leading and that only through the example of action can others be motivated to join the process.

Mobilization. Mobilization involves the influencing of people to voluntarily engage and move into the leadership process with you. Mobilization refers to the movement of people from one place to another; from being inactive to becoming active, from non-leading to leading. It is a word that includes the subconcepts of influence and motivation but moves beyond them to emphasize the active movement of people toward change. Burns' phrase "leadership *mobilizes*, naked power *coerces*" (as cited in Rost 1993, p. 121) presents a critical truth. People are mobilized by the leader's vision and example of action. This is not a coercive process. To the level that coercion is used true leadership is diminished.

Change. Change is an outcome achieved as a result of intentional action toward the preferred reality. Rost (1993) contends that "change is the most distinguishing characteristic of leadership" (p. 115). Without vision, action, and the mobilization of people toward change, leading does not occur. Leading always moves toward change.

So, as our definition states, a leader is a person who sees a vision, takes action toward the vision, and mobilizes others to become partners in pursuing change.

Reflection Questions

- *How well, in your opinion, does this definition deal with the seven confusion points?*
- *In what ways can this definition be used to determine if you are, or are not, leading in a specific situation?*
- *How might you use this definition to help identify emerging young leaders?*

For leading to occur, these four key essentials of vision, action, mobilization, and change must exist and work together in an integrated fashion. It is not enough to have one, two, or even three of the essentials. All four must exist together.

For example, vision apart from the other three essentials is mere dreaming. The world is full of dreamers who never pursue and produce change. The dream itself is a powerful beginning, but it cannot remain a dream alone if something of worth is to be accomplished. Greenleaf (1977) spoke to the power of a dream when he said that

> Not much happens without a dream. And for something great to happen, there must be a great dream. Behind every great achievement is a dreamer of great dreams. Much more than a dreamer is required to bring it to reality; but the dream must be there first. (p. 16)

Action apart from the other three essentials is impulsive and reactionary. It has no direction and no controlling boundaries to guide it forward. Action without a positive powerful vision can do more harm than good. At the least, it is arbitrary good intention. At the worst, it produces man's worst inhumanity to man. Action guided by vision is purposeful and powerful.

Mobilization without the other three essentials becomes misdirected busyness. How many times have our organizations expended incredible energy in misguided efforts that end up nowhere? How many times have you attended a long-drawn-out meeting that began with no clear intention and ended with no definite accomplishment? It isn't enough just to get people together or to move them for the sake of movement alone. Mobilization is purposeful shared action toward a common vision.

Change without the other three essentials is haphazard and arbitrary. It is something that happens to us instead of something that we pursue and create. When change happens to us, we feel powerless. We become victims. People in this situation find themselves hopeless without the personal power exercised to create change in their life. Change toward a shared vision pursued through purposeful group action is the result of leaders and followers together creating the dynamic of leadership.

Leadership is an intentional change process integrating leaders with the mobilized action of people who desire change and are willing to take the risk to pursue it.

Defining the Term: Leadership

Napoleon said that "a general's most important talent is to know the mind of the soldier and gain his confidence, and in both respects the French soldier is more difficult to lead than another. He is not a machine that must be made to move, he is a reasonable being who needs leadership" (as cited in Roberts, 2014, p. 74). The concept of leadership is different than *leading* or being *a leader*. This is challenging to grasp since we commonly use these terms interchangeably. Leadership refers to the process through which leaders and followers engage to produce change. The definition proposed here includes the four essential elements that form the definition for the term *leader* but it expands to include the *leadership process*. The concept of mobilization is assumed in this definition now that followers have responded to the initiation of the leader.

Definition of Leadership—Leadership is an intentional change process through which leaders and followers, joined by a shared purpose, initiate action to pursue a common vision.

Now, let's consider the essential elements of this definition:

An intentional change process. A process is "a particular course of action intended to achieve a result" (Merriam-Webster Collegiate Dictionary, 1998). Leadership is an intentional process, a process that follows from a compelling vision to pursue change. It is a dynamic process that is affected by more than the leader's original intentions. Once the leader and follower engage in this process the vision can shift, the action become redirected, and the change reconsidered. Seeing the need for change creates the vision of leadership. Pursuing change is the action of leadership. Mobilized leaders and followers engage in this process to create change and therefore serve as change agents together. Change is always the intended outcome of leadership. Leaders and followers may not get the change they desire, but the reason for entering this leadership partnership is to pursue change. The purpose of leadership is to move (to change) the world.

... Through which leaders and followers. For leadership to take place leaders must initiate the process and followers must then voluntarily engage. Remember, we are not talking in any way about positional leadership. The original leaders in this process, those who initiate the process of vision and action, may take on the role of follower during different stages of the process. Those who initially engaged the process as followers may then provide initiation and ideas that place them into the role of leader. A new idea is shared and the process is challenged. Leadership is a dynamic process in which roles are functional versus positional and the motivating force is the common desire to see the vision realized through change. The number of leaders and followers is not essential to this definition, but both roles must be present for leadership to occur.

... Joined by shared purpose. Leaders and followers engage in this process due to a shared sense of mission and purpose. This purpose is the foundation that provides them a strong place to stand to engage in the pursuit of change together. They are linked by a common set of values and mutual beliefs that join them in a community of commitment around the shared vision. This purpose sets the stage to consider multiple change scenarios while giving both leaders and followers a reason and motivation to engage in the leadership process.

… Initiate action. Action is always essential to the leadership process. Leadership does not begin until action is taken, normally initiated by the leader, but soon joined by mobilized followers in a dynamic process of pursuing change. Non-leadership is the absence of action, the unwillingness to engage issues, to speak up, to take the risk, to make a difference. The leadership change process is made possible through a shared purpose directed by the vision, continuing to operate on the mutual action of leaders and followers.

… To pursue a common vision. The vision originates with a leader, or leaders, and then is picked up by followers who share a common purpose with the leader. The vision then is owned by the leaders and followers together through the process. The vision is also dynamic. It continues to take shape and clarity as everyone engages in the process, speaks to it, and owns it. This mutual ownership of the vision becomes a powerful motivator to action. Vision is the change already realized in the mind's eye of the leader. This vision gives leaders and followers reason and motivation to act even when the vision leads them into dangerous and risky territory. The vision must be valued more than the risk is feared.

Let's consider the usefulness and accuracy of this definition by applying it to the scenario of Tara Church. As a young girl she sees a need in the world that requires correction. This inspired annoyance drives her to move beyond the first act of planting Marcy the Marvelous Tree. Tara takes action to plant more trees. She mobilizes children to get involved and initiates a critical mass of shared effort resulting in literally millions of trees planted. Her vision is joined with others who begin to see the potential of harnessing the incredible energy of children to move their world to a better place through the planting of trees. Through this process, thousands of children are challenged to become leaders to pursue their own vision of societal change. Yes, Tara Church was a leader. Not because she built an organization or serves as Chair of a board of directors (these are vehicles to allow leadership vision to flourish) but because she acted on a vision of change and mobilized others to become part of a leadership process.

Reflection Questions

- *What does this definition of leadership add to the earlier definition of leader?*
- *According to this definition, is leadership observable? Could it be measured?*
- *What is the significance of leadership being defined as "a process"?*

Defining the Term: Follower

The concept of *follower* is essential to the definition and understanding of the term leadership. Both leaders and followers provide essential functions while overlapping efforts and roles within the leadership process. This is different from the emphasis on followership in leadership studies that essentially is a study of the *position* of following and how those who are followers by position or role can be the most effective and useful followers possible. In contrast, with this definition we are looking at following as a function or set of actions that anyone, leaders included, should be willing and able to display in order to fully participate in the process of leadership. Let's look together at the definition of the term follower.

Definition of Follower—Followers voluntarily and actively engage in the leadership process by responding to the leader's initiative to identify shared purpose, vision, and action toward change.

Now, let's consider the essential elements of this definition:

Voluntarily and actively engage in the leadership process. Followers engage in the leadership process voluntarily and actively. This draws a clear distinction between followers and mere employees or members of a group. This also distinguishes what happens in the leadership process from the transactional nature of most employment contracts. As a true follower, I chose to engage in the leadership process. I am active, not passive, in the process. Leadership itself will not occur without my willing involvement. A leader may initiate a vision and act on that vision but without the follower's will to engage, leadership will not occur. At this point the reader may be asking, what if the follower offers compliance due to the force or threat of punishment from the leader? Doesn't leadership often occur where followers are forced to obey rather than respond voluntarily? This situation, though common in power-over relationships, by this definition is not leadership. It is something else, a different human interaction. You can call it intimidation or coercion, but you cannot call it leadership according to this definition. The leadership process requires the voluntary engagement of the follower.

Respond to the leader's initiative. The leader initiates action based on a vision which creates the opportunity for the leadership process to occur. The follower's willing response allows for the process to continue moving toward the desired change. This follower response is crucial. Without it the leader has failed to mobilize others to action and therefore has failed to lead effectively. Leadership always begins with the individual leader but is fulfilled within community. Within this understanding, the one who originally functions as a follower, the one who voluntarily responses and engages, can at any time assume the functions of a leader by becoming the one who envisions and acts. This can be done by suggesting a change in direction or process. This new idea, then, can be agreed to by the original leader who now takes on the functions of follower as he or she decides whether or not to voluntarily engage in the new idea or direction. This becomes a fluid and dynamic process where leading and following are defined by what a person is doing (function) at any given time within the process. Leading and following are functions (not positions) and are both critical to the leadership process.

Identify a shared purpose. Community becomes possible through the supportive framework of shared purpose. We agree on why we are together. We are aligned and going in the same direction. There is a reason why we exist together and this reason allows us to communicate, trust, commit, and labor toward a common vision. The more explicit we are in identifying this common purpose the stronger the leadership process will be and the greater our potential for pursuing change. Shared purpose does not mean uniformity. The most diverse groups can share a focus, passion, and set of values—a purpose. The combination of a unity of purpose with a diversity of gifts and viewpoints is a powerful mixture. Both leaders and followers work to enhance this mixture by facilitating an understanding and appreciation of their shared purpose.

Identify a shared vision. The vision that originates with the leader is shared with potential followers. When the followers voluntarily and actively engage in the leadership process they are motivated by a compelling vision. However, what is compelling about the vision is usually very personal and individual. Each person who hears it begins to reshape it according to their own view of reality. The process of leadership allows for this refinement, even a redirecting of an original vision based on the shared wisdom of the group. This protects the leadership process from being derailed by a single leader's ego and self-absorption. It allows the most preferred change to be pursued by those who desire it and are willing to own it fully.

Pursue shared action toward change. There is incredible power in a common vision pursued by the shared coordinated action of a group. This power will result in change, even if the change is not what was originally envisioned. Sometimes the change is an increased awareness of the need for change. Sometimes the change is in the resolve of the leaders and followers to continue increased change efforts. Rost's (1993) definition of leadership focuses on the leaders and followers who "intend real changes" (p. 102). The word *intend* is too weak for an action-based model of leadership. Leaders and followers actually *pursue* shared action toward change. The change must be more than intended; it must be actively pursued (through action) in order for leadership to occur.

Thus far, we have worked to define the key terms essential to our understanding of leadership. We have defined the terms leader, leadership, and follower since they are all part of clearly understanding what leadership is at its core. We now move to a related but distinct term that we will use in contrast to leadership.

Defining the Term: Management

In continuing to develop this typology of definitions we must deal with the concept of management since it is one of the key confusion points in the use of leadership terms. Daft's (2008) definition for management is used since it presents the traditional and generally accepted meanings of the term while showing a clear contrast with the definitions offered in this text of leadership terms. Leadership is not a subset of management.

It is a separate process altogether with different functions and outcomes. As Harter (2006) has suggested on leadership, "the word is not so broad and malleable as to include *every* instance of social or interpersonal change. If it means anything at all, it has to mean something in contradistinction to something else" (p. 4). Viewing leadership in contradistinction to management will help to clarify both concepts.

Definition of Management—"Management is the attainment of organizational goals in an effective and efficient manner through planning, organizing, staffing, directing, and controlling organizational resources" (Daft, 2008, p. 14).

This definition identifies that management is less about long-term vision and more about operational goals that must be attained to move toward the vision. These goals are pursued effectively and efficiently through five key functions: planning, organizing, staffing, directing, and controlling.

In Table 3.1 the two definitions for management and leadership are contrasted and key distinctions between the two concepts are provided from Kotter (as cited in Northouse, 2016).

Leadership is about action toward change while management is about making things run well and stabilizing them to work more efficiently. Leading and managing are both essential processes in any organization and one is not more valuable than the other. To be sure, they sometimes

Table 3.1 Management contrasted to leadership

Management	Leadership
Definition: Management is the attainment of organizational goals in an effective and efficient manner through planning, organizing, staffing, directing, and controlling organizational resources—(Daft, 2008, p. 14)	*Definition*: Leadership is an intentional change process through which leaders and followers, joined by a shared purpose, initiate action to pursue a common vision—Laub
Produces: Order and consistency	Produces: Change and movement
Includes:	Includes:
• Planning/budgeting • Organizing/staffing • Controlling/problem solving (Northouse, 2016, p. 14)	• Vision building/strategizing • Aligning people/communicating • Motivating/inspiring (Northouse, 2016, p. 14)

seem to be working at odds with each other since the key outcome of leading is *change* while the key outcome of managing is *stability*. This tension is healthy and must be maintained to allow for complete and healthy organizational function. Unfortunately, some leadership writers have denigrated management in order to ennoble leadership. For instance, Daft (2008) contrasts the personal qualities of management and leadership in a way that shows leadership with stronger qualities of "listening," "character," and "courage" while management is portrayed as exhibiting the personal qualities of "talking" (in contrast to listening), "conformity" and "emotional distance." (p. 15). This is an unfortunate way of drawing the distinction between the two valuable concepts since it reinforces a positive stereotype of leaders and a negative stereotype of managers. We should agree to affirm that leading and managing are both important and different functions that bring value to an organization.

Reflection Questions

- *Identify three clear distinctions between leadership and management.*
- *What does leadership offer an organization that management does not?*
- *What does management offer an organization that leadership does not?*

Keep in mind that we are not addressing these terms as *positions* of leadership or management in any way. Instead, leading and managing promote different functions that people choose to do or not to do. If I happen to be a *positional* leader (the president of my company, for instance) that is an issue of title and role. It says absolutely nothing about whether or not I am leading or managing or doing either one effectively.

Leadership and Management: Contrasting Formulas for Different Functions

The definitions proposed for both leadership and management can be presented in the following two formulas. For leadership, the formula is $V + A + M = C$ (Vision + Action + Mobilization = Change). Leading begins with a vision of a preferred future and is initiated through the action of the leader who mobilizes others to join to pursue change. The management formula can be stated as $P + O + D = S$ (Planning + Organizing + Directing = Stability). The managing functions begin with planning toward the vision, creating a pathway toward the vision the group is pursuing followed by organizing people and things so that movement toward the vision can be pursued in the most efficient and effective way possible. This involves critical managing tasks like creating business plans, budgets, gathering resources, and the assignment of tasks and teams. Then management calls for the function of directing or supervising the work of others. This includes tasks such as job descriptions, performance expectations and reviews, reporting and supporting the work of each person, and holding individuals and teams accountable for work performance. The outcome of these actions or functions is to create stability for the organization. Leading pursues change while managing pursues stability. The change sought by leading creates instability related to the status quo. The stability sought by managing resists change and sees it as a challenge to the smooth functioning of the organization. This tension, though uncomfortable, is necessary and good for the organization and the healthy organization learns how to appreciate and live productively with this ever-present tension between leading and managing.

Assess Your Leadership and Management Strengths

At the website, servantleaderperformance.com you can complete the free Leader-Manager Assessment to assess your relative strengths in leading and managing along with your relative strengths in the four functions of management and the four functions of leadership. If you determine that you are by preference more inclined and perhaps more skilled in leading, you will want to build your managing skills while recruiting people for your team who possess these managing functions in greater strength. If you by personality, values, or experience fall more toward the managing functions then you will want to increase your leading skills and recruit others who will more naturally represent the functions of leading. Then, you must accept the inevitable tension that will ensue. Leaders with a preference for the managing functions will focus more on things that will bring stability to the organization while those with a preference for leading functions will be continually inclined toward change. Understanding the difference between these two sets of functions, and when they should best be implemented, allows you to understand the need for and value of both sets of functions while developing an appreciation for your less preferred functions.

Defining leadership terms in this way sets the stage for creating definitions for key subsets of leadership and we will do that, in this text, for the concept of servant leadership. Servant leadership can only be clearly understood if leadership is clearly defined.

Defining Servant Leadership

Servant leadership is best understood as a mindset of leading, an understanding and practice of leading that is distinct from other leadership mindsets. If leading is about vision, action, mobilization, and change, then how does the servant leader address these four functions differently than other ways of leading?

Laub's (1999) initial definition of servant leadership, "an understanding and practice of leadership that places the good of those led over the self-interest of the leader" (p. 83), will be expanded in Chap. 7 where we present the contrasts between three mindsets of leadership—autocratic, paternalistic (parental), and servant.

Conclusion

In this chapter we have done the foundational work of definition making for key leadership terms. In the next chapter we will present a foundational model of servant leadership that includes the leadership disciplines of displaying authenticity, valuing people, developing people, building community, providing leadership, and sharing leadership. This servant leadership model provides a comprehensive understanding of the disciplines and actions of servant leadership and how this way of leading works to create healthy leadership and healthy organizations.

References

Daft, R. L. (2008). *The leadership experience* (4th ed.). Mason, OH: Thompson South-Western.

Greenleaf, R. K. (1977). *Servant leadership: A journey into the nature of legitimate power and greatness*. New York: The Paulist Press.

Harter, N. (2006). *Clearings in the forest: On the study of leadership*. West Lafayette, IN: Purdue University Press.

Laub, J. A. (1999). *Assessing the servant organization: Development of the servant organizational leadership assessment (SOLA) instrument*. Doctoral dissertation for Florida Atlantic University.

Maxwell, J. (1998). *The 21 irrefutable laws of leadership*. Nashville, TN: Thomas Nelson Publishers.

Northouse, P. G. (2016). *Leadership: Theory and practice* (7th ed.). Thousand Oaks, CA: Sage Publications.

Process. (1998). *In Merriam-Webster's collegiate dictionary*. Springfield, MA: Merriam-Webster.

Roberts, A. (2014). *Napoleon: A life*. New York, NY: Penguin Books.

Rost, J. C. (1993). *Leadership for the twenty-first century*. London: Praeger.

Terry, R. W. (1993). *Authentic leadership: Courage in action*. Hoboken, NJ: Jossey-Bass Publisher.

Yukl, G. A. (2001). *Leadership in organizations* (5th ed.). Upper Saddle River, NJ: Pearson Publishing.

Zufi, J. (2013). *Iconic: A photographic tribute to Apple innovation*. Atlanta: Ridgewood Publishing.

4

Explaining the Servant Mindset: The OLA Servant Leadership Model

In this chapter we introduce the Organizational Leadership Assessment (OLA) servant leadership model developed by Laub (1999) along with the development of the OLA instrument. This is the first model of servant leadership developed through a research-based approach providing an operational and measureable set of constructs to describe what servant leadership looks like in practice. The six central disciplines of servant leadership are described along with three descriptors for each discipline. The OLA model of servant leadership provides a framework for understanding the unique mindset a servant leader possesses and how this mindset is lived out through the servant leader's behavior.

The Servant Leader Mindset

Since Greenleaf introduced the name and concept of servant leadership in 1970 there have been several major leadership writers who have given credence to this paradoxical approach to leadership. When authors like Steven Covey (1994), Meg Wheatley (1994), Ron Heifetz (1994), Peter Senge (1997), and Peter Northouse (2016) cite the influence of servant leadership we know that Greenleaf's ideas have gained a wide audience

© The Author(s) 2018
J. Laub, *Leveraging the Power of Servant Leadership*, Palgrave Studies in Workplace Spirituality and Fulfillment, https://doi.org/10.1007/978-3-319-77143-4_4

among leadership theorists. Spears (1995) developed, from Greenleaf's writings, the ten characteristics of the servant leader which helped to codify the tenets of Greenleaf's thought and was the first conceptual model offered on the servant leadership approach. Laub (1999) recognized that if servant leadership was to grow as a key leadership theory and approach, the term must be clearly defined, a research-based conceptual model must be developed, and an instrument to measure the perceptions of servant leadership should be created. In other words, a research base was needed and this chapter presents the work done to set the stage for that research base. This chapter will focus on Laub's research and model while the next chapter will present and contrast other key servant leadership models that have preceded and followed Laub's work providing a rich research base for servant leadership. Here is a list of the servant leadership models considered (Table 4.1).

Though each of these models adds something new and distinct to the servant leadership discussion it is clear that a consistent understanding is emerging about what servant leadership is and what it looks like in leadership practice and organizational life. These models, and for some, the assessment tools developed from them, are used by researchers to establish a growing research base and business case for the value of using the servant leadership approach to build high performing organizations. To be sure, servant leadership is a morally based concept, what Patterson (2003) calls a "virtuous theory," and therefore can be presented as a *right* way to lead, but more and more we can state with confidence that servant

Table 4.1 Servant leadership model authors 1991–2016

Graham	1991
Spears (Greenleaf)	1995
Laub	1999
Russell & Stone	2002
Patterson	2003
Dennis & Bocarnea	2005
Barbuto & Wheeler	2006
Wong & Davey	2007
Sendjaya, Sarros, & Santora	2008
Liden, Wayne, Zhao, & Henderson	2008
van Dierendonck & Nuijten	2011
McCarren, Lewis-Smith, Belton, Yanovsky, Robinson, & Osatuke	2016

leadership also *works* (Millard, 1995) in that it serves to develop healthier and higher performing organizations. We know that the practice of servant leadership correlates positively with key organizational health factors such as job satisfaction, organizational and leader trust, team effectiveness, student and employee performance, while negatively corresponding to employee attrition and employee absenteeism (Laub, 2010). When people review these models, including the OLA servant leadership model shared in this chapter, they hopefully gain a higher level of confidence in a leadership approach that at first glance may appear too idealistic to work in the hard-driving reality of current organizations but in fact is the best way to leverage leadership power to move the world to a new and better place.

Defining Servant Leadership

What is servant leadership and what does it look like in practice? What do servant leaders do and how do they display this approach in their leadership? A clearly stated definition and model is necessary to provide a strong foundation for how we talk about servant leadership and how we end up assessing it in organizations.

The OLA Research Process

Laub's first step to address these questions was to determine the characteristics of the servant leader in order to establish a working definition of the term. Then a research-based conceptual model was developed to guide the creation of an assessment tool to measure the concept of servant leadership within organizations. A Delphi research process was employed through which 14 experts in the field of servant leadership responded to three separate questionnaires to develop a consensus list of criteria to describe the servant leader. This list of experts included people who had published or taught at the university level on servant leadership or were considered to be key practitioners of the concept; Jim Kouzes, Larry Spears, Ann McGee-Cooper, Lea Williams, and Ted Ward were among the participating experts. In the first step of the process, the experts were asked a foundational question; what are the characteristics of the servant leader? They first had the opportunity to respond openly to this question and then were provided a list of characteristics drawn from the servant leadership literature. Then they were asked to add any of these characteristics to their initial list. Through this a beginning list was compiled of the characteristics of the servant leader. Then, in the second phase of the Delphi research process, all characteristics collected from phase one were placed in a semantic rating scale and the experts were asked to rate each characteristic as to whether it was *essential, necessary, desirable*, or *unnecessary*. After collecting the results from the second questionnaire, a third and final survey step was taken. Each of the characteristics was again provided on the same semantic scale with the results from the second questionnaire plus the average response and interquartile range for each characteristic. The experts were then asked to provide a final rating for each characteristic along with an explanation of why any of their responses fell outside the average responses from the total expert group. Through this three-phase Delphi process the group of experts came to a consensus on 60 criteria to describe the servant leader. A sign test was run on the interquartile ranges from phase two and three of the process confirming significant movement toward consensus by the expert panel. The final list of 60 approved characteristics was then clustered into the 6 disciplines and 18 descriptors that are used to inform the definition and conceptual model of servant leadership presented in this chapter. A panel of six judges reviewed the clustering that produced the OLA model and also reviewed the final items that composed the OLA survey instrument.

The Definition of Servant Leadership

The initial definition developed from this research process was "servant leadership is an understanding and practice of leadership that places the good of those led over the self-interest of the leader" (Laub, 1999, p. 83). This definition has several essential elements. First, *servant leadership is an understanding and practice of leadership*. This places servant leadership clearly within the larger concept of leadership. Leadership is defined as "an intentional change process through which leaders and followers, joined by a shared purpose, initiate action to pursue a common vision" (Laub, 2004, p. 83). Leadership, according to this definition, is about vision, action, mobilization, and change. There are no ethical or moral assumptions built into this definition. Leaders can be moral or immoral, ethical or unethical, good or evil, and of course they are. When the qualifier, *servant*, is added to leadership it suggests that this is a particular and unique *understanding and practice of leadership* that can be distinguished from other understandings and ways of leading. These differences can be viewed in terms of different leadership theories (i.e. Transformational Leadership, Situational Leadership, Authentic Leadership, Leader-Member Exchange) or in terms of different mindsets of leadership (i.e. autocratic, parental, servant). Servant leadership is a particular way of leading, a unique mode of thinking about leading that creates a mindset unique to this understanding and practice of leadership. Secondly, servant leadership, in this definition, presents an understanding and practice of leadership that *places the good of those led over the self-interest of the leader.* Servant leadership is the only leadership approach that recognizes the danger of leader self-interest and counters that self-interest with a clear other focus directed toward the followers; to *those led.* The focus of the servant leader on those led is a critical point that distinguishes this approach from somewhat similar approaches like Transformational Leadership. Servant leadership then is best understood as an understanding and practice of leadership where the leader works for the good of those led over and above his or her self-interest.

This definition of servant leadership was expanded through the Delphi process to create the OLA conceptual model which identifies specific ways that leadership is modified by the term servant. What does leadership look like when it is lived out through a servant mindset? The OLA model of servant leadership holds that "servant leadership promotes the valuing and developing of people, the building of community, the practice of authenticity, the providing of leadership for the good of those led and the sharing of power and status for the common good of each individual, the total organization and those served by the organization" (Laub, 1999, p. 83). This conceptual model presents six disciplines, each with three descriptors, which show what a servant leader does when displaying the actions of leading (vision, action, mobilization, and change) through a servant mindset. This model creates an effective way to help leaders and organizations develop a healthier, more servant-oriented practice of leadership. This model also serves as the basis for the Organizational Leadership Assessment (*OLA*), an instrument that measures perceptions of servant leadership in organizations (Laub, 1999–2018). Parris and Peachey (2013) in their systematic literature review of servant leadership theory determined that this definition and the OLA conceptual model was the third most referred to definition and model for servant leadership research studies in the literature after Greenleaf and Spears. The OLA has been used in over 85 research studies to date revealing multiple positive and powerful effects of the model when used in organizations.

The OLA Servant Leadership Model: Six Disciplines of the Servant Leader

If servant leaders put their followers first, how is that done? What does it look like? Is there an observable and measurable set of criteria that can clearly describe the servant leader in action? The OLA servant leadership model was drawn from the 60 characteristics identified through a Delphi research process. These characteristics were then clustered into six key disciplines of servant leadership with three descriptors each. A model was sought that would resonate with leaders and workers in the workplace who could clearly observe when these disciplines were present or absent and could report on the level to which they saw them practiced within their organization. This created a model that was not only useful for researchers but also understandable and usable by leadership practitioners. Through the OLA, assessment can be conducted according to this model and we can use the model to provide targeted leadership training and development. Through this definition and model, we can understand what servant leadership is and what it looks like when practiced by leaders and observed within organizational life.

According to the OLA servant leadership model, servant leaders:

1. Value People

   (a) By trusting and believing in people
   (b) By serving other's needs before their own
   (c) By receptive, nonjudgmental listening

2. Develop People

   (a) By providing opportunities for learning and growth
   (b) By modeling appropriate behavior
   (c) By building up others through encouragement and affirmation

3. Build Community

   (a) By building strong personal relationships
   (b) By working collaboratively with others
   (c) By valuing the differences of others

4. Display Authenticity

   (a) By being open and accountable to others
   (b) By a willingness to learn from others
   (c) By maintaining integrity and trust

5. Provide Leadership

   (a) By envisioning the future
   (b) By taking initiative
   (c) By clarifying goals

6. Share Leadership

   (a) By facilitating a shared vision
   (b) By sharing power and releasing control
   (c) By sharing status and promoting others

Value People: Servant Leader Discipline #1

Servant leadership requires a different view of others. People are to be valued and developed not *used* for the purposes of the leader. Servant leaders accept the fact that people have present value, not just future potential. Each person exists to fulfill a God-given purpose and our role as leaders is to assist them in that quest. Workers seem to have an innate ability to know whether or not they are truly valued by others; whether or not they are trusted. As a servant leader we need to accept and believe in a person's value up-front. We give them trust as a gift without demanding that they earn it first. Jackson (2002) states that "policies and practices developed in the West along instrumental lines see people primarily as a means to an end. This may be directly opposed to a humanistic view of human value that sees people as having a value in themselves" (p. 1). Yes, there is a strong tendency to see people as a means to our own ends and grant them instrumental value rather than the inherent value they possess. What happens when a person of influence decides to believe in you even before you have earned the right to be believed in? Consider a time when that happened for you. It may have been a parent, a teacher, a coach, or a boss who saw something in you that you did not yet see in yourself. When someone believes in you, they create a positive vision for your life and future. Servant leaders not only believe in the value of their workers but they speak value into them. They see potential that is not yet evident. They cast a vision on behalf of the worker's potential and help move that worker toward that potential. As servant leaders we value people by serving others first, by believing and trusting in others and by listening receptively (Fig. 4.1).

Value People by Serving Others First

This is the essence of the servant leader: putting others before self. The servant leader first sees himself or herself as a servant—a servant first, rather than a leader first. "It begins with the natural feeling that one wants to serve, to serve first. Then conscious choice brings one to aspire to lead" (Greenleaf, 1970, pp. 13–14). Greenleaf saw this concept of ser-

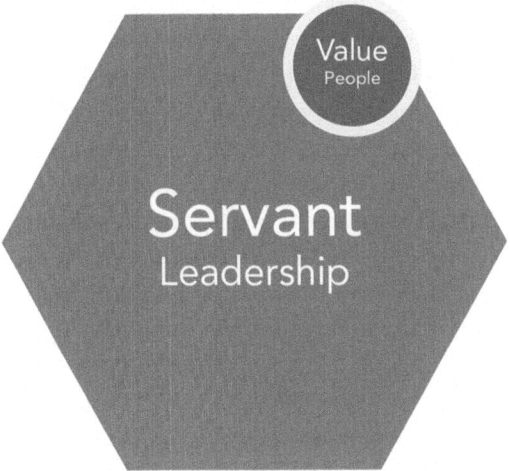

Fig. 4.1   OLA servant leadership model—value people

vant first as one clear distinction between a servant leader and a nonservant leader. He believed that a leader with a leader-first mindset focuses primarily on their own interests and privileges while a leader with a servant-first mindset focuses on the needs of the led over their own self-interest. Servant leaders focus on the needs of their workers and how they can best meet those needs. They know that true joy and health only come through serving and giving rather than seeking to be served by others.

Grant (2013) introduces three categories of people revealed through his research: givers, takers, and matchers. Givers are people whose default motivation is to give to others with no expectation of a gift given in return. Givers love to give; it is natural to them and they are not concerned about keeping a ledger to make sure that their service is reciprocated. Giving, for givers, is its own reward. Takers on the other hand are motivated to win over others and will do whatever it takes to come out on top. One thinks of the ethical approach of egoism that suggests that if everyone simply takes care of themselves first all will be well. Takers view the world as a zero-sum game with winners and losers and they relate to others in ways that ensure they will end up on the winning side. Matchers are Grant's third category referring to those who view life as a set of transactions that should ultimately be fair to all. Reciprocity is the highest goal for matchers with fairness and justice as the highest values. Matchers have no problem serving, but they see a fair return as a natural expectation. Grant contends that givers sometimes perform at a lower level than takers and matchers due to their propensity to give freely to others at personal cost to themselves; at least in the short term. However, it is the givers who outperform the others over the long term due to the inherent power of giving and serving. His argument is a strong endorsement of the leveraged power of serving others over self. Might there be an inherent motivation to serve others over self, serving others first over our own self-interest? This requires giving with no expectation of return and "making sure that other people's highest priority needs are being served" (Greenleaf, 1977, p. 27). This is the motivation of the servant leader who values others over self and seeks to give what is needed to each worker. Imagine the power and freedom one would experience, if valued and served in this way.

Value People by Believing and Trusting in Them

The Trust Game was developed by Berg, Dikhaut, and McCabe (Seidman, 2007) to determine if people are more apt to trust or distrust others. Here's how the game works. People who do not know each other are paired randomly and connected remotely through computers. Each participant is paid a sum of money they are free to use as they choose within the game. The first decision maker (DM1) is instructed to send any amount of money they choose to the other person (DM2) knowing that the amount they send will be tripled in the others' (DM2's) account. DM2 then may share whatever he or she chooses in response to the gift from DM1. In the game, there is no obligation to give any money away or to give any money back and both DM1 and DM2 are aware of this. The trust issues are clear. Will a person give freely to a stranger who may or may not give anything in return? The research revealed that 75% of DM1s sent money to their partner (DM2) and an even higher ratio of DM2s sent money back. Seidman put it this way, "It would seem that humans, at a very early stage of mental development are hardwired with the ability and desire to connect with and help others, despite the fact that doing so engenders great risk and returns no obvious reward" (2007, p. 69).

Servant leaders make a conscious choice to give others their trust knowing full well that this trust may not be reciprocated. They choose to believe in the possibilities of another person's abilities, motivation, and potential. They look beyond the immediate externals to find the true value of the other and in this value they discover incredible possibilities. Consider these two statements. Which one do you agree with more? Which statement rings most true to you?

1. Trust is something that must be earned
2. Trust is something that should be given as a gift

Which one do you agree with most? The answer you choose may reveal something important about your own motivation in trusting others. Most people tend to choose the first statement and do so because the statement is true. Our experience tells us that trust is earned over time by exhibiting trustworthy behaviors. We also know that trust is easily broken and very difficult to rebuild. Others, however, choose the second statement, that trust should be given as a gift. These are people who know that trust is ultimately a gift, something each of us can give or withhold and that giving it can create a powerful response from the recipient. When someone gives us the gift of trust, even before we have earned it, we tend to respond with trustworthy behavior. We want to give back. The reverse is also true. If I am suspicious of a person and I am withholding my trust until it is sufficiently earned, the tendency of the person is to draw back and withhold their own trusting response. We as leaders are to take the first step. We make a conscious choice as to who we will trust and who we will not trust. Joseph and Winston (2005) propose that "managers and leaders can improve organizational performance through the practice of servant leadership behaviors that increase trust in the manager and in the organization" (p. 16). Servant leaders choose to believe in others and to give them the gift of trust believing that this will create the sense of being fully valued and will create optimal conditions for trustworthy behaviors from both leaders and followers. Servant leaders value others and they do so by believing in them and giving them the gift of their trust.

Value People by Listening Receptively

How do you know when someone is truly listening to you? There are techniques for effective listening that we are all familiar with—look the person in the eyes, nod your head in supportive response, and provide verbal feedback to show that you are engaging them and their comments. The best way to know that you are listened to, listened to receptively, is when you perceive that the person listening truly values you. They value you for who you are, not for something they may gain from you. They want to listen to what you are saying because they care about you and they value your thoughts and ideas. They believe in you and trust you and therefore are listening beyond your words for your meaning and your heart. Listening receptively is listening to learn from someone you value and respect. When we truly listen to another we will *hear* them if we listen nonjudgmentally, when we listen to learn and to understand. One of Covey's seven habits of highly effective people is "seek first to understand and then to be understood" (1989, p. 235). This kind of deep understanding requires humble, receptive listening.

Ward shares that "we must be silent before we can listen. We must listen before we can learn. We must learn before we can prepare. We must prepare before we can serve. We must serve before we can lead" (1970). This discipline of listening receptively presumes another key action required of the servant leader. The servant leader asks questions because they truly want to learn; they ask more than they tell. When a leader asks a follower for their ideas and recommendations value for the person is communicated. The servant leader truly values others and views himself or herself as a learner who needs the insights of others. They know they don't know everything and they truly want to learn from others regardless of the person's position in the organization. They value the opinions and insights of their followers knowing that workers likely know more about day-to-day work functions than does the leader. To become a receptive listener, learn how to ask questions that convey value to the one being asked. Here are some examples:

- What should we do to improve as an organization?
- What is working well? What is not working well? How can we do better?
- What are we missing? Where do we need to give more attention?
- What do you recommend to make this a better place to work?

When a leader asks a follower to share their ideas, they offer them the opportunity to lead, to take the initiative in the conversation. This shows respect and conveys a sense of obligation that the leader has toward the follower. The leader acts out of humility admitting that he or she needs something from the worker believing the worker has something valuable to contribute. Servant leaders listen because they know it is one of the best ways to show value to others.

Yes, servant leaders value people. Servant leaders have developed a mindset that allows them to serve others, trust others, and listen receptively. This requires an outward focus while shifting our view away from ourselves and our own needs as leaders toward those we lead. Through this we leverage a whole new level of interpersonal power and unleash the potential of our followers to bring benefit to themselves, the organization, and those the organization serves.

Develop People: Servant Leader Discipline #2

Our responsibility as servant leaders is to help others grow toward their potential as servants and leaders. Therefore, we should seek to create a dynamic learning environment that encourages growth and development. We focus on strengths more than weakness. As we interact with others we are conscious of what we are learning together. In this mindset, our mistakes and those of others become opportunities to learn. Failure leads to new growth and we become attuned to the habit of seeking new learning rather than seeking someone to blame. We know that people have both present value *and* future potential. As leaders, we are part of helping our followers realize that potential. As you work with people within organizations you will serve them if you display the qualities of developing people (Fig. 4.2).

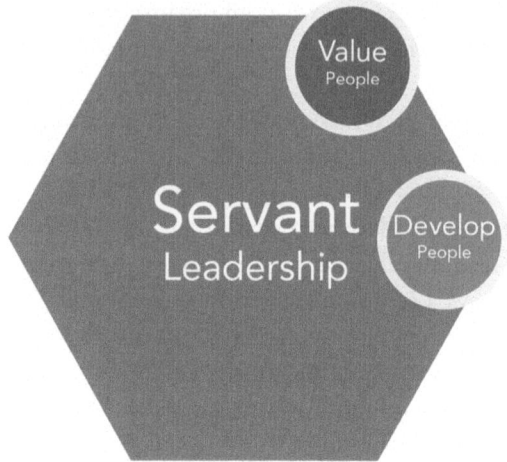

Fig. 4.2 OLA servant leadership model—develop people

Develop People by Providing for Learning

Servant leaders offer people opportunities for new learning. They provide an atmosphere where mistakes can lead to new insights. They join others in the learning. Having a learning mindset totally changes the atmosphere in a relationship from casting blame to seeking new learning. The leader with this mindset does not ask *who is at fault here* but rather asks *what are we to learn from this?* This shift of thinking allows a complete refocus related to errors and mistakes of our own and others by creating an environment of constant cycles of learning. Blaming pits people against each other and creates a negative environment that shuts down learning and forces people into a defensive self-protective mode. When the leader pursues learning and withholds blame he or she is modeling a new way of thinking and acting for the organization.

Think of how a child learns. They learn in a very short time to walk, to speak, to explore. They love to learn and they are masters at it. Consider then how this natural drive to learn can be replaced by a fear of making mistakes. Instead of learning, the child is expected to know—to repeat the right answer and to see learning as a series of right or wrong responses. The joy of learning and therefore the effectiveness of learning is lost. We know instinctively and from experience that learning something new is exciting and energizing. The thrill of exploration allows us to transcend our daily existence to consider things beyond the horizon. We need to recapture this commitment and excitement for learning, this ability to wonder. Servant leaders resist the idea that positional leaders are supposed to know more than others. They resist this illusion because it imprisons us in a right or wrong mindset instead of a questioning, inquisitive mindset. Servant leaders become adept at asking questions and they are open to anyone who might have helpful answers. By providing this learning environment and allowing each person to be both a teacher and a learner, the servant leader, through his or her own desire to learn, creates the opportunity for others to learn.

Develop People by Modeling Appropriate Behavior

The servant leader does not just tell others what to do. They model the behavior they desire to see from others. They help people to develop by working alongside them so they are able to learn from them and alongside them. When Les Cochran took over as President at Youngstown State University he faced a daunting challenge. The university was in the middle of a depressed crime-prone neighborhood aggravated by the shutdown of Youngstown's steel mill and the ensuing economic downturn. How could President Cochran communicate his commitment to the university and the struggling community? His first action was to purchase an abandoned building on the edge of the campus where he would build his new residence. He worked alongside the construction crews and once the residence was completed, he moved his family in. He wanted to encourage a new attitude that would not give in to fear and hopelessness. His motto—*Together we can make a difference*—became empowered through his bold and fearless action. It wasn't enough for President Cochran to have personal positive values or even to back up these values with his words. He needed to *act* on his values and model the behavior he desired to see in others (Kouzes & Posner, 2003). How often have leaders demanded that their workers respond quickly to any and all requests for information? Sometimes these requests come in the middle of the night or during a weekend off. However, these same leaders feel it is their right not to respond to similar requests from their followers. Why this double standard? Servant leaders hold themselves accountable to the same standards and expectations they have of others, and they are willing to go beyond these expectations to model behaviors that fully comply with their values and the shared values of their organization.

Ulysses S. Grant, former US president and general of the northern army during the Civil War, while an army officer was leading a group of men with the challenging but mundane task of clearing oyster beds and removing obstacles so that boats could navigate a river pass. Grant tried to lead the men through his words, but the message was not getting through. So, he jumped into the water up to his waist and began working side by side with his men. This created the direction and motivation he was seeking. While the other officers, high and dry on the shore made fun of Grant's behavior, his commanding officer at the time, Zachery Taylor commented "I wish I had more officers like Grant who would stand ready to set a personal example when needed" (as cited in White, 2017, p. 68). This kind of example derives from a particular mindset of leadership that is directly related to the leader's character. Grant was a humble man who also happened to be an introverted leader. He hated to draw attention to himself even as later he was given leadership of the entire Union army and eventually served two terms as president of the United States. When Grant was being evaluated by President Lincoln and Secretary of War Stanton, Charles Dana from the *New York Tribune* was sent to provide an assessment of the new general. Dana reported back that he had never met a leader like Grant. His report referred to Grant as "an uncommon fellow—the most modest, the most disinterested, and the most honest man I ever knew, with a temper nothing could disturb." He went on to describe Grant as "not an original or brilliant man, but sincere, thoughtful, deep, and gifted with courage that never faltered" (as cited in White, 2017, p. 259).

Servant leaders do not draw attention to themselves. They instead model behavior they expect from others. They do not see themselves as higher than or more important than those they lead; instead, they work with their followers as partners to show them not only the tasks to be performed and how best to perform them but also the values and character expected.

Develop People by Building Them Up Through Encouragement

The servant leader encourages others, honors others, accepts others, and builds up others. They catch others doing things right. They recognize accomplishments and celebrate creativity. They use words of encouragement and affirmation. Rath and Clifton report on a Gallup survey of more than 4 million employees worldwide finding that "individuals who receive regular recognition and praise:

- increase their individual productivity
- increase engagement among their colleagues
- are more likely to stay with their organization
- receive higher loyalty and satisfaction scores from customers
- have better safety records and fewer accidents on the job" (2004)

This same study referred to a study by Fieldman who discovered a statistically and clinically significant rise in blood pressure and hypertension in workers who did not receive this kind of encouragement. The lack of praise and encouragement "could increase the risk of coronary heart disease by one-sixth and the risk of *stroke* by one-third" (Rath & Clifton, 2004). Refusing to offer encouragement and praise can have negative health effects that should not be ignored.

When you believe in people, and tell them that you do, you create a virtuous cycle, "you believe in your constituents' abilities; your favorable expectations cause you to be more positive in your actions; and those encouraging behaviors produce better results, reinforcing your belief that people can do it" (Kouzes & Posner, 2012, p. 279). In light of the incredible benefits of providing this kind of encouragement and affirmation to our workers, why do we not do it when it costs us nothing but our time and minimal effort?

Developing a discipline of encouragement not only benefits the workers but it also brings benefit to the leader by developing a habit of gratitude and appreciation. The simple, yet profound act of saying thank you becomes a recognition of our true role as a leader and serves to keep us humble and rightly related to those we serve. As Depree (1989) states, "the first job of the leader is to define reality, the last job is to say thank you. In between the two, the leader must become a servant and a debtor" (p. 11).

As servant leaders we are to develop those we lead—by providing opportunities for new learning, by modeling appropriate behavior, and by providing encouragement, praise, and affirmation. Through these disciplines we provide what people need to be most productive and to become leaders themselves.

Build Community: Servant Leader Discipline #3

Servant leaders have a different way of thinking about how people do their work. Servant leaders build community—a sense that we are all part of a loving, caring team with a shared goal to accomplish. Leaders resist the tendency to *just get the job done*. They are just as concerned with the relationships of the people doing the job. Leaders know that people will be as impacted by the quality of relationships as they will be by the accomplishment of tasks; therefore, they will intentionally work to build a community that works together and learns to serve one other in the process (Fig. 4.3).

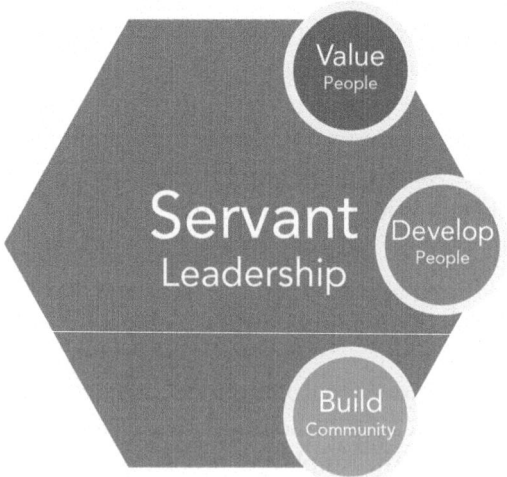

Fig. 4.3 OLA servant leadership model—build community

Greenleaf spoke on this sense of building community when he described his view of institutions, which he called

> a gathering of persons who have an accepted common purpose, and common discipline to guide their pursuit of that purpose, to the end that each involved person reaches higher fulfillment as a person, through serving and being served by the common venture, more so than would be achieved alone or in a less committed relationship. (as cited in Chamberlain, 1995, p. 170)

This sense of shared purpose, people serving and being served at all levels, speaks to a deep commitment to partnership, people working together to produce something that none of them could do alone. Partnership suggests a shared commitment to each other based on a covenant, rather than a contract, between them. It is transformational rather than transactional where each person willfully accepts a high level of accountability to all partners (both leaders and followers). Jack Lowe, Jr., past president of TDIndustries in Dallas, Texas, shared about the necessity of mutual trust to create a community of partners. In fact, TDIndustries, a mechanical construction and service company, is owned by its employees who call each other *partners*. This deep organizational value was significantly challenged in 1989 when the company was nearly lost due to a major economic downturn. It was their first loss as a company in more than 30 years and the leaders had no immediate solution. TDI's bank had gone under and the organization owed significant money and other banks were not in a position to lend. Lowe stated that "much was required for us to survive this situation, but the essential ingredient was the trust and the spirit of our partners" (as cited in Spears, 1998, p. 73). He appealed to his employees offering them the opportunity to invest their Defined Benefit Retirement Earnings into the company. They were asked to take a risk on the future of the company as well as their own financial well-being. Had every partner invested in the new plan they would have raised $1,500,000. They raised $1,250,000 and, as Lowe says, "the rest is history" (p. 74). TDIndustries is more than an organization. They are a community of trust, partners that work, invest, and risk together. They invested in building a community of partnership that ultimately allowed the company to survive and prosper and several floor-level workers became millionaires in the process.

Build Community by Building Relationships

People need the time and space to be together to share, to listen, and to reflect. They need to get to know one another. Servant leaders do not encourage lone-ranger success over team accomplishment; instead, they encourage friendships to emerge and deepen. Desmond Tutu writing on the Act of Law that set up the Truth and Reconciliation Commission in South Africa stated,

> The Act says that the thing you're striving after should be 'Ubuntu' rather than revenge. It comes from the root [of a Zulu-Xhosa word], which means "a person." So it is the essence of being a person. And in our experience, in our understanding, a person is a person through other persons. You can't be a solitary human being. We're all linked. We have this communal sense, and because of this deep sense of community, the harmony of the group is a prime attribute. (as cited in Spears & Lawrence, 2004, p. 238)

What Tutu recognized is that South Africa, coming out of a desperate time of oppression, racism, violence, and atrocity, could never survive unless people viewed each other as persons rather than objects. A person is like me, is part of me, connected to me. An object can be dismissed and rejected or even misused. Leadership is never a solitary endeavor. It assumes relationship and partnership with those we lead. Servant leaders work to build strong positive relationships with others and relationships of this kind must accept the need for offering forgiveness and grace even to those who do not deserve it. The Truth and Reconciliation Commission offered perpetrators of violence a pathway to amnesty if they would tell the whole truth about their crimes and seek forgiveness. This was an amazing step for a new government to take and it led to a mostly bloodless change of power at the highest levels of government. Through this governmental act of servant leadership, South Africa was able to create a forum where relationships could be healed and renewed out of the most difficult of circumstances.

Build Community by Working Collaboratively

Servant leaders do not allow competitiveness between individuals to define the culture of the group. They refuse to *win* at the expense of the team. They emphasize collaboration over competition because they know it fosters the open sharing of information and ideas. The team succeeds or fails together and collaboration gives the team the best chance for success. Servant leaders create a language around collaboration and partnership. Consider the power of language on the tendency to either collaborate or compete. Kouzes and Posner (2012) share the results of an experiment in which participants were told that they were playing either the Community Game or the Wall Street Game. Both games were played by the same rules; in fact, they were exactly the same game except for the different titles. Interestingly, 70% of those who played the game under the title *Community Game* played cooperatively from start to finish while those who played the game under the name of the *Wall Street Game* reacted in an opposite manner. Seventy percent did *not* cooperate and when the 30% who started to play cooperatively saw the lack of cooperation from the larger group, they also stopped cooperating. The mere suggestion from giving the game two different names made a difference in people's willingness to collaborate or compete.

Servant leaders know that competition can motivate some workers to higher performance, but they also know that competition serves to highlight individual performance over the team. Collaboration allows for the contribution of each person and their unique strengths while minimizing weakness. The team serves to balance out each person's contribution to mitigate collective weakness while maximizing strengths. Servant leaders believe in the team and this includes the leadership team. Greenleaf (1977) shared how the top leader serves best from a position of first among equals, primus inter pares, leading with a leadership team rather than leading from the lone spot at the top of a hierarchical structure. He shared that "there is still a 'first,' a leader, but that leader is not the chief … it is important that the *primus* constantly test and prove that leadership among a group of able peers" (p. 61). This is true leadership collaboration that makes full use of the skills of other leaders while protecting the top leader from the problems inherent in leading from a lone premier position.

Build Community by Valuing Differences

Servant leaders respect and celebrate differences in ethnicity, race, gender, age, and culture. They are aware of their own prejudices and biases and are willing to confront them so that no individual or group feels less valued by the organization. Consider the words of Sun Tzu from the fifth century BC in China writing on the beauty of diversity as illustrated by music, colors, and tastes.

> There are not more than five musical notes, yet the combinations of these five give rise to more melodies than can ever be heard.
> There are not more than five primary colors, yet in combination they produce more hues than can ever been seen.
> There are not more than five cardinal tastes, yet combinations of them yield more flavors than can ever be tasted. (Sun Tzu & Griffith, 1964, p. 37)

The servant leader sees the amazing potential of bringing together unique personalities, gifts, and passions to create new possibilities that would never emerge if people were forced to work in isolation. Servant leadership is a paradigm, a mindset, that encourages diversity (Chin & Trimble, 2015) and it does this by valuing and developing people not just for what they produce for the company but toward benefit for the people themselves. Servant leaders, and the people they lead, are encouraged to see difference as a strength because they are learners who realize they can gain from anyone and insights come from any direction.

Much has been made of seeking a cultural fit when hiring new workers and leaders. We want people to share in our common mission, vision, and values. This kind of commitment culture believes that striving for cohesion will produce a team that works together most effectively. A problem with this common wisdom is that our search for alignment may devolve into a placid conformity where everyone is expected to be the same, think the same, and agree on everything. Bridgewater Associates, a financial investment company, challenges this idea of easy agreement with a commitment to encouraging dissenting opinions throughout the organization. Even the founder and president, Ray Dalio, is not immune from this aggressive honesty as he can be (and is) challenged by those below him in the organization. Instead of marginalizing the dissenter, Bridgewater rewards them and has made honest critique part of their culture and a key expectation for employee performance. This works to prevent groupthink (everyone agreeing even though they don't really agree) and promotes an honest exchange of ideas. This has worked for them. "In 2010, Bridgewater's returns exceeded the combined profits of Google, eBay, Yahoo, and Amazon" (Grant, 2016, p. 188). A commitment to diversity is too often seen as seeking a general appreciation for differences while rewarding compliance and comfortable conformity. True diversity requires an acceptance and encouragement of dissent and the servant leader intentionally creates ways for this dissent to be heard. As we have seen, a servant-minded culture that truly values people and seeks to develop them is in the best position to accept the dissenting voice. So, instead of only hiring people who fit the culture, the servant leader will seek people who can improve the culture and will provide forums for these dissenting views to be heard.

Provide Leadership: Servant Leader Discipline #4

Leadership is defined, in this text, as "an intentional change process through which leaders and followers, joined by a shared purpose, initiate action to pursue a common vision" (Laub, 2004, p. 5) so leadership involves the leader's initiative, influence, and impact. However, when servant leaders lead, they do so for the good of those being led over the self-interest of the leader. Servant leadership then becomes a *way* of leading others, a commitment to put the needs of others first before the needs of the leader while working to serve and create other empowered leaders. The servant leader will not neglect to take appropriate action; in fact, all leaders have a bias for action but their action is other-directed and designed for the common good rather than serving the leader's interests. This initiative-taking comes not from being driven to personal ambition but by being called to serve the highest needs of others. Servant leaders are committed to pursuing change, change that seeks the benefit of others. One misconception of servant leadership is that it is only about serving

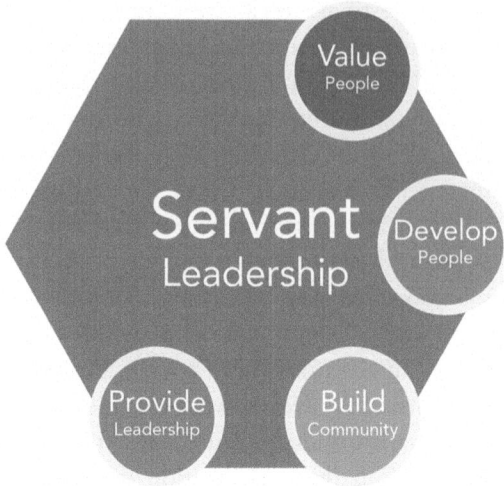

Fig. 4.4   OLA servant leadership model—provide leadership

and not about leading. The servant leader is sometimes viewed as a high-level follower of others (due to understandable confusion surrounding the title of servant leadership) allowing others to dictate what is done in the organization and how the leader acts. This and other misconceptions of servant leadership will be addressed in a later chapter but suffice it to say that servant leaders both serve *and* lead and are not hesitant to bring their own vision and courageous action into the leadership process. Through serving, leaders act out of a strength of personal character and humility that creates unity, commitment, and empowerment throughout the organization (Fig. 4.4).

Provide Leadership by Envisioning the Future: Vision

Leadership is always future oriented; in fact, it exists to create and shape the future. The servant leader looks ahead to envision what *could* be, and *should* be, but the servant leader creates the future through the lens of serving others. The vision that servant leaders create is not for their own benefit or for the benefit of the organization they serve, but it is a vision first for the people they lead. What can each of our workers become?

What can we accomplish together if we consider first the future development of our employees and their unique potential? Servant leaders recognize that they serve as partners with other leaders and followers who also are looking ahead to the future. Servant leaders share their vision openly with the goal of creating a new shared vision developed with others and this requires a high level of trust in the workforce. Servant leaders mobilize others to rally around this shared and collaborative vision, a vision that everyone has worked to shape. A vision like this is owned by each person at all levels of the organization and therefore is more likely to create organizational alignment and follow-through. It all begins with the dream of a preferred future. As Greenleaf (1970) tells us, "not much happens without a dream and for something great to happen, there must be a great dream. Behind every great achievement is a dreamer of great dreams. Much more than a dreamer is required to bring it to reality, but the dream must be there first" (p. 16). Servant leaders create a vision for the development of their workers as well as the entire organization.

Provide Leadership by Taking the Initiative: Action

Leadership requires action. It doesn't hold back in order to protect the leader from making mistakes. The servant leader moves out boldly to serve others and the agreed-upon mission of the group. Greenleaf states that "the essence of leadership ... is that the leader makes the effort first. The leader takes the first step in the belief that, if it provides a clear demonstration of the intent to build a more honest relationship, followers will respond" (as cited in Spears, 1998, p. 85).

In *Servants of the People* (1996) Lea Williams tells the story of Fannie Lou Hamer, who during the civil rights Freedom Summer of 1962 decided that continuing to live in fear was no longer an option. Hamer decided to take action to help the black citizens of Mississippi register to vote. In response, she was evicted from her home, beaten and put in jail, but she would not be deterred. She crusaded throughout the state to address poverty, education needs, and equal rights for blacks at a time when oppression was strong and opposition fierce. She exemplified what Williams called "a rarer type" of leadership. Taking the initiative and pursuing leadership action requires courage and the willingness to step into uncharted territory. When you are serving a great cause and seeking to help those most oppressed there are those who will oppose you. The servant leader must be willing to act through this fear to lead through the resistance that will certainly come. Williams (1996) states, "the servant-leader is committed to serving others through a cause, a crusade, a movement, a campaign with humanitarian not materialistic, goals" (p. 143). Fannie Lou Hamer's favorite spiritual *This Little Light of Mine* became her theme song. She believed that the little light she produced would make a difference in the darkness of rural Mississippi. "I grew up believin' in God," she shared, "but I knew things was bad wrong, and I used to think, 'Let me have a chance, and whatever this is that's wrong in Mississippi, I'm gonna do somethin' about it'" (p. 159). Yes, leadership is about doing something to make a difference in the world. Servant leaders lead. They have a bias for action and are not willing to let others suffer without moving boldly toward a vision for change.

Provide Leadership by Clarifying Goals: Mobilization

A vision is a vivid and compelling picture of a desired future state. It paints an image of a future that exists initially in the mind's eye of the leader, but for leadership to occur we move past the dream and the initial action of pursuing the dream. We create a pathway to the vision; one that everyone can understand while identifying the critical part each person will play. Leadership must be clear on where it is headed. Servant leaders use well-defined and open communication to point the direction the group will pursue together. They determine, with the followers, steps to take to move meaningfully toward the agreed-upon vision. Then, the leader encourages mutual accountability to the goals, for themselves and for others. Servant leaders create a stairway to the vision and then walk up the stairs alongside their partners (fellow leaders and workers) who share the commitment together to see the vision become a reality.

Servant leaders serve and servant leaders lead. They dare not abdicate the power invested in them to create and share vision, act courageously and mobilize others to pursue change. The leadership they provide is first and foremost for others including those they lead and not for their own benefit. The servant leader leads but also allows others to lead so that leadership power can multiply through the lives of other potential leaders.

Share Leadership: Servant Leader Discipline #5

Every leader possesses power and must continually make choices as to how that power is used. Servant leaders share the power they possess so that others can lead, thus increasing the potential influence and impact of their leadership. This sharing of vision, power, and status is a hallmark of the servant leader approach and clearly distinguishes it from other theories and approaches to leadership (Fig. 4.5).

Ulysses S. Grant evaluated two of the commanders he served under years before he himself rose to the level of general of the Union army. He described the first leader, Zachary Taylor, as simply dressed, moving throughout the field of battle without staff to guide him, and confident of his ability to evaluate the situation and direct his men without needing to draw attention to himself. The other leader, Winfield Scott, wore the

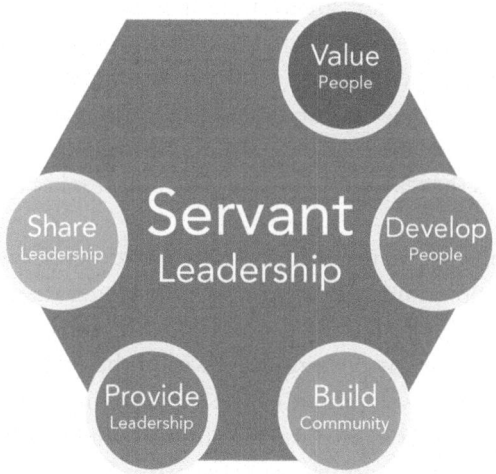

Fig. 4.5 OLA servant leadership model—share leadership

prescribed uniform of the commander, traveled with a large staff, and always sent ahead notification as to when he would arrive so that his troops could salute their leader. Grant's comment is telling as he compares these two very different commanders, "both were pleasant to serve under—Taylor was pleasant to serve with" (as cited in White, 2017, p. 95). Servant leaders allow and expect others to lead with them and it is this partnership that helps create the leveraged power of servant leadership. Servant leaders bring out the power, influence, and creativity of each person creating a critical mass of leadership influence and possibilities. Servant leaders share power. They expect others to lead and share in the leadership process creating an increase in both power and performance.

Share Leadership by Sharing the Vision

The vision of a group does not belong to a single leader. A clear vision of the future shared by the entire group becomes a powerful magnet to draw together the resources, skills, and abilities of the team. Vision comes to leaders who are willing to *see*, and a shared vision occurs when our individual visions align toward an agreed-upon future. Senge (1990) shares that "a shared vision is not an idea … it is, rather a force in people's hearts, a force of impressive power" (p. 206) When people have this deep caring for a vision, when they are truly committed to it, the vision itself is empowered; it becomes a true guiding force that pulls the group and the individuals forward toward the future. The group desires to see this future realized so they are willing to do whatever it takes to see the vision become reality.

"When visions are shared, they attract more people, sustain higher levels of motivation, and withstand more challenges than those that are singular" (Kouzes & Posner, 2012, p. 104). Servant leaders realize that vision can come from any position level within the organization and that those closest to the development of the product or the service provided have the best perspective on how key improvements should be made. When we work to share vision we create spaces for sharing and refining the vision. We talk with people at all levels of the organization especially those closest to our customers and those we serve. We, as leaders, then articulate the shared nature of our vision that derives from these creative forums. We contribute to the vision, to be sure, but only contribute. We seek a vision that emerges from the shared experience and collaborative intelligence of the entire team.

Share Leadership by Sharing Power

Power can be defined as the ability to *do* ... the ability to act in a given situation. In organizational terms it becomes the ability to make important decisions, allocate resources, moving things forward to create new realities. Shared leadership empowers all people at all levels to act, for the good of the group and the shared mission of the organization.

Consider the story of David Marquet (2012) who determined that truly great leaders give control to their followers rather than take control. When Marquet became captain of the nuclear submarine *Santa Fe* it was the poorest-performing sub in the fleet. Over the previous year he had studied the details of a different sub he was scheduled to lead and he knew that ship backward and forward, but at the very last minute, his assignment was changed to the *Santa Fe.* When he boarded as captain he knew less about the ship than anyone else on board and he quickly realized how dependent he was on others. He tried to be the bold, commanding leader but knew that wouldn't work for long. He knew how to command, but he didn't know the ship. The officers under him knew the ship but only understood compliance to orders. It was a disaster waiting to happen. Marquet gathered his men and told them they would all need to become leaders and do the jobs they were trained to do. By allowing others to lead, he opened up their creativity and commitment. People stepped up because they knew they were called on to provide the leadership and expertise only they could provide. The *Santa Fe* moved from a commander with compliant followers to a team of leaders. No excuses, no blaming others; everyone was expected to lead and lead they did. The *Santa Fe* moved from worst to first in the fleet in all categories and several officers ended up commanding nuclear subs after their time on the *Santa Fe.*

Servant leaders give away their power so that all can become more effective leaders. They expect people to act within their areas of expertise and do what is needed to bring improvement to the organization. When servant leaders give power away they end up increasing their own level of power as well as the power of those they serve. They leverage the limited power they possess as a single leader by sharing it with others allowing them to use that power to make important decisions, take necessary action, and work meaningfully for the good of the enterprise. Shared power is never lost. It multiplies as it is used over and over again by those in the best position to act. Servant leaders are willing to take the risk of letting others lead and make critical decisions.

Share Leadership by Sharing Status

Leadership is not about position, status, or prestige. Servant leaders resist the tendency to accept special perks and privileges often granted to leaders in high positions. They know that all people need to be affirmed and recognized for their inherent value and for what they can contribute to the success of the team. Keith (2008) speaks to the willingness of the servant leadership to share status.

> To thrive as a servant-leader, you don't need symbols of success. You need to get material results for your organization, but you need spiritual returns for yourself. You need the personal meaning that will feed your spirit and your soul and give you deep happiness. You need the kind of happiness that cannot come from power, wealth, or fame. You need the happiness that can only come from a life of service. (p. 70)

The symbols of success Keith speaks of may include the large, top-floor, corner office or the special parking space or dining privileges or other perks your followers do not have access to. These symbols often serve to separate leaders from those they serve while creating a false sense of personal and leadership entitlement. When we share status we reject this special privilege and acknowledge that status, prestige, and special perks given to positional leaders can be barriers to the kind of partnership and community we seek with our fellow leaders and workers. Servant leaders desire and seek a happiness that can only come from a life of service to others and nothing, even the special perks of top leadership position, is allowed to get in the way of that higher goal.

Display Authenticity: Servant Leader Discipline #6

Servant leadership begins with a different view of yourself as leader. Servant leaders are open, real, approachable, and accountable to others. They do not consider themselves more valuable than others due to role or position. In fact, a leader's position speaks to responsibility not value or level of contribution. Servant leaders reject the elitism that creeps into organizations as exemplified by Lee Iacocca, former CEO of Chrysler Motors, who was known to pay low wages and provide poor working conditions while spending 2 million dollars renovating his corporate suite when the company was struggling to survive (Dweck, 2016). This kind of autocratic (self-rule) approach to leadership causes much abuse to workers and organizations. It is impossible to value people, develop people, and build community when you create different privileged and non-privileged levels within the organization. Servant leaders work to create an environment that is open and transparent, where information is shared (in appropriate ways) and where workers know that their interests are fully considered and addressed by their leaders (Fig. 4.6).

Display Authenticity by Being Open and Accountable

Servant leaders resist the tendency to protect themselves at all cost. When they make mistakes, they admit them. They recognize that they are accountable to others and not just those who are *over* them positionally in the organization. A servant-minded leader has nothing to prove and does not need to be validated by others and so can fully risk being open and transparent with those they lead. To do this the servant leader is open to criticism and will seek it from those they lead. They accept the warning from Gardner (1990) who states, "pity the leader caught between unlov-

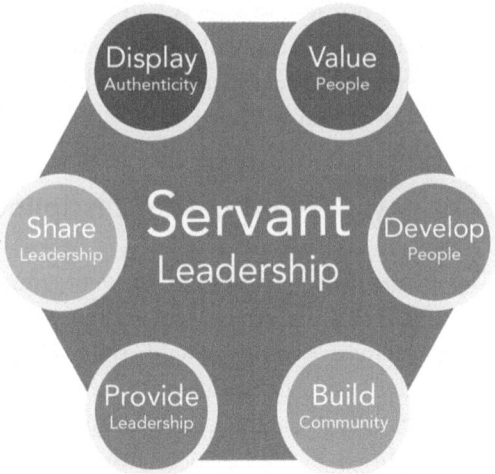

Fig. 4.6 OLA servant leadership model—display authenticity

ing critics and uncritical lovers" (p. 135). Leaders are often insulated from the reality of what is really going on in their organizations and therefore need to receive honest feedback from their followers. The failure to get this kind of input creates a danger for any leader and any organization. As Gardner shared in his commencement address at Cornell University,

> On the one side, those who loved their institutions tended to smother them in an embrace of death, loving their rigidities more than their promise, shielding them from life-giving criticism. On the other side, there arose a breed of critics without love, skilled in demolition, but untutored in the arts by which human institutions are nurtured and strengthened and made to flourish. Between the two, the institutions perished. (1969, p. 4)

All leaders have power over others and this power becomes a block to receiving the kind of honest feedback required. There always will be unloving critics but the leader's worst enemies are the uncritical lovers who tell the leader what he or she wants to know rather than the truth they desperately need to hear. Servant leaders work to create an environment that welcomes honest feedback and truthful analysis. They do this because they lead to serve others not to protect their own image and leadership position. Servant leaders are willing to make themselves accountable to others from all levels of the organization and from people from all roles and positions in order to learn the truth and to give people a voice in speaking to the needs and direction of the organization. They do this because they have a deep willingness and desire to learn.

Display Authenticity Through a Willingness to Learn

Servant leaders approach others from the role of a learner. Servant leaders know that they have much to learn and that each person can be their teacher. They, as leaders, do not always know what is needed and what to do. They are willing to listen before making decisions. They ask a lot of questions and are sincerely interested in the answers. Most important of all, they are willing to admit their mistakes because they see mistakes and failure as pathways to new learning. Though we generally agree that honesty is the best policy we often find reasons to obscure the truth or stonewall against its open expression. Nowhere is this more challenging than in the field of healthcare. Consider the actions taken by the University of Michigan Hospitals and Health System (UMHS). In 2001 they had to pay out $18 million dollars to fight or settle lawsuits. When considering how to decrease their liability they looked to their stated organizational values. They valued respect, compassion, trust, integrity, and leadership, values they truly believed in; so they began a program called *The Michigan Model* designed to promote a new level of honesty and transparency. "The goal of the 'Michigan model' is to limit errors by acknowledging and learning from them. Apologizing to patients and offering follow-up care and sometimes financial compensation also makes them less likely to sue" (Alexander, 2014). Yes, doctors and staff were encouraged to readily admit mistakes and to apologize for these mistakes. What was the result? Within three years of this kind of authenticity, their medical malpractice claims and lawsuits decreased by nearly 50%.

When leaders are willing to admit mistakes and respond honestly to challenges, they engender trust in others, but this requires a mindset that views mistakes as opportunities to learn and grow not as failures to hide and explain away.

Display Authenticity Through Honesty and Integrity

Servant leaders refuse to cut corners on the truth. When they make a promise they do everything they can to fulfill it. When they cannot they quickly communicate openly and honestly to those they made the promise to. Followers learn they can trust what their leaders say and that the leader's actions fit their words. Establishing trustworthiness is a nonnegotiable goal for the servant leader because he or she knows that trust cannot be demanded; it must be earned each and every day. Machiavelli provided an odd twist on this by recommending that the leader do everything to *appear* trustworthy to followers since that would create value and trust for the leader in the minds of the followers. For Machiavelli, honesty of course was not required, only the appearance of it. Servant leaders know that this kind of charade cannot be maintained and that our followers can see through false integrity very efficiently. Our workers want honesty from their leaders and it seems that they want that one quality more than any other. Kouzes and Posner (2012) conducted a multiyear research project with respondents from six continents to determine what people want most from their leaders. The results from 1987 to 2012 changed somewhat from year to year and country to country, but the top characteristic leading the list every year was that of honesty. People want their leaders to be honest with them. They also want their leaders to be forward-looking, competent, and inspiring but honesty is always the number one choice. When leaders are honest they are perceived as trustworthy and people want to follow them.

Janet Cooke, as a young reporter, won acclaim during her tenure at the *Washington Post*. Her article series on an eight-year-old drug addict won her the Pulitzer Prize. Stephen Glass was the young wunderkind reporter at the *New Republic* who rose to prominence due to powerful investigative stories that drew attention to his rising star, but there was a problem. None of these stories were true; they were fabrications made up to make the reporters look good (Dweck, 2016). Their editors were so enamored by the reporter's success that they overlooked, or failed to pursue, the truth of their stories. Success and recognition were the primary driving values and both reporters ended up resigning in shame and the publications took a well-deserved hit on their integrity. Leaders must be honest with their workers, boards, customers, and the public. Leaders who fail this basic test of authenticity will lose the trust of their constituents and find their moral standing compromised.

This kind of authenticity by leaders requires a mindset of humility, acknowledging that others are the priority and that you as a leader do not have all of the answers and that you have much to learn. You cultivate this mindset by taking an accurate view of your strengths and weaknesses and freely admitting mistakes. Yes, authenticity by a leader is risky, but a greater risk is to build a self-protective wall that seriously limits your leadership effectiveness.

Conclusion

The OLA servant leadership model contains six foundational disciplines, each with three descriptors, to guide our understanding and practice of servant leadership. These disciplines are learnable behaviors that can improve with practice but require a change of leadership mindset to practice consistently. This framework provides a way of assessing your own leadership practice while gaining clarity on areas to improve. Servant leadership does not describe a certain type of personality but rather presents a set of actions to help leaders to put others first. Though the practice of this leadership may look different, as it is lived out by leaders with different personalities, we affirm that servant leadership should not be characterized (as it sometimes has been) as introverted, mild-mannered, soft-spoken, and leaderless. Rather, servant leadership presents a leadership of strength and leveraged power that requires a unique courage and drive to trust and empower those we lead, to welcome and draw new learning from failure (our own and others) while creating effective and engaged organizations that fulfill our mission and pursue our shared vision. Servant leadership presents a humble strength that unleashes a stunning powerful response from followers who are for the first time are allowed, even expected, to become leaders themselves.

Assess Your Own Leadership Mindset

To assess your own leadership mindset, go to the website servantleader-performance.com to complete the free Servant Leader Performance (SLP) *Self-Assessment* instrument. Through this you can assess your own relative strengths and weaknesses in the six key disciplines of servant leadership.

References

Alexander, D. (2014, May). The honesty policy. *Ann Arbor Observer*. Retrieved from http://annarborobserver.com/articles/printable/printable_the_honesty_policy.html

Barbuto, J. E., Jr., & Wheeler, D. W. (2006). Scale development and construct clarification of servant leadership. *Group and Organizational Management, 31*, 300–326.

Chamberlain, P. (1995). Team-building and servant-leadership. In L. C. Spears & M. Lawrence (Eds.), *Reflections on leadership: How Robert K. Greenleaf's theory of servant-leadership influenced today's top management thinkers* (pp. 169–178). New York, NY: John Wiley & Sons, Inc.

Chin, J. L., & Trimble, J. E. (2015). *Diversity and leadership*. Los Angeles, CA: Sage Publications.

Covey, S. R. (1989). *The 7 habits of highly effective people: Powerful lessons in personal change*. New York, NY: Free Press.

Covey, S. R. (1994). Serving the one. *Executive Excellence, 11*(9), 3–4.

Dennis, R. S., & Bocarnea, M. (2005). Development of the servant leadership assessment instrument. *Leadership & Organization Development Journal, 26*, 600–615.

DePree, M. (1989). *Leadership is an art*. New York, NY: Dell Publishing Group.

Dweck, C. S. (2016). *Mindset: The new psychology of success* (2nd ed.). New York, NY: Ballantine Books.

Gardner, J.W. (1969). Uncritical lovers, unloving critics. *The Journal of Educational Research, 62*(9), 396–399. Retrieved from https://www.jstor.org/stable/27532243

Gardner, J. W. (1990). *On leadership*. New York, NY: The Free Press.

Graham, J. W. (1991). Servant-leadership in organizations: Inspirational and moral. *Leadership Quarterly, 2*(2), 105–119.

Grant, A. (2013). *Give and take: A revolutionary approach to success*. New York, NY: Penguin Group.

Grant, A. (2016). *Originals: How non-conformists move the world*. New York, NY: Penguin Group.

Greenleaf, R. (1970). *The servant as leader*. Westfield, IN: Greenleaf Center for Servant Leadership.

Greenleaf, R. K. (1977). *Servant leadership: A journey into the nature of legitimate power and greatness*. Mahwah, NJ: Paulist Press.

Heifetz, R. A. (1994). *Leadership without easy answers*. Cambridge: Harvard University Press.

Jackson, T. (2002). The management of people across cultures: Valuing people differently. *Human Resource Management, 41*(4), 455–475. https://doi.org/10.1002/hrm.10054

Joseph, E. E., & Winston, B. E. (2005). A correlation of servant leadership, leader trust, and organizational trust. *Leadership & Organization Development Journal, 26*(1), 6–22.

Keith, K. M. (2008). *The case for servant leadership*. Westfield, IN: The Greenleaf Center for Servant Leadership.

Kouzes, J. M., & Posner, B. Z. (2003). *The Jossey-bass academic Administrator's guide to exemplary leadership*. San Francisco, CA: Jossey-Bass.

Kouzes, J. M., & Posner, B. Z. (2012). *The leadership challenge: How to make extraordinary things happen in organizations* (5th ed.). San Francisco, CA: The Leadership Challenge, A Wiley brand.

Laub, J. A. (1999). *Assessing the servant organization: Development of the servant organizational leadership (SOLA) instrument*. Unpublished doctoral dissertation, Florida Atlantic University.

Laub, J. A. (1999–2018). *The Organizational Leadership Assessment instrument (OLA)*. Jupiter, FL: The OLAgroup.

Laub, J. A. (2004). Defining servant leadership: A recommended typology for servant leadership studies. *Proceedings of the Servant Leadership Research Roundtable*. Retrieved August 20, 2009, from http://www.regent.edu/acad/global/publications/sl_proceedings/2004/laub_defining_servant.pdf

Laub, J. A. (2010). The servant organization. In D. van Dierendonck & K. Patterson (Eds.), *Servant leadership: Developments in theory and research* (pp. 105–117). Hampshire: Palgrave Macmillan.

Liden, R. C., Wayne, S. J., Zhao, H., & Henderson, D. (2008). Servant leadership: Development of a multidimensional measure and multi-level assessment. *Leadership Quarterly, 19*, 161–177.

Lowe, J. (1998). Trust: The invaluable asset. In L. C. Spears (Ed.), *Insights on leadership: Service, stewardship, spirit, and servant-leadership* (pp. 68–76). New York, NY: John Wiley & Sons, Inc.

Marquet, L. D. (2012). *Turn the ship around: How to create leadership at every level.* Austin, TX: Greenleaf Book Group Press.

McCarron, H. S., Lewis-Smith, J., Belton, L., Yanovsky, B., Robinson, J., & Osatuke, K. (2016, February). Creation of a multi-rater feedback assessment for the development of servant leaders at the veterans health administration. *Servant Leadership: Theory & Practice, 3*(1), 12–51.

Millard, B. (1995). *Servant-leadership – It's right and it works!* Colorado Springs, CO: Life Discovery Publications.

Northouse, P. G. (2016). *Leadership: Theory and practice* (7th ed.). Thousand Oaks, CA: Sage Publications, Inc.

Parris, D. L., & Peachey, J. W. (2013). A systematic literature review of servant leadership theory in organizational contexts. *Journal of Business Ethics, 113,* 377–393.

Patterson, K. A. (2003). *Servant leadership: A theoretical model.* Doctoral dissertation, Regent University, ATT 30882719.

Rath, T., & Clifton, D. O. (2004, July). *The power of praise and recognition.* Retrieved August, 2017, from http://www.gallup.com/businessjournal/12157/power-praise-recognition.aspx

Russell, R. F., & Stone, A. G. (2002). A review of servant-leadership attributes: Developing a practical model. *Leadership & Organization Development Journal, 23,* 145–157.

Seidman, D. (2007). *How: Why how we do anything means everything … in business (and in life).* Hoboken, NJ: John Wiley & Sons, Inc.

Sendjaya, S., Sarros, J. C., & Santora, J. C. (2008). Defining and measuring servant leadership behavior in organizations. *Journal of Management Studies, 45*(2), 402–424.

Senge, P. M. (1990). *The fifth discipline: The art & practice of the learning organization.* New York, NY: Doubleday.

Senge, P. M. (1997). Creating learning communities. *Executive Excellence, 14*(3), 17–18.

Spears, L. (Ed.). (1995). *Reflections on leadership: How Robert K. Greenleaf's theory of servant-leadership influenced today's top management thinkers.* New York: Wiley.

Spears, L., & Lawrence, M. (Eds.). (2004). *Practicing servant leadership: Succeeding through trust, bravery, and forgiveness*. San Francisco, CA: Jossey-Bass.

Spears, L. C. (Ed.). (1998). *The power of servant-leadership: Essays by Robert K. Greenleaf*. San Francisco, CA: Berrett-Koehler Publishers.

Sun Tzu, & Griffith, S. B. (1964). *The art of war*. Oxford: Clarendon Press.

van Dierendonck, D., & Nuijten, I. (2011). The servant leadership survey: Development and validation of a multidimensional measure. *Journal of Business and Psychology, 26*, 246–267.

Ward, W. A. (1970). *Fountains of faith: The words of William Arthur Ward*. Anderson, SC: Droke House Publishers.

Wheatley, M. J. (1994). *Leadership and the new science: Learning about organizations from an orderly universe*. San Francisco: Berrett-Koehler.

White, R. C. (2017). *American Ulysses: A life of Ulysses S. Grant*. New York, NY: Random House Trade Paperback Edition.

Williams, L. E. (1996). *Servants of the people: The 1960's legacy of African American leadership*. New York, NY: St. Martin's Press.

Wong, P. T. P., & Davey, D. (2007). *Best practices in servant leadership*. Paper presented at the Servant Leadership Research Roundtable, Regen University, Virginia Beach, VA.

5

Model Building for Servant Leadership: 1991–2016

The OLA model of servant leadership presented in the previous chapter is one of 11 servant leadership models put forward by writers and researchers over the years seeking to build from and expand Greenleaf's original work. These models reveal a progression of learning while affirming common themes to help us understand more clearly what servant leadership is, what it looks like, and how it functions within organizations. Most of these models are research based and several have developed reliable and valid assessment tools to measure servant leadership for ongoing research and organizational consulting. Here is the list of the 11 models followed by an explanation and review.

1. The Graham model (1991)
2. The Spears model (1995) (drawn from Greenleaf's writings)
3. The Laub model (1999)—with the OLA
4. The Russell and Stone model (2002)
5. The Patterson model (2003)—with the *Servant Leadership Assessment Instrument* (Dennis & Bocarnea, 2005)
6. The Barbuto and Wheeler model (2006)—with the *Servant Leadership Questionnaire* (SLQ)

© The Author(s) 2018
J. Laub, *Leveraging the Power of Servant Leadership*, Palgrave Studies in Workplace Spirituality and Fulfillment, https://doi.org/10.1007/978-3-319-77143-4_5

7. The Wong and Davey model (2007)—with the *Revised Servant Leadership Profile* (RSLP)
8. The Sendjaya, Sarros, and Santora model (2008)—with the *Servant Leadership Behavior Scale* (SLBS)
9. The Liden, Wayne, Zhao, and Henderson model (2008)—with the *Servant Leadership Scale* (SLS)
10. The van Dierendonck and Nuijten model (2011)—with the *Servant Leadership Survey* (SLS)
11. The McCarren, Lewis-Smith, Belton, Yanovsky, Robinson, and Osatuke model (2016)—with the *VHA Servant Leadership 360-Degree Assessment* (VHA SL360)

Ten of these models are compared and contrasted in Table 5.1 toward the end of the chapter to show commonalities and contrasts between models and to summarize the learning gained over the past two decades of study. Before viewing that summary, let's first walk through an analysis of each of these important models and how each one adds to the growing body of servant leadership research.

The Graham Model (1991)

Just two decades after Greenleaf's initial essay (1970), Graham evaluated servant leadership in contrast to charismatic leadership. Her concern was that charismatic leadership as a subset of Transformational Leadership (Bass, 1985, 2000; Burns, 1978) did not provide a moral base since leaders as disparate as Hitler and Mother Teresa could be viewed as charismatic leaders. Graham was drawn to the servant leadership approach due to its explicit ethical and moral foundations and she proposed the following five characteristics of servant leadership:

1. Humility
2. Relational power
3. Autonomy
4. Moral development of followers
5. Emulation of leaders' service orientation (Graham, 1991)

Graham's list was collected through a review of the literature including original work from Greenleaf. This was the beginning of servant leadership model building and it was up to Spears, Director of the Greenleaf Center for Servant Leadership at the time, to put together the first official list of servant leadership characteristics drawn specifically from the work of Greenleaf.

The Spears Model (1995): Ten Characteristics of the Servant Leader Drawn from Greenleaf

Greenleaf was the first to coin the term servant leadership and introduce the concept to a modern audience. Servant leadership, of course, has a rich history in classical literature as reviewed in Chap. 2, but it was Greenleaf who developed the philosophical underpinnings of the concept and it was Spears who codified the list of ten characteristics drawn from the work of Greenleaf. Greenleaf served at the AT&T organization for 40 years before retiring in the 1960s when the concept of servant leadership began to coalesce in his mind. Spears relates the influence a story in Herman Hesse's novel *Journey to the East* had on Greenleaf's thinking about servant leadership. Spears (1995) shares the story about

a mythical journey by a group of people on a spiritual quest. The central figure of the story is Leo, who accompanies the party as the servant and who sustains them with his caring spirit. All goes well with the journey until one day Leo disappears. The group cannot manage without Leo. After many years of searching, the narrator of the story stumbles upon Leo and is taken into the religious order that sponsored the original journey. There, he discovers that Leo, whom he had known as a servant, was in fact the head and guiding spirit of the order—a great and noble leader. Greenleaf concluded that the central meaning of this story is that great leaders must first serve others, and that this simple fact is central to his or her greatness. True leadership emerges from those whose primary motivation is a desire to help others. (p. 3)

From this conviction, Greenleaf moved on to clarify a distinction between what he saw as the one who is leader first versus one who is servant first and how that commitment to serve first moves to a desire to lead from the heart of a servant.

It begins with the natural feeling that one wants to serve, to serve first. Then conscious choice brings one to aspire to lead. The difference manifests itself in the care taken by the servant—first to make sure that other people's highest priority needs are being served. The best test is: Do those served grow as persons; do they, while being served, become healthier, wiser, freer, more autonomous, more likely themselves to become servants? (as cited in Spears, 1995, p. 4)

From the foundational works of Greenleaf, Spears (1995), then the Director of the Greenleaf Center for Servant Leadership, drew this list of ten characteristics of the servant leader.

1. Listening
2. Empathy
3. Healing
4. Awareness
5. Persuasion
6. Conceptualization
7. Foresight
8. Stewardship
9. Commitment to the growth of people
10. Building community (pp. 4–7)

Spears affirms that these ten characteristics "are by no means exhaustive" (p. 7) so he foresaw the ongoing development of multiple servant leadership models seeking to bring clarity to this age-old concept of servant leadership.

The Laub (OLA) Model (1999)

Laub's OLA servant leadership model is presented in this book as the central model for our discussion on leveraging the power of servant leadership. The OLA model was the first research-based servant leadership approach and was developed through a Delphi research process and used as the basis of the development of the *Organizational Leadership Assessment* (*OLA*) instrument. This instrument, the first research-based assessment tool on servant leadership, has been used in over 85 studies contributing to the growing field of servant leadership research as described in Chap. 9.

According to the Laub (OLA) servant leadership model, servant leaders:

1. Value People

    (a) By trusting and believing in people
    (b) By serving others' needs before their own
    (c) By receptive, non-judgmental listening

2. Develop People

    (a) By providing opportunities for learning and growth
    (b) By modeling appropriate behavior
    (c) By building up others through encouragement and affirmation

3. Build Community

    (a) By building strong personal relationships
    (b) By working collaboratively with others
    (c) By valuing the differences of others

4. Display Authenticity

    (a) By being open and accountable to others
    (b) By a willingness to learn from others
    (c) By maintaining integrity and trust

5. Provide Leadership

    (a) By envisioning the future
    (b) By taking initiative
    (c) By clarifying goals

6. Share Leadership

    (a) By facilitating a shared vision
    (b) By sharing power and releasing control
    (c) By sharing status and promoting others. (1999, p. 83)

These six disciplines of servant leadership, each with three descriptors, provide a description of what servant leadership looks like when displayed by leaders within an organization or team setting. These characteristics are observable and therefore can be assessed by people within the organization (top leaders, managers, and the workforce). The OLA instrument is a single-score assessment with high reliability scores yet was not able to support a multidimensional model like those produced in later studies. In addition to the high number of studies on servant leadership conducted with the OLA, the instrument has also been used in hundreds of organizations for assessment and consulting to help measure their level of organizational health and then pursue ways to improve their servant mindset.

The Russell and Stone Model (2002)

Russell and Stone (2002) developed their model after a review of the servant leadership literature with the hope of developing a researchable model. For them, "servant leadership takes place when leaders assume the position of servant in their relationships with fellow workers. Self-interest should not motivate servant leadership; rather, it should ascend to a higher plane of motivation that focuses on the needs of others" (p. 145). Russell and Stone claim that this list of servant leadership attributes "includes all of the Greenleaf characteristics in some form or another" (p. 146) since most of the literature at the time was developed from Greenleaf's writings. They identified nine *functional* attributes, called this due to their common use in the literature, viewing them as "operative qualities, characteristics and distinctive features belonging to leaders and observed through specific leader behaviors in the workplace" (p. 146). In addition to the functional attributes they identified 11 additional attributes they called *accompanying* attributes which serve to complement the functional attributes.

Functional Attributes

1. Vision
2. Honesty
3. Integrity

4. Trust
5. Service
6. Modeling
7. Pioneering
8. Appreciation of others
9. Empowerment

Accompanying Attributes

1. Communication
2. Credibility
3. Competence
4. Stewardship
5. Visibility
6. Influence
7. Persuasion
8. Listening
9. Encouragement
10. Teaching
11. Delegation

Utilizing this attribute list as a base, the authors proposed two conceptual models of servant leadership to show the interrelationship of the functional and accompanying attributes, values, organizational culture, employee attitudes, work behaviors, and organizational performance.

The Patterson Model (2003)

Patterson (2003) presents a "theoretical model that specifically addresses phenomena not fully explained in the literature" (p. 1) and presents what she calls seven virtuous constructs of servant leadership. Patterson contrasts servant leadership with Transformational Leadership suggesting that the latter does not account for altruism of the leader toward the follower or for the servant-oriented humility of the leader and its affects. "Servant leadership is about focus. The focus of the leader is on followers and his/her behaviors and attitudes are congruent with this follower focus" (2003, p. 2). Patterson contrasts this view with Transformational Leadership where the focus is on organizational outcomes and workers are viewed as a means to an end that ultimately benefits the organization first. Patterson's model "is based on virtues that comprise servant leadership and consists of qualities of the leader, actions a leader takes, and the internal state of the leader" (McCarren et al., 2016, p. 25). She proposes seven characteristics in her model:

1. Agapao (unconditional) Love
2. Humility
3. Altruism
4. Vision
5. Trust
6. Empowerment
7. Service

These seven virtuous constructs are seen as working in a progression. First, the leader has a moral, unconditional love for others that compels them to serve. They possess an accurate estimation of themselves in relation to others and a humble spirit that allows them to focus on others instead of their own self-interest. This results in acts of altruism to serve other's needs. Vision, in Patterson's view, refers to a leader's vision for their followers and how each person has future potential the leader can help them realize. This focus on the follower engenders trust between leader and follower and that trust allows for empowerment to occur leading ultimately to all, both leaders and followers, providing service to others continuing the servant leadership procession. In 2005, Dennis and Bocarnea developed the *Servant Leadership Assessment Instrument* based on Patterson's model. Through exploratory factor analysis, five factors were found: empowerment, love, humility, trust, and vision. The altruism and service factors were not supported directly by the factor analysis, but remain an important part of the model.

The Barbuto and Wheeler Model (2006)

Barbuto and Wheeler (2006) assembled 11 characteristics of servant leadership taken from a review of the literature and submitted this list to a research testing of internal consistency, factor analysis and validity. The result of this study produced the following five factors. This list was then used to develop the *Servant Leader Questionnaire (SLQ)* instrument.

1. Altruistic calling
2. Emotional healing
3. Persuasive mapping
4. Wisdom
5. Organizational stewardship

An additional finding from this study was that "servant leadership was a better predictor of LMX quality than was transformational leadership. This finding supports the premise that servant leaders create serving relationships with their followers, which contrasts with transformational leaders, who transcend follower interest toward organizational goals" (p. 319). This supports the finding of Patterson that servant leadership focuses first on the followers while Transformational Leadership focuses first on the organization (Stone, Russell, & Patterson, 2004). Barbuto and Wheeler (2006) share that "the excitement surrounding servant leadership may be justified, as it appears strong relationships with positive outcomes such as employees' extra effort, employees' satisfaction, and perceptions of organizational effectiveness were found" (p. 322).

The Wong and Davey Model (2007)

To Wong and Davey (2007), servant leadership

represents a radical approach—it is humanistic and spiritual rather than rational and mechanistic; it puts workers rather than shareholders at the center of concentric circles; and it motivates workers primarily through creating a caring and supportive workplace rather than through individual systems. (p. 3)

Wong originally worked with Page to identify seven factors for a servant leader profile (Wong & Page, 2003). Through the use of their instrument, the *Revised Servant Leadership Profile* (RSLP), they trimmed this list down to "five meaningful and stable factors" (2007, p. 6).

1. Serving and developing others
2. Consulting and involving others
3. Humility and selflessness
4. Modeling integrity and authenticity
5. Inspiring and influencing others

They claim that "this five-factor theory of SL captures the essential aspects of servant leadership and provides a useful conceptual framework for practice and leadership training" (2007, p. 6). The model continues the development of a clear and growingly consistent approach to understanding servant leadership.

The Sendjaya, Sarros, and Santora Model (2008)

These authors, two from Australia and one from the United States, reveal a growing global interest in servant leadership research. They collaborated to develop the *Servant Leadership Behavior Scale* (SLBS) which presents the following six dimensions for measuring servant leadership.

1. Transforming influence
2. Voluntary subordination
3. Authentic self
4. Transcendental spirituality
5. Covenantal relationship
6. Responsible morality

To explain the characteristics of voluntary subordination, which could sound like a negative term, the authors state, the Bible where seven key Greek words are often used to denote the term 'servant' while referring to leaders, namely *diakonos, doulos, huperetes, therapon, oiketes, sundoulos,* and *pais* (Getz, 1984). None of these words insinuates a lack of self-respect or low self-image. Instead, voluntary subordination is manifested in the willingness to assume the lowliest of positions and endure hardship and suffering on behalf of other people. (2008, p. 406)

The authors see servant leadership not as a set of behaviors but rather a description of who the servant leader is at his or her core. It is the essence, or nature, of the servant leader that this list is focused on. "Servant leaders portray a resolute conviction and strong character by taking on not only the role of a servant, but also the nature of a servant, which is demonstrated by their total commitment to serve other people" (2008. p. 406). This particular model, more than the others, brings out the concept of spirituality or what they call transcendental spirituality believing that the servant leader is "imbued with spiritual values" by bringing together service and meaning (2008, p. 408). By adding the spiritual and moral-ethical dimensions to previous models the authors believe that they have presented "a more holistic model of servant leadership than existing models" (2008, p. 410).

The Liden, Wayne, Zhao, and Henderson Model (2008)

Liden, and associates, created a model that moved beyond servant leadership characteristics or behaviors to include both antecedent conditions that affect servant leadership application and the outcomes of those servant leadership behaviors. Three antecedent conditions were identified: context and culture, leader attributes, and follower receptivity (Northouse, 2016). This suggests that the organizational context and culture impacts how servant leadership is displayed and received by followers. In addition, leader traits and attributes affect how servant leadership is displayed by different leaders. Follower receptivity refers to the follower's desire to work with a servant leader and suggests that not all do and that this match between servant leadership and the follower's desire for it impacts servant leadership effectiveness. Seven servant leader behaviors constitute the heart of the model indicating what servant leaders do.

Servant Leader Behaviors

1. Conceptualizing
2. Emotional healing
3. Putting followers first
4. Helping followers grow and succeed
5. Behaving ethically
6. Empowering
7. Creating value for the community

Three servant leadership outcomes are also considered within the model: follower performance and growth, organizational performance, and societal impact. These are anticipated or expected outcomes from servant leadership behaviors being applied and moderated by the antecedent conditions. To develop this model and to test its implications the *Servant Leadership Scale* (SLS) was developed. "A consistent criticism across the many servant leadership models is their blending of antecedents, behaviors, and outcomes of servant leadership" (McCarren et al., 2016, p. 29). The Liden model works to address this criticism.

The van Dierendonck and Nuijten Model (2011)

This multidimensional model by van Dierendonck and Nuijten (2011) was "based on literature review and expert judgment" (p. 249) and through this study a new assessment tool was developed called the *Servant Leadership Survey* (SLS). "The SLS primarily focuses on the leader-follower relationship measured from the perspective of the follower" (2011, p. 251). The authors felt that too much emphasis in past models had been on the *servant* side of servant leadership and not enough on the *leadership* side. They provide a helpful analysis of the strengths and weaknesses of previous models and assessment tools. "Based on an analysis of the servant leadership literature and interviews with servant leaders, these eight aspects were selected as the best indicators of servant leadership" (2011, p. 252).

1. Empowerment
2. Humility
3. Standing back
4. Authenticity
5. Forgiveness
6. Courage
7. Accountability
8. Stewardship

In comparing this approach to previous models, areas that stand out as unique are accountability, stewardship, and courage. The SLS assessment developed through this study is a strong addition to the field and is currently used in multiple research studies to further the foundational base of servant leadership understanding.

The McCarren, Lewis-Smith, Belton, Yanovsky, Robinson, and Osatuke Model (2016)

This study from McCarren and associates was specifically designed to develop an assessment tool for use in the Veteran's Health Administration (VHA) in the United States to support the development of a more servant-oriented culture. The authors also desired to provide "a blueprint for other organizations seeking to embed servant leadership principles in their culture" (McCarren et al., 2016, p. 14). They reviewed multiple servant leadership models and assessment tools and settled on the *Seven Pillars of Servant Leadership model* developed by Sipe and Frick (2009). The seven pillars are further extended by the addition of 20 behavioral characteristics.

Pillar 1: Person of Character

1. Maintains integrity
2. Demonstrates humility
3. Engages in value-driven behavior

Pillar 2: Puts People First

4. Service driven
5. Mentor-minded
6. Shows care and concern

Pillar 3: Skilled Communicator

7. Empathetic listening
8. Invites and delivers feedback
9. Communicates persuasively

Pillar 4: Compassionate Collaborator

10. Builds teams and communities
11. Psychological safety
12. First among equals

Pillar 5: Foresight

13. Visionary
14. Anticipates consequences
15. Takes courageous, decisive action

Pillar 6: Systems Thinker

16. Comfortable with complexity
17. Effectively leads change
18. Stewardship

Pillar 7: Moral Authority

19. Shares power and control
20. Creates a culture of accountability

The authors of this model sought to move away from viewing servant leadership as a philosophy to viewing it as "a learnable and teachable set of practices" (2016, p. 29). From this model, the *VHA Servant Leadership 360-Degree Assessment* (VHA SL360) was developed to give leaders in the VHA feedback on their performance based on the criteria of this model. The VHA is intentionally implementing servant leadership even to evaluating managers on servant leadership behaviors in performance reviews. Senior managers in the VHA are held accountable for modeling servant leadership throughout the organization and new hires are screened and selected according to these servant leadership traits.

Summary of Servant Leadership Models Review

Each of these 11 models provides unique perspectives while a set of common characteristics can be seen. Common characteristics shared through these models are serving others/selflessness, humility, authenticity, integrity/trustworthiness, developing people, empowerment/sharing leadership, building community/relationships, stewardship, valuing people/love, and providing leadership/vision/influence. Some characteristics that are unique to select models are consulting and involving others (Wong & Davey, 2007), emotional healing, persuasive mapping, wisdom (Barbuto & Wheeler, 2006), transcendental spirituality (Sendjaya et al., 2008), and forgiveness, courage, and accountability (van Dierendonck & Nuijten, 2011). Though there are differences in the models there are more commonalities, suggesting a developing and consistent understanding of servant leadership through the current research literature.

A further and deeper comparison is available from a review of the *Comparison of Servant Leadership Models* (1995–2016) where all models are compared and contrasted (see Table 5.1).

Comparison Chart of Multiple Servant Leadership Models (1995–2016)

Table 5.1 A comparison of servant leadership models (1995–2016)

Laub (1999)	Spears (Greenleaf) (1995)	Russell and Stone (2002)	Patterson (2003), Dennis and Bocarnea (2005)	Barbuto and Wheeler (2006)	Wong and Davey (2007)	Sendjaya et al. (2008)	Liden et al. (2008)	van Dierendonck and Nuijten (2011)	McCarren et al. (2016)
Value people	Empathy							Interpersonal acceptance—forgiveness	Shows care and concern
Trusting & believing in others		Trust Appreciation of others	Trust			Trust			
Serving others	Healing	Service	Altruism Service	Altruistic calling Emotional healing		Voluntary subordination Being a servant Acts of service	Putting followers first Emotional healing	Standing back	Service driven
Receptive listening	Listening	Listening							Empathetic listening
Develop people					Serving and developing others	Transforming influence	Helping followers grow and succeed		Invites and delivers feedback
Opportunities for learning	Commitment to the growth of people	Teaching				Mentoring			Mentor-minded
Modeling behavior		Modeling Visibility				Modeling			
Encouragement		Encouragement							
Build community	Building community								Builds teams and communities
Build relationships			Covenantal relationship			Covenantal relationship			Psychological safety

Collaborative work Valuing differences						Collaboration			First among equals
Display authenticity	Awareness		Humility	Wisdom	Humility and selflessness	Authentic self Humility Responsible morality Security Vulnerability Accountability	Behaving ethically	Authenticity Humility	Engages in value-driven behavior Demonstrates humility
Accountable								Accountability	Creates a culture of accountability
Learning from others					Consulting and involving others				
Integrity & Trustworthiness		Honesty Integrity Credibility Trust			Integrity and authenticity	Integrity			Maintains integrity
Provide leadership	Persuasion	Influence Competence Persuasion		Persuasive mapping	Inspiring and influencing others			Courage	Communicates persuasively Effectively leads change
Envision the future	Conceptualization foresight	Vision				Vision	Conceptualizing		Visionary Anticipate consequences
Taking initiative		Pioneering							Takes courageous decisive action
Clarifying direction		Communication							

(continued)

Table 5.1 (continued)

Laub (1999)	Spears (Greenleaf) (1995)	Russell and Stone (2002)	Patterson (2003), Dennis and Bocarnea (2005)	Barbuto and Wheeler (2006)	Wong and Davey (2007)	Sendjaya et al. (2008)	Liden et al. (2008)	van Dierendonck and Nuijten (2011)	McCarren et al. (2016)
Share leadership	Stewardship	Stewardship		Organizational stewardship				Stewardship	Stewardship
Sharing vision									
Sharing power		Empowerment Delegation	Empowerment			Empowerment	Empowering	Empowerment	Shares power and control
Sharing status						Transcendental spirituality	Creating value for the community		Comfortable with complexity
Servant Leadership Assessment Instruments									
Organizational Leadership Assessment (OLA)			Servant Leadership Assessment Instrument	Servant Leader Questionnaire (SLQ)	Revised Servant Leadership Profile (RSLP)	Servant Leadership Behavior Scale (SLBS)	Servant Leadership Scale (SLS)	Servant Leadership Survey (SLS)	VHA Servant Leadership 360-Degree Assessment (VHA SL360)

An Argument in Favor of Multiple Models

A common concern shared within and outside the servant leadership literature is the lack of a consistent definition and model for presenting and training in servant leadership. "A comprehensive review of the existing literature revealed a lack of a theory-based framework for how to intentionally develop an organization's servant leadership culture" (McCarren et al., 2016, p. 14). Also, "the field is lacking consistency and consensus in the definition, measurement, and application of the construct" (McCarren et al., 2016, p. 14) (van Dierendonck & Nuijten, 2011). The characterization of the state of servant leadership studies is considered by Brown and Bryant to be "muddled … because scholars are speaking different languages as they continue to define and redefine servant leadership" (as cited in McCarren et al., 2016, p. 44).

This author takes a different view, especially after reviewing each of these models. Servant leadership is an age-old concept yet is relatively new in the study of leadership. The same criticism we hear about the muddle of servant leadership definition, model building, and research is also cast at the study of leadership itself. All of these models are needed. All of these studies bring something valuable to the growing understanding and clarity of what servant leadership is, how it should be defined and operationalized, and how it can be taught to bring greater health to organizations.

There is immense value in these models and one would expect scholars to disagree and even speak different languages as they come at this concept from multiple lenses and viewpoints. However, we can celebrate a growing clarity as we continue to work through the defining, measurement, and application of servant leadership. Learning is sometimes a messy and imprecise business yet we can benefit from taking a more appreciative approach to the learning we have and the opportunity this creates for greater clarity in the future.

Conclusion

We have seen, in this chapter, a 25-year effort to clarify the meaning and application of servant leadership. Each of these models provides a unique lens for viewing this dynamic approach to leadership and all of them taken together provide a set of common characteristics that bring clarity to our understanding. We are learning what it means to be a servant leader and we have discovered multiple ways these constructs can be measured within organizations. There is much work remaining, but we certainly have a rich and valuable heritage of servant leadership model building to guide us. Another pathway we can take to understand the concept of servant leadership better is to address objections and misconceptions that come from those who challenge the validity or usefulness of the concept. We move now to consider the most common misconceptions and objections that people have about servant leadership as a viable understanding and practice of leadership.

References

Barbuto, J. E., Jr., & Wheeler, D. W. (2006). Scale development and construct clarification of servant leadership. *Group and Organizational Management, 31*, 300–326.

Bass, B. M. (1985). *Performance beyond expectations*. New York: Free Press.

Bass, B. M. (2000). The future of leadership in learning organizations. *The Journal of Leadership Studies, 7*, 18–40.

Burns, J. M. (1978). *Leadership*. New York: Harper and Row.

Dennis, R. S., & Bocarnea, M. (2005). Development of the servant leadership assessment instrument. *Leadership & Organization Development Journal, 26*, 600–615.

Graham, J. W. (1991). Servant-leadership in organizations: Inspirational and moral. *Leadership Quarterly, 2*(2), 105–119.

Greenleaf, R. K. (1970). *The servant as a leader*. Indianapolis, IN: Greenleaf Center.

Laub, J. A. (1999). *Assessing the servant organization: Development of the servant organizational leadership (SOLA) instrument*. Unpublished doctoral dissertation, Florida Atlantic University.

Liden, R. C., Wayne, S. J., Zhao, H., & Henderson, D. (2008). Servant leadership: Development of a multidimensional measure and multi-level assessment. *Leadership Quarterly, 19*, 161–177.

McCarren, H. S., Lewis-Smith, J., Belton, L., Yanovsky, B., Robinson, J., & Osatuke, K. (2016, February). Creation of a multi-rater feedback assessment for the development of servant leaders at the Veterans Health Administration. *Servant Leadership: Theory & Practice, 3*(1), 12–51.

Northouse, P. G. (2016). *Leadership: Theory and practice* (7th ed.). Los Angeles, CA: Sage.

Patterson, K. A. (2003). *Servant leadership: A theoretical model*. Doctoral dissertation, Regent University, ATT 30882719.

Russell, R. F., & Stone, A. G. (2002). A review of servant-leadership attributes: Developing a practical model. *Leadership & Organization Development Journal, 23*, 145–157.

Sendjaya, S., Sarros, J. C., & Santora, J. C. (2008). Defining and measuring servant leadership behavior in organizations. *Journal of Management Studies, 45*(2), 402–424.

Sipe, J. W., & Frick, D. M. (2009). *Seven pillars of servant leadership: Practicing the wisdom of leading by serving*. New York, NY: Paulist Press.

Spears, L. (Ed.). (1995). *Reflections on leadership: How Robert K. Greenleaf's theory of servant-leadership influenced today's top management thinkers*. New York: Wiley.

Stone, A. G., Russell, R. F., & Patterson, K. (2004). Transformational versus servant leadership: A difference in leader focus. *Leadership & Organization Development Journal, 25*, 349–361.

van Dierendonck, D., & Nuijten, I. (2011). The servant leadership survey: Development and validation of a multidimensional measure. *Journal of Business and Psychology, 26*, 246–267.

Wong, P. T. P., & Davey, D. (2007). *Best practices in servant leadership*. Paper presented at the Servant Leadership Research Roundtable, Regen University, Virginia Beach, VA.

Wong, P. T. P., & Page, D. (2003). *Servant leadership: An opponent-process model and the Revised Servant Leadership Profile*. Paper presented at the Servant Leadership Research Roundtable, Regent University, Virginia Beach, VA. Retrieved from http://www.drpaulwong.com/wpcontent/ uploads/2013/09/Wong-Servant-Leadership-An-Opponent-Process-Model.pdf

6

Responding to Misconceptions and Objections to Servant Leadership

In May, 2013, James Heskett posted a question on his leadership blog that provoked a rich and varied response. The question, and blog title, was *Why Isn't Servant Leadership More Prevalent?* The question is posed at the end of an article that extolls the many credible authors who have spoken in favor of the concept, authors such as Robert Greenleaf, William Pollard, Max DePree, and more currently Adam Grant who Heskett quotes as suggesting "that servant leaders are not only more highly regarded than others by their employees and not only feel better about themselves at the end of the day *but are more productive as well*" (para. 12). Heskett ends his article by stating that "if servant leadership is as effective as portrayed in recent research, why isn't it more prevalent?" (para. 13). To this article and the question posed, the responses poured in. Here is a summary of some of the many comments:

- "A majority of leaders as agents of principals see themselves as maniacally focused on getting short term results."
- "The organizational model is not geared to move the 'servant' person to the top"
- Servant leadership is "a risky proposition … within organizations."

© The Author(s) 2018
J. Laub, *Leveraging the Power of Servant Leadership*, Palgrave Studies in Workplace Spirituality and Fulfillment, https://doi.org/10.1007/978-3-319-77143-4_6

- Servant leadership is "a long and hard road for someone" and "where do you go to learn how to lead this way?"
- Servant leadership "requires qualities that are all too rare" … "making it very challenging for younger people to be servant leaders."
- "The term itself may pose an obstacle for the concept … these terms do not fit together—Servant & Leader."
- "Our need to be led is far more important than our need to be served" (para. 3, 4, 6).

There were more comments like these attacking the practicality and usefulness of servant leadership as well as the inability of leaders today to embrace this approach to leadership. Underlying assumptions about servant leadership were evident throughout this exchange and it is clear that there are many objections and misconceptions about servant leadership that make it a confusing topic for students of leadership. Where do we begin to sort through the conflicting thoughts and opinions about this approach to leadership? First, we can begin by stating clearly what servant leader is and what it is not. Then we can address the most common misconceptions that make this approach misunderstood and too often rejected out of hand.

Understanding Servant Leadership as a Mindset

Servant leadership is "an understanding and practice of leadership that places the good of those led over the self-interest of the leader" (Laub, 1999, p. 81). Servant leadership is best understood not as a competing *theory* of leadership but as an underlying *mindset* of leadership theory and practice. As a competing theory one may line it up next to other theoretical approaches to leadership—transformational, situational, leader-member exchange, path goal, and other approaches—to determine which theory is the strongest in light of theoretical concerns as well as application to leadership practice. One can also determine that servant leadership is just one of many good leadership approaches to be considered useful only as far as it fits into particular leadership situations. This is all well and good and servant leadership, as a leadership approach, must measure up to the same research expectations and review as other leadership approaches, but what if we considered servant leadership as more of a mindset of leadership, a way of thinking about those being led, about the purpose of leadership and about the role of the leader? What if servant leadership is better conceived of as a set of assumptions that drive our leadership behavior in certain directions, not a set of prescriptions of how a leader must act but a mindset that shapes a leader's attitudes and behaviors? With this different way of thinking about servant leadership it is possible for the servant leader to utilize any or all of the other leadership approaches to greater effect, think of Transformational Leadership driven by a servant mindset, or think of situational leadership practiced as a way to put the followers first over the leader's self-interest, or think of charismatic leadership tempered by a focus of the servant leader mindset toward the interests and well-being of the followers. Servant leadership is an understanding and practice (a mindset) of leadership that focuses on the well-being of the followers above the self-interest of the leader.

What servant leadership is not, then, is just one more style of leadership. Rather, it is foundational to how we view our understanding and practice of leadership while remaining inclusive of various leadership theories and approaches. With this in mind, let's look at eight common misconceptions of servant leadership and how each one might be better understood through the lens of a servant mindset. We will then explore the dark side of servant leadership or areas in which this approach may cause leaders to face particular struggles.

Misconceptions of Servant Leadership

With a paradoxical and provocative name like servant leadership, there are bound to be reactions and concerns to cast doubt on the usefulness of this leadership approach. Where that doubt is warranted, we need to own it honestly, but when an objection is based on a misconception then that error should be confronted openly. There simply is too much to gain from the servant leadership mindset to leave it too easily dismissed. Each of these misconceptions, as misconceptions often are, are based on some level of truth, but unwarranted conclusions are often drawn keeping us from realizing the full power of this mindset and how it can transform our leadership, our followers, and our organizations.

Misconception #1: Servant Leadership Describes an Unreachable Ideal State

Within this misconception, servant leadership is seen as requiring too much of the leader since it describes an unreachable ideal state. Servant leadership, in this view, becomes an unrealistic target especially considering that virtuous leaders like Mother Teresa, Nelson Mandela, Gandhi, and Jesus are often referred to as examples of servant leaders we should emulate. Also, the servant leadership models we have presented in the previous chapter certainly feed this view since the qualities and characteristics of the various models call for a high level of personal character, virtue, and selflessness. Does servant leadership require too much? Is it so utopian a view that it becomes unattainable and ultimately unusable in real-life organizations?

In response to this misconception, servant leadership certainly raises a high mark, but not one that is unreachable. The central issue of servant leadership is to break away the focus of our leadership from ourselves to those that we lead. This other-focus mindset, so central to what servant leadership is all about, is not easily attained, but it is possible. It requires that we challenge our assumptions about what leadership is and what leadership is for, in order to empower others to lead, bring out the creativity of our followers, admit to mistakes and authentically present ourselves to others, and it does not have to be done perfectly. When the servant leader leads for others first, she or he can fall short in many ways and in humility can admit to errors and join with others in being imperfect leaders and followers. Servant leadership does not require an ideal state of leadership practice, but rather an authentic striving for a mindset and set of behaviors that put the needs of others ahead of the self-interest of the leader. Every leader can do this if he or she chooses that mindset. Research has shown that leaders and organizations can attain this high level of servant leadership behavior. In one study by Laub (2010) it was discovered that almost 12% of the organizations were identified as servant-led while in Herman's study (2008) that figure was over 16%. Certainly servant-led organizations are in the minority but they do exist and it must be recognized that it is not easy to change deeply implanted mindsets of autocratic or paternalistic leadership. We certainly do the servant leadership approach a disservice to claim it as a utopian ideal since we are all too human and mistake prone so by setting a bar of near perfection we likely will not even try to develop a healthier servant-minded approach to our leadership. When we consider the negative alternatives of practicing from less healthy leadership mindsets, that is, autocratic or parental, then we must give this approach full consideration.

Misconception #2: Servant Leadership Is (or Appears to Be) Weak

The fear that servant leadership is weak, or even if it merely *appears* to be weak, is enough for many to cast it aside as an ineffective way to lead. After all, leaders are expected to get results, make hard decisions, and move the organization forward through the power and influence of their individual vision and personality. The misconception here is that servant leaders do not actually lead and are averse to using their power as leaders. If this were the case, then one should conclude that servant leadership is weak and cannot therefore stand up to the demands of leadership in today's organizations, but this is not the case. It is a misconception that servant leaders do not use power or exercise their leadership to move the organization forward. Yes, the servant leader serves, but the servant leader also leads. Servant leaders cannot abdicate their authority or responsibility to make the hard decisions that leadership often demands. Servant leaders must not merely follow the crowd and do whatever their followers desire. Yes, servant leaders refuse to use others to fulfill their own needs as leaders, but instead they choose to act to benefit the followers. This might seem to put the leader at the mercy of the follower and the fear is that servant leadership would then be harmful to the leader where they might be abused by their own followers.

The reality is that servant leaders, as all leaders must, use their power and authority to do the jobs they have been hired to do and this sometimes means that the hard decision of firing an ineffective employee or holding followers accountable for their performance is a part of what servant leaders do. Yes, they use their power, but within a servant mindset. The well-being of the followers is always at the forefront but the servant leader is also committed to organizational interests and goals and they will not sacrifice the organization on the altar of group opinion.

An example of this misconception comes from Lussier and Achua (2001) when they state that "servant leadership calls for the highest level of selflessness—a level some doubt exists in the real world. The leader completely assumes the role of follower at the lowest rung of the ladder and serves others in the accomplishment of organizational goals" (p. 391). In response to this, the servant leader does not assume the role of the follower at the lowest rung of the ladder; rather, they serve from the positional level they have been granted and they serve not from a position of weakness but from a position of strength. What is stronger than a person who serves from a high position who is not required to serve? What is more powerful than a leader who chooses to serve his or her followers to empower them, support them, and expect the best from them? The idea that servant leadership is weak is an imposed assumption from those who just see someone serving another as an act of weakness. It is not. Serving others out of a firm belief that others should be our main focus (over self) is a value-laden act that comes out of a strength of character and virtue that cannot be matched by a different kind of power used to serve self and the leader's own vision at the expense of others.

Servant leadership is not about being nice. People often have the impression that servant leadership is only about making people happy or treating them kindly no matter what they do. Remember, one of the characteristics of the servant leader is displaying authenticity which requires a high level of honesty even if that honesty causes discomfort or pain for the listener. The servant leader will not hedge on the truth in order to make their employee feel better. Yes, servant leaders value people and develop people, build community, and share leadership, but they also provide leadership and display authenticity so just being nice is not an option for any leader. The servant leader must lead and they must use the power granted to them but how they use that power is the unique offering of the servant leader.

Servant leadership is not about always being democratic. There are times that a servant leader will make a unilateral decision for the good of the company and the employees as a whole and that decision may not be perceived as positive by all followers. Servant leaders do bring a democratic and participative spirit to their leadership, to be sure, but this does not require that they are subject to the whims of their followers. The servant leader must use wisdom to know how to make the most ethical decisions while maintaining a servant mindset and a focus on follower needs while, at the same time, meeting the demands and needs of the organization. No one claimed that leadership is easy.

The idea that servant leaders are not strong enough or powerful enough to do what needs to be done as a leader is simply not true. The servant leader mindset requires a deep commitment to serving others first while maintaining a bold honesty and expectation level for those we lead. It is an approach to leadership that does not take the easy way of authoritarian, power-over leadership. It is easy to tell people what to do and then manipulate the behavior of others through punishment and reward. The servant leader knows that these techniques of power over others do not match up to the true power of high expectations and mutual partnership that comes from a servant mindset. Servant leadership is not weak. Power is exercised, but primarily for the good of others and the good of the organization and the mission they serve. Wong and Davey (2007) share that "a Christian University President told the faculty that the university's core value of servant leadership was intended for faculty and staff, not for the President, because the President often had to make tough decisions" (para. 31), the implication being that servant leaders cannot make tough decisions. This clearly presents an example of this misconception in action. We cannot ignore our responsibility to serve those we lead because we know we are called on to make difficult decisions. Servant leaders can make these hard decisions but they make them within a servant mindset.

Misconception #3: Servant Leadership Is Situationally Limited

There are three ways that people may find servant leadership to be a limiting approach to leadership and we will address each of these misconceptions separately.

1. Servant leadership is just one style of leadership among many styles
2. Servant leadership fits only leaders with particular personalities
3. Servant leadership only works in certain types of organizations

Servant Leadership Is Just One Style of Leadership Among Many Styles

Servant leadership is best viewed not as one leadership style among many, but is a mindset, a set of underlying assumptions that guide our leadership philosophy and behavior. If we choose to see servant leadership as a style, or just another approach to leadership, we will look at it as one of many different ways of leading and will tend to see it as situationally driven and applied. This leads to the misconception that servant leadership should be used only if the situation is right, and should not be used if power and authority are called upon. This is a foundational error in seeing servant leadership as averse to using power and authority. If we see it as a mindset we will not limit the concept in this way. We will see it as a foundational set of assumptions, a belief system that shapes how we view our role as leader, our perceptions about those we lead, and our understanding of the purpose and outcomes of leadership. If we view servant leadership as a style, we reduce it to a set of prescribed behaviors that we assume will always be required of the servant leader. This in turn leads to the problem of seeing servant leadership as requiring leaders to give in to followers, always acting in ways that make others feel better while struggling to distinguish between the good of one employee against the good of the entire group. Viewing servant leadership as a mindset allows the servant leader to use multiple approaches and theories of leadership while serving to shape how those theories are applied.

An example of this would be how a servant leader deals with an ineffective follower. Greenleaf (1977) believed that servant leaders will look within and evaluate themselves before they evaluate their followers. They will, based on a servant mindset, consider if they have provided what the follower needs in terms of job definition, clarity of task assignments, support, resources, and training. The servant leader will provide opportunities for the worker to develop in deficient areas, but will not tolerate a worker who refuses this opportunity for development. Once the servant leader determines that the worker is either not able to do the work or unwilling to develop their competencies to perform better, they will terminate the employee as a way to better serve the worker, the team, and the organization. They will provide transition assistance for this worker since the mindset of serving underlies the leader's actions and concern for the worker will continue, but servant leadership in no way demands that the leader avoid acting in ways needed by the organization. Servant leadership is not just one style of leadership among many styles. It is a servant, other-oriented mindset that informs our day-to-day leadership decisions and shapes our ongoing leadership philosophy.

Servant Leadership Fits Only Leaders with Particular Personalities

There is a perception that servant leadership only fits and can be displayed by leaders with soft, introverted, and passive personalities. This belief connects to the misconception of servant leadership as a *nice* approach to leading and assumes that only those with quiet and sensitive natures will be able to pull off this unique way of leading. There may be some truth to the observation that hard-driving Type A personalities may be drawn to more transformational approaches due to their focus on the influence of strong charismatic leaders (Northouse, 2016), while leaders of a more reflective and quiet personality may be drawn to the supportive, giving side of servant leadership. However, there is nothing in the concept of servant leadership that restricts any personality type from effectively adopting a servant mindset. A strong charismatic personality, like Nelson Mandela, can choose to act from a servant mindset as can a quiet introverted leader like Mother Teresa. They will lead differently, of course, due to differences in personality, talents, and strengths, but their ability to choose a servant mindset is in no way limited by their personality. Susan Cain in her book *Quiet: The Power of Introverts in a World that Can't Stop Talking* (2015) makes a strong case for the strength of introverted leaders and how they display a different yet firm kind of power. Extroverts, it seems, get most of the attention in leadership, but there is no limitation for introverts to use power, make decisions, cast vision, or exercise any other key leadership skill. The point is that both introverts and extroverts, both quieter and louder personalities can adopt a servant leadership mindset and benefit, along with their followers, from this choice.

Servant Leadership Only Works in Certain Types of Organizations

This false assumption is based on the true belief that different organizational situations call for different kinds of leadership emphasis. For instance, sometimes an organization needs a clear dynamic vision to move it beyond the status quo. This vision may require significant changes in how the organization functions and how employees are expected to work. This organizational situation requires leaders who are bold, decisive, and provide clear and unambiguous direction. Servant leaders in this situation are able to provide this kind of direction because that is how they can best serve. Sometimes an organization finds itself in a stable, growth-oriented position and a different leadership of encouragement, team building, and stability is called for. The servant leader can also provide this kind of leadership. The point is that the mindset of servant leadership calls for putting the needs of the followers ahead of the leader's own self-interest and the focus of servant leadership is primarily (though not exclusively) on the followers. With this mindset the servant leader uses his or her wisdom to best discern what leadership actions and decisions are most needed to meet the organization's needs.

Another false assumption is that servant leadership will work only for people-oriented organizations (non-profits, education, community service) and will not work in profit-oriented organizations like business. In research conducted by Laub (1999) there was no significant difference found in servant leadership scores between these different types of organizations. If a leader has an autocratic (self-focused) mindset and oversees a community service agency providing help to people in need, they will view their workers as a means to an end, as servants to fulfill the leader's goals and not as partners in the enterprise. They may serve their constituents well, but with this mindset they will not serve their employees well. If a leader has a servant (other-focused) mindset and oversees a government or business organization, they will see their primary role as a servant as they act in ways that benefit their workers and the organization's mission. This mindset will enhance service to both customers and employees.

Bowie (2000) suggests that servant leadership is unrealistic and impractical and would never work within the military or prisons systems. This is a false assumption about the values of servant leadership because these values can and have been implemented in the military and in prison systems. Consider McKean, a federal correctional institution medium-security prison in Bradford, Pennsylvania, led for several years by Warden Dennis Luther. Luther brought a servant-minded approach to this prison back in the 1990s with a firm belief in a "founding principle that an unconditional respect for prisoners as people leads to a positive, rehabilitating culture, in which prisoners have a stake in the prison as a community and ultimately reenter the world as engaged community members" (Editorial Page Board, 2014, para. 3). Luther also believed that this unconditional respect for prisoners required specific principles and beliefs about how inmates should be treated. This credo of beliefs included 28 guiding statements that include the following:

1. Inmates are sent to prison *as* punishment and not *for* punishment.
2. You must believe in a man's *capacity* to change his behavior.
3. *Be responsive* to inmate requests for action and information. Respond in a timely manner and respond the first time an inmate makes a request.
4. *Be dependable* when dealing with inmates. If you say you are going to do something, do it.

5. It is important for staff to *model* the kind of behavior they expect to see duplicated by inmates.
6. Inmates are to be treated *respectfully and with basic dignity*. Staff can treat inmates respectfully without compromising the essential element of professional distance.
7. Be courteous, polite, and professional in all dealings with inmates, regardless of their behavior.
8. Never, *never lie* to an inmate.
9. Punish behavior that threatens order and security—swiftly and harshly.
10. Inmate discipline must be consistent and fair. (Peters, 1992, pp. 254–255)

Certainly, this is a different way to conduct prison leadership and Warden Luther found himself resisted by politicians who called for a harder line of punishment for prisoners, as well as those above him who saw him as a maverick going against the culture of no-frills prisons accusing him of coddling prisoners and creating a country club atmosphere rather than a place where inmates are expected to do hard time. "Yet, McKean, by several measures, may well be the most successful medium-security prison in the country" (Worth, 1995, para. 3). Keeping prisoners at McKean cost the taxpayers about 72% per inmate compared to other federal institutions and the incident record had "No escapes. No homicides. No sexual assaults. No suicides. In six years there have been three serious assaults on staff members and six recorded assaults on inmates" (Worth, 1995, para. 3), about the number of assaults other federal prisons see in one week.

Servant leadership is a mindset that values people, develops people, builds community, provides and shares leadership, and displays authenticity. These behaviors, based on a servant mindset, can be displayed in any type of organization because people should always be respected and supported by their leaders whether in business, government, the military, the paramilitary, or corrections work.

Misconception #4: Servant Leadership Is Too Religious, Too Christian, and Too Western

There is no doubt that servant leadership connects to a rich religious and Christian background. It is a philosophy based on values consistent with the highest religious traditions as well as the virtue-based philosophies of Aristotle, Plato, and others (McCloskey, 2014). Greenleaf who popularized the concept in the twentieth century did not hide his Quaker roots, but did not present servant leadership in the context of religion or spiritual belief but rather through positive human values. Greenleaf sought to present a values-based way of leading that took into consideration how positive leader behaviors bring about corresponding positive follower behaviors that in turn benefit all in the organization as well as all served by the organization. So, though there certainly is much for people of faith to connect to in servant leadership, the concept itself does not require an adoption of faith or religious belief. Statements like "Greenleaf wanted the corporate world to be infused with and regulated by religious doctrine" (Eicher-Catt, 2005, p. 23) are simply not true and are not a fair representation of Greenleaf's writings. Eicher-Catt goes on to claim that "S-L is clearly rooted in the meaning systems of a Judeo-Christian ideology that has sought to 'bind' Western U.S. society to androcentric principles" (2005, p. 23). This statement makes unsupported claims and says more about Eicher-Catt's assumptions on religious belief and gender than it does about the claims of Greenleaf or the servant leadership concept. Though servant leadership fits well with religious assumptions it does not require these assumptions from leaders who do not espouse a particular faith. Servant leadership has been implemented by many organizations that have no religious base or purpose, such as Southwest Airlines, the Container Store, the Toro Company, and others.

Is servant leadership too Western in its cultural assumptions? Or, is servant leadership drawn from broad values that transcend culture? The Global Leadership & Organizational Behavior Effectiveness (GLOBE) studies collected data from 62 countries, collected into ten-country clusters searching for preferences on six different styles of leadership—Autonomous, Self-Protective, Charismatic/Value-Based, Team-Oriented, Humane-Oriented, and Participative—revealing that workers in different cultures desired different approaches to leadership (Northouse, 2016). Servant leadership connects to several of these different leadership styles (Value-Based, Team-Oriented, Humane-Oriented, and Participative) so it clearly can apply to these different cultures and how they view and prefer leadership. The GLOBE studies also identified a set of universal leadership attributes that included the following positive characteristics of leaders:

- Trustworthy
- Honest
- Encouraging
- Dependable
- Team builder
- Positive
- Just (Northouse, 2018, p. 8)

In addition to these positive attributes, the study also identified universal negative attributes; characteristics that people worldwide do not want in their leaders:

- Ruthless
- Dictatorial
- Non-cooperative
- Egocentric (Northouse, 2018, p. 8)

Clearly, servant leadership values as represented in these lists transcend culture and country boundaries. "Servant-leadership has been applied successfully in various companies all over the world. With all of their diversity, these companies have one thing in common: they are better because of it" (Trompenaars & Voerman, 2009, p. xvi). People from all cultures and ethnicities share foundational desires in common related to leadership. They want to be led with respect, trust, honesty, and competence. Though they may desire some leadership styles over others, they all will respond to a leader who puts them and their well-being first. They tend to respond positively to a leader with a servant-minded leader mindset.

Misconception #5: Servant Leadership Is Too Long-Term Oriented

This misconception, rooted in truth, believes that servant leadership takes too long to establish itself since it is so dependent on strong working relationships and a culture that is built over time to become servant oriented. Certainly, it takes time to change a culture, but there is no doubt that after years of self-focused and autocratic leadership that even short-term gains can be realized if someone brings a new type of leadership to the organization. A good example of this is when the Campbell's Soup Company, the most iconic brand of soup in the world, was going through a drastic downturn in profits and market share due to an oppressive and toxic culture brought on by its leaders. In one year, 2000, the company lost 54% of its market value. The response by Campbell's leaders focused only on short-term fixes including cuts in employees and employee benefits and training. To stem the tide of the downturn, the board at Campbell's brought in Doug Conant, who had found success previously at Kraft and Nabisco, to change the culture and that is exactly what he did. First he used the Gallup engagement survey to determine how employees viewed the company and their work. The survey revealed an employee engagement ratio of 1:1 which meant that out of 20,000 total employees only half were engaged in their work while the others were not. So, Conant's first focus was on the employees of the company. For the first three years he determined to "tangibly demonstrate to our employees that we value their agenda before we can ever expect them to value our agenda. It simply doesn't work any other way" (as cited in Galagan & Bingham, 2011, para. 13). At the same time, Conant began to create a leadership expectation built on trust and valuing of people. This culture shift resulted in 300 of the top 350 leaders leaving, some of whom left freely since they could not embrace the new philosophy while others were asked to leave. To replace these top leaders 150 leaders were brought up from within the company while another 150 were brought from the outside. All leaders were trained in the new Campbell's Leadership Model which included the following six expectations:

1. Inspire trust
2. Create direction
3. Drive organization alignment
4. Build organization vitality
5. Execute with excellence
6. Produce extraordinary results (Galagan & Bingham, 2011, para. 19)

What were the results of this relatively quick organizational change effort? Remember, most of this change was initiated in just the first three years. Employee engagement moved from 1:1, meaning that for every worker engaged one was disengaged, to an astounding 23:1 with 23 employees engaged for every employee not engaged. This amazing change led to Campbell's Soup Company eight years later being "ranked on lists of Best Places to Work, Most Ethical Companies, Best Employers for Healthy Lifestyles, Best Corporate Citizens, and Best Global Brands" (Galagan & Bingham, 2011, para. 3). As far as financial performance goes, the company, in the midst of the great recession, posted a profit of $800 million in 2009 and more in 2010. Putting employees first and serving their needs ahead of the leaders created the best foundation for high performance even during the most challenging financial times.

Now certainly the three to nine years it took to realize this turnaround can be considered long term when compared to viewing the next quarterly report, but Campbell's was facing economic disaster and most of the turnaround was instituted by Conant within the first three years. The concepts of a servant leadership mindset can be implemented by leaders who are determined to state their values, model those values, create accountability around those values, and build a new and healthier organizational culture. No, it can't be accomplished in a single quarter or a single year, but in a reasonably short time a new organization can emerge from the ashes of past dysfunction. Arguments are often made that it takes an authoritarian approach to get short-term results, but it can also be argued that those short-term results are not ultimately in the best interest of the company, its leaders, and certainly not its employees.

Misconception #6: Servant Leadership Lacks a Strong Research Base

Many writings on servant leadership mention that there is a lack of a research base to support the concept (Northouse, 2016). Fortunately, this has been changing over the past few years as more studies and more rigorous research is conducted on servant leadership. Servant leadership research is continuing to grow as valid and reliable instrument tools have been created, beginning with Laub's Organizational Leadership Assessment (OLA) (1999), to developing research-based conceptual models while exploring how servant leadership actually works in organizations. To date, servant leadership research has focused more on the development of assessments and models but is now expanding into studies on how servant leadership relates to key organizational health factors like job satisfaction, trust, team effectiveness, employee safety, student performance, profitability, employee tenure, and turnover and bottom-line financial performance.

For several years Regent University has conducted an annual Servant Leadership Roundtable, creating a platform for servant leadership research. An international servant leadership research roundtable was also conducted with the most recent occurring in 2016 in Iceland. Servant leadership researchers from the United States, Spain, Finland, South Africa, Turkey, New Zealand, Denmark, Germany, the Netherlands, Iceland, Belgium, and Sweden came together to share their latest research and learning on servant leadership.

There is much to do to build a strong research base for servant leadership especially in the relationship of this model to leader and organizational performance. Of course, more needs to be done, but we now possess a foundational research base to build from to support servant leadership as a credible and usable mindset of leading that can make a significantly positive difference in organizations.

Misconception #7: Servant Leadership Has a Problematic, Confusing, and Contradictory Name

In response to Heskett's blog post and his question "why isn't servant leadership more prevalent?" one respondent shared that "the Servant Leadership approach is one that is so schizophrenic that it is an entirely unhealthy approach for a leader to take ... our need to be led well is far more important than our need to be served ... The more correct notion is that of a serving leader—and it's more than just semantics" (2013). The name *servant leadership* has been a tripping point for many since Greenleaf coined the term in 1970. The contradictory nature of the term is part of the perceived problem. The term servant leadership can come across as ambiguous and unappealing. How can one be both a servant and a leader? Clearly, Greenleaf saw the value of this paradoxical title and the tension it creates, but does the name servant leadership add to the problem of the unwillingness of leaders to accept this approach? Some, as the quote suggests, recommend a different title like the serving leader (Jennings & Stahl-Wert, 2016) since it speaks to the leader's behavior rather than their identity as a servant. What about other titles—values-based leadership, relational leadership, service-oriented leadership, caring leadership, humble leadership, and so on. At one level there certainly is no problem using a different title for this kind of leadership. Jim Collins called it Level 5 leadership (2001). Adam Grant referred to it as givers versus takers (2013). If the name is problematic, as it certainly is to some, shouldn't we jettison it for a less controversial term?

The recommendation of this author is that the name servant leadership be maintained and that the paradoxical nature of the term is actually a strength. There is no doubt that adding the word servant to the word leader and thereby asking the leader to consider himself or herself to be identified as a servant (a humble term to be sure) can create a hindrance, but taking away the tension of the term is not ultimately in the best interest of our understanding of the unique power of this approach to leadership. When leaders, from a position of power and influence, choose willfully to put their own self-interest aside to focus on the best interests of their followers, they are intentionally accepting a humble position, one that stands out more by nature of the fact that it is unexpected and may even be unappreciated. Also, when leaders do this without relinquishing the authority and power of their leadership role it is even more effective. When a leader's power combines with a commitment to support their followers, they are able to empower them with the power they have been granted as leader. They are free to lead, free to act, free to serve, and it is this freedom that makes the choice of servant leadership so potentially life-changing for the followers. We can bypass the natural tendency for people to resist our power and influence when they realize that this power, which they fully acknowledge and respect, is targeted not to their detriment but to their good. Senge (1995) addresses the value of the title of servant leadership when he states that

> servant-leadership is an interesting phrase, a juxtaposition of apparent opposites, which immediately causes us to think freshly. But, I actually think that the phrase is a sort of gateway … it leads us into a different universe … a universe in which most of us, I believe, have a deep hunger to participate. (p. 221)

So, call it what you will (a rose by any other name) but realize that there is a unique power in the leveraging of joining the word servant to the word leader. Servant leadership has a rich and long tradition that provides much value if we are willing to live within the healthy tension it creates.

Misconception #8: Servant Leadership Does Not Allow a Leader to Make Unilateral Decisions and Exercise Personal Leadership Power

This misconception comes from a misunderstanding of the term autocratic. Autocratic comes from two Greek terms, *autos* meaning self and *kratos* meaning power. In light of this foundational meaning of the term autocratic is used to designate a leadership mindset that is self-focused on the interests and needs of the leader over those led. It is a mindset that sees power as something to be used over others to impose the leader's will against the best interests of the followers. So, when defined this way autocratic leadership is not an appropriate or healthy mindset for leadership. However, this does not mean that servant leaders do not use the power or authority granted to them through their leadership roles and sometimes the servant leader will be called on to make unilateral decisions that he or she feels is in the best interest of the organization and most of the workers. No leadership decision pleases everybody and leaders must make decisions that will bring harm to some of their workers. The servant leader does not make these decisions lightly or without serious consideration of the needs of the followers, but it is a misconception to think that servant leadership does not allow for the leader to make these kinds of hard and difficult decisions. In fact, these decisions must be made in order to fulfill our leadership responsibilities to the organization. That being said, the servant leader will always focus on the well-being of his or her followers. The good of those led will always be foremost in the servant leader's mind but when a decision is called for, a decision that will be favored by some and resisted by others, the servant leader will not shrink from making that decision.

Again, it is important to repeat that servant leaders use power. They make decisions. They lead. As they lead, they never forget why they are leading and for whom they are leading. To clarify this further, it may be helpful to contrast certain terms that often get confused. As we have seen, the term autocratic is leading for the leader himself or herself over the well-being of the followers. Autocratic leadership uses power to get what the leader wants while exploiting the followers. Authority, in contrast, is the given right to use power. It is granted to the leader through their leadership position and leaders are expected to use this authority (power) to benefit the organization. Autocratic leaders use their authority to benefit themselves while servant leaders use their authority to benefit others. Another term—authoritarian—is a view of leadership (similar to autocratic) that uses power to exercise control over the will of others. It is a power-over approach to leadership power and applies to both autocratic and paternalistic leadership. Servant leaders are not autocratic or authoritarian, but they do use their authority and power to serve others and the organization they have been called to lead.

The Dark Side of Servant Leadership

Is there a dark side to servant leadership? At first glance it would appear not. Servant leadership is a mindset of leadership that holds to a selfless approach, putting the needs of others first and placing the self-interest of the leader last. What limitations might this create for the leader pursuing such an approach? By nature of its own strengths, servant leadership has tendencies that must be acknowledged and brought to awareness since these can become potential blind spots for the servant leader.

Servant Leaders Struggle with Holding People Accountable

Due to the common misconception of the servant leader always being *nice*, it is sometimes difficult for the servant leader to hold people accountable for poor performance. It is difficult and often painful to tell a follower that they are not doing what they should be doing and that they need to change. We as leaders may feel that we must move from a servant mindset to a parental mindset to hold others accountable since that is our common understanding of how someone is corrected or disciplined. The servant leader needs to be aware of this dark-side tendency and must be willing to serve not only through giving encouragement but also authentically by telling the truth about a worker's performance, the good, the bad, and the ugly. Giving correction can still be done in a servant (or adult) mindset but this must be intentional by the leader to avoid parental attitudes when dealing with workers. If the servant leader truly values others and is committed to developing them and being honest with them, they will move past their own self-protective tendencies to tell their workers the truth. They will hold them accountable for poor performance because leaving this unaddressed will do harm to the organization, the team, and ultimately the worker. The servant leader serves even when it is most difficult to do so and even when they may be perceived as anything but a servant by the action of holding their followers accountable.

Servant Leaders Struggle with Delegating to Others

While it may seem obvious that servant leaders will delegate to others in order to empower them to lead, there can be a tendency to protect or nurture the followers and therefore resist challenging them with tasks and responsibilities that will take them to the next level of development. This desire to protect and nurture is actually more an expression of a parental mindset rather than that of a servant and this points out the common error of seeing positive parental leadership as servant leadership. As a positive parent I take care of my children. I protect them from harm or difficulty. I provide for them emotionally so they do not despair of a challenge too big for them. As a servant-minded leader, I see this as it is, a limiting of the development of the follower, keeping them in a child role and not allowing them to move into their own potential as a leader with all of the corresponding pain and discomfort that demands. Servant leaders refuse to take the role of parent and see themselves instead as partners who are willing to provide the challenging but essential role of building up others as leaders.

Servant Leaders Struggle Being Firm and Authoritative

Servant leaders are very susceptible to the misconception of the niceness that seems to be required of their role. They want to be viewed as a servant and will do anything to reinforce this perception. The problem is that by doing so, they undercut their own effectiveness as leaders. Leaders must be authentic and firm with their honesty. They must speak the truth as one partner will share with another in an adult-to-adult exchange. They will not hedge on the truth in order to protect their own image as a nice-guy leader. Servant leaders will resist this tendency to play to type and will be willing to serve others even when it is likely that the others will not see them as servants due to the difficulty and messiness of the situation. Yes, it is possible for a leader to serve a worker authentically yet appear to that worker as autocratic or parental. It is also possible for the servant leader to lead autocratically or parentally when they think that they are responding as a servant. Mindsets are tricky to deal with and it requires a growing level of self-awareness and personal accountability for the leader to discern when they are acting authentically out of a particular mindset.

Servant Leaders Struggle to Achieve Short-Term Results

Sometimes we as leaders are called on to create short-term results and sometimes that is exactly what the organization needs. Though servant leadership builds for the long term it does not shrink away from getting the results needed in the short term. However, the servant leader will continue to serve the needs of the workers first as they, at the same time, address organizational needs. All workers are aware that there will be times in the life cycle of an organization when special sacrifices are required. Mature workers may not like the extra demands put on them but they will not resist it as unnatural or abusive especially if they are working for a leader who values them and is willing to communicate clearly and often as to what is needed and what resources are provided. The servant leader certainly will challenge an organizational culture that lives from crisis to crisis and abuses the goodwill of its workers to get short-term results at the expense of the worker's health and life balance but they also are willing to challenge their followers to go beyond expectations and comfort levels when that challenge is required.

Servant Leaders Struggle with Leaders Misusing the Concept

Some leaders desire to be seen as servant, but operate as autocrats or parental leaders. They may espouse the values of servant leadership but their values in practice tell a different story. This should come as no surprise and certainly is not a weakness in the servant leader concept itself but if servant leadership is misunderstood, leaders can talk about caring for workers first while living out leadership behaviors that are self-focused and self-guided. Servant leaders must constantly be on guard against being blinded to their own self-interest and their own parental tendencies in leadership. This requires a high level of self-awareness and the willingness to be held accountable by others. The servant leader provides for ongoing evaluation and feedback on their own performance as leader and how they live out the principles they espouse. They use assessment tools, like the OLA, on a regular basis to determine how people are experiencing the organization and their leadership. As we know, talk is cheap and words alone are never enough. As leaders, we must act in line with our stated values consistently enough to lay claim to a true servant leader mindset.

Conclusion

While servant leaders must acknowledge the darker tendencies that may come with this mindset of leading, they should not be distracted by misconceptions that others hold wrongly and unfairly. Servant leadership is best understood as a mindset and a clearer understanding can be gained by contrasting it with the two competing mindsets of autocratic and paternalistic leadership. That is where we go next—to an exploration of the three mindsets of leadership (Autocratic, Paternalistic, and Servant) to create clear distinctions between these three ways of understanding and practicing leadership.

References

Bowie, N. (2000). Business ethics, philosophy, and the next 25 years. *Business Ethics Quarterly, 10*(1), 7–20.

Cain, S. (2015). *Quiet: The power of introverts in a world that can't stop talking.* New York, NY: Crown Publishing Group.

Collins, J. (2001). *Good to great: Why some companies make the leap … and others don't.* New York, NY: Harper Collins Publishers.

Editorial Page Board. (2014). *Editorial: Fixing the prison problem.* Brown Daily Herald. Retrieved from http://www.browndailyherald.com/2014/11/06/editorial-fixing-prison-problem/

Eicher-Catt, D. (2005). The myth of servant-leadership: A feminist perspective. *Women and Language. Urbana: Organization for the Study of Communication Language and Gender, 28*(1), 17–25.

Galagan, P., & Bingham, T. (2011). *M'm m'm good: Learning and performance at Campbell Soup Company.* Association for Talent Development. Retrieved from https://www.td.org/Publications/Magazines/TD/TD-Archive/2011/03/MM-MM-Good-Learning-and-Performance-at-Campbell-Soup-Company

Grant, A. (2013). *Give and take: A revolutionary approach to success.* New York, NY: The Penguin Group.

Greenleaf, R. K. (1977). *Servant leadership: A journey into the nature of legitimate power and greatness.* Mahwah, NJ: Paulist Press.

Herman, R. (2008). *Servant leadership: A model for organizations desiring a workplace spirituality culture.* Doctoral dissertation, Capella University.

Heskett, J. (2013, May 5). *Why isn't servant leadership more prevalent?* Retrieved from http://hbswk.hbs.edu/item/why-isnt-servant-leadership-more-prevalent

Jennings, K., & Stahl-Wert, J. (2016). *The serving leader: Five powerful actions to transform your team, business, and community.* Oakland, CA: Berrett-Koehler, Inc.

Laub, J. A. (1999). *Assessing the servant organization: Development of the servant organizational leadership (SOLA) instrument.* Unpublished doctoral dissertation, Florida Atlantic University.

Laub, J. A. (2010). The servant organization. In D. van Dierendonck & K. Patterson (Eds.), *Servant leadership: Developments in theory and research* (pp. 105–117). Hampshire: Palgrave Macmillan.

Lussier, R. N., & Achua, C. F. (2001). *Leadership: Theory, application, skill development.* Cincinnati, OH: South-Western College Publishing.

McCloskey, M. W. (2014). *Learning leadership in a changing world: Virtue and effective leadership in the 21st century.* New York, NY: Palgrave Macmillan.

Northouse, P. G. (2016). *Leadership: Theory and practice* (7th ed.). Los Angeles, CA: Sage.

Northouse, P. G. (2018). *Introduction to Leadership: Concepts and practice* (4th ed.). Los Angeles, CA: Sage.

Peters, T. (1992). *Liberation management: Necessary disorganization for the nanosecond nineties.* New York: Alfred A. Knopf.

Senge, P. (1995). Robert Greenleaf's legacy: A new foundation for twenty-first century institutions. In L. C. Spears & M. Lawrence (Eds.), *Reflections on leadership: How Robert K. Greenleaf's theory of servant-leadership influenced today's top management thinkers* (pp. 217–240). New York, NY: John Wiley & Sons, Inc.

Trompenaars, F., & Voerman, E. (2009). *Servant-leadership across cultures: Harnessing the Strength of the world's most powerful management philosophy.* Oxford: Infinite Ideas Limited.

Wong, P. T. P., & Davey, D. (2007). *Best practices in servant leadership.* Paper presented at the Servant Leadership Research Roundtable, Regen University, Virginia Beach, VA.

Worth, R. (1995). A model prison: McKean, a federal correctional institution, does everything that "make 'em bust rocks" politicians decry—Imagine, educating inmates!—And it works. *The Atlantic.* Retrieved from https://www.theatlantic.com/magazine/archive/1995/11/a-model-prison/308518/

7

The Three Mindsets of Leadership: Autocratic, Paternalistic, and Servant

A review of research from the past 10 to 15 years reveals that the most prevalent mindset of leadership practiced in the world today is paternalistic (Jackson, 2016). This view of the leader as parent and the followers as children goes mostly unrecognized and therefore unaddressed, particularly in the West. By understanding the implications of this paternalistic (parental) mindset we can address its benefits and limitations and how it compares to and helps us better understand the servant mindset of leadership. This chapter provides an overview of the three main mindsets of leadership with a focus on the paternalistic leadership approach. Contrasting paternalistic to servant leadership provides for greater clarity in defining key terms to differentiate between these two mindsets.

The autocratic-paternalistic-servant (A-P-S) model shown in Fig. 7.1 presents three distinct mindsets of leadership. Within these mindsets, leaders choose how they view themselves as leaders, how they view those led, and how they view the role and purpose of leadership. Servant leaders see themselves as stewards of the organization and its people. They put the needs of the led first, before their own self-interest, and they treat workers as adult partners. Autocratic leaders see themselves as dictators over others. They put their own needs, as leaders, first and treat their workers as their servants.

© The Author(s) 2018
J. Laub, *Leveraging the Power of Servant Leadership*, Palgrave Studies in Workplace Spirituality and Fulfillment, https://doi.org/10.1007/978-3-319-77143-4_7

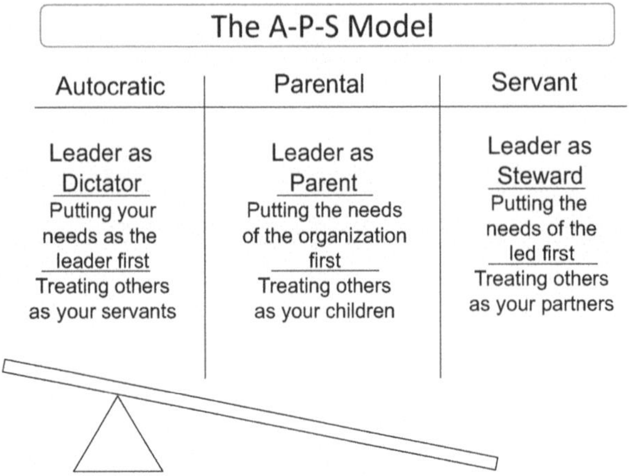

The A-P-S Model		
Autocratic	Parental	Servant
Leader as Dictator	Leader as Parent	Leader as Steward
Putting your needs as the leader first	Putting the needs of the organization first	Putting the needs of the led first
Treating others as your servants	Treating others as your children	Treating others as your partners

Fig. 7.1 The A-P-S model

Paternalistic (parental) leaders view themselves as parents over their followers. They put the needs of the organization first and treat their workers as children. Parental leaders can be either negatively parental or positively parental in their approach. It is the contention of this author that many of the organizations that view themselves as servant organizations may be, in fact, a positive version of a paternalistic organization. Servant leadership is more than treating people kindly with benevolence. Getting to the level of servant organization requires a mindshift where leaders see themselves differently, view the led differently, and reshape their entire view of the purpose and meaning of leadership.

The Autocratic Leadership Mindset

The autocratic mindset brings together the exploitive use of power over followers to support the self-interest of the leader. Kellerman (2004) catalogs the various ways leaders can be bad: through incompetence and rigidity, intemperance and callousness, or corruption. Hornstein (1996) discusses how brutal bosses act toward their employees while living out what he calls the eight daily sins—"deceit, constraint, coercion, selfishness, inequity, cruelty, disregard and deification" (pp. 15–16). Deification references the brutal bosses' belief that he or she is the master and the employee is the servant with positions of superiority and subordination firmly maintained. Adams and Balfour (2009) explore what they term administrative evil providing the example of the National Aeronautics and Space Administration (NASA) during the time of the Space Shuttle disasters of the *Challenger* and then the *Columbia*. The authors trace a dangerously unhealthy leadership culture that began with Wernher van Braun's deeply controlling leadership approach leading to Dr. William Lucas developing what the authors referred to as "a persecutory organizational identity" (p. 100), where workers feel powerless to act and are disrespected by NASA's leaders. Lucas was known for publicly and abusively reprimanding those under him who made a mistake. Mistakes were not allowed; therefore mistakes were covered up. People were afraid to speak the truth. This unhealthy leadership culture created a work environment that significantly impacted the Space Shuttle disasters and the subsequent loss of life. Certainly, our mindset of leadership and the corresponding leadership behaviors matter and the results of our mindset choice can cause great danger and harm.

Defining Autocratic Leadership: Authoritarian Power + Exploitation

Autocratic leadership is a mindset through which the leader uses authoritarian power to control followers with an exploitative approach to serve the needs and desires of the leader at the expense of the well-being of the followers. The term autocratic comes from two Greek words: *autos* meaning self and *kratos* meaning power. Autocratic then, at its core, refers to a mindset of leadership that is focused on the self-interest of the leader with all power centralized at the top of the organization. Autocratic leaders use power and authority over others to seek the good the leader envisions for himself or herself. Some see this as necessary to make needed changes in the organization, but the toxic nature of this kind of exploitive leadership creates significant and lasting damage to the culture and people of the organization.

Contrasting the Autocratic and the Servant Leader Mindsets

One of the key determinants of our mindset is where we place our focus and this presents, for leaders, a foundational ethical issue. Will my central focus of my life and leadership be on others or on self? Figure 7.2 shows the continuum from the self-focus of the autocratic leader to the other focus of the servant leader.

Instead of valuing people, autocratic leaders abuse others and devalue them by withholding trust while creating an oppressive atmosphere of suspicion and doubt. Instead of developing people they *use* others for their own purposes and once the workers have been used up they are easily discarded. Instead of building a culture of community and belonging, autocratic leaders isolate people from each other, creating a negative atmosphere of cut-throat competition. In place of openness, transparency, and honesty, autocratic leaders seek to protect themselves and their leadership position at all costs by projecting an image of trustworthiness while not backing it up with trustworthy behaviors. To these leaders, truth is pliable and adjusted as needed to gain what the leaders want. Often, these leaders fail to provide accurate and clear direction for their followers. Workers are kept on a need-to-know basis and information is shared only at a time and place the leader chooses. Leadership is provided,

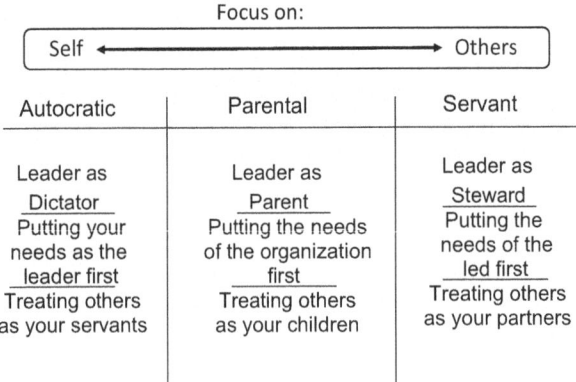

Fig. 7.2 The A-P-S model (focus on self vs. others)

not for the good of those led, but for the good of the leader and power is hoarded and dispersed from the top levels of the organization. Workers are seen as implementers of strategy and not creators of strategy, and a clear and subordinate distinction exists between leaders and followers. Position levels are rigidly maintained and used to designate value as well as responsibility. Workers do not feel empowered under this mindset of leadership. They exist only to serve the organization and the whims and desires of the leaders.

Types of Autocratic Leadership

Autocratic leadership combines the authoritarian use of power with the exploitation of the followers. Palmer (1998) tells us that a leader is

> a person who has an unusual degree of power to project onto other people his or her shadow, or his or her light. A leader is a person who has an unusual degree of power to create the conditions under which other people must live and move and have their being, conditions that can either be as illuminating as heaven or as shadowy as hell. (p. 200)

Since leaders possess this awesome power, we must become aware of this mindset and how it manifests itself in the workplace. There are three types of leaders that display this autocratic mindset.

Self-focused leaders. At the most foundational level, autocratic leadership is about leading for the benefit of the leader at the expense of others. It is a selfish and self-focused mindset that ends up exploiting the followers for the benefit of the leader. Workers are viewed as a means to an end and the end in mind is whatever the leader desires. Even the needs of the organization ultimately become secondary to the needs of the leader. Another common problem connected with this mindset is that it often accompanied by a high lack of self-awareness by the leader, who is unable or refuses to see the truth of the underlying mindset that guides his or her behavior. This focus on self can deepen into a dysfunctional self-absorption leading to abusive relationships and unaddressed blind spots.

Narcissistic leaders. "At the heart of leadership lies narcissism … which Freud … summarized as behaviors that range from a normal self-interest to a pathological self-absorption" (Northouse, 2016, p. 305). It should come as no surprise that the foundational self-focus of autocratic leaders can become an expression of the deeper more dysfunctional personality of narcissism. Narcissism is present when "an individual has an inflated self-view and craves affirmation of that self-view." These leaders tend to be "excessively confident about their intelligence and judgment and to be arrogant and disagreeable. They also seek continuous affirmation of their inflated self-view by exhibiting their superiority, devaluing others, and reacting aggressively to criticism" (Zhu & Chen, 2015, p. 32). This combination of inflated self-view with the need for constant affirmation from others and the obsessive focus on self leads to an organization that is self-, rather than other-, focused, and uses followers as a means to an end to satisfy the deep needs of the leader. Narcissistic leaders with their outsized self-confidence are often looked to as the heroic leader who will save the organization and solve all of its problems. When an organization is in deepest despair, there is often a willingness to accept dependence on this kind of powerful leader, but that is a dangerous bargain to make. The narcissistic leader is never satisfied by their latest huge acquisition, or recent praise from subordinates. They always require more. Top leader roles are attractive to narcissistic leaders and they seek them since these positions provide a place where these leaders can meet their self-focused needs and are affirmed as long as they bring success to the organization.

Addictive leaders. Schaef and Fassel (1988) contend that "many of our organizations are addictive organizations embedded in an addictive society. By this we mean that many organizations are affected by addictions and an addictive worldview and even themselves function exactly like an active individual addict" (p. 11). The authors identify several characteristics of addictive leaders: denial of reality, failure to take responsibility for actions, controlling others, dishonesty, manipulation, blaming others, and self-centeredness.

The company Uber, when going through its chaotic leadership transition in 2017, exhibited many of these characteristics.

For years, one former operations person said, the intensity and camaraderie at Uber was fulfilling; the harder he worked, the more quickly he was promoted, and the larger his bonuses were. The culture was brutal but efficient, and high performers were always rewarded; as the company grew, his sense of validation swelled. The experience, he said, was not dissimilar to being an addict. The highs were incredible ... but no addiction turns out to be good. (O'Donovan & Anand, 2017, para. 98–99)

Uber, as a company, found out that endorsing addictive behaviors such as these creates an unhealthy organizational culture where employees feel marginalized, depleted, and abused and this kind of culture ultimately leads to a serious lack of organizational focus and success.

Yes, autocratic leadership can be dangerous for followers, and it also creates serious risk for the organization. In autocratic, toxic organizations, not only is the leader focused on himself or herself but the rest of the organization is as well. Dweck (2016) in sharing the research of Collins found that in the companies that did not go from good to great, the leader became the main focus and "the minute a leader allows himself to become the primary reality people worry about, rather than reality being the primary reality, you have a recipe for mediocrity, or worse" (p. 124). Autocratic leadership and organizations are alive and well in our world today, but there is a better way, a healthier way to lead.

The Paternalistic/Parental Leadership Mindset

Paternalistic leadership is the most prevalent mindset of leadership in the world but it is rarely discussed at least in the Western world. "We hear little about paternalistic leadership despite its prevalence in the majority world. Its absence is likely because of its denigration in the minority (Western) world" (Jackson, 2016, p. 3). This negative attitude toward paternalistic leadership in the West is due to the carryover from autocratic leadership of an authoritarian approach to leadership. The West tends to espouse a more individualistic and egalitarian culture that views authoritarian leadership with suspicion. Northouse (2013) refers to the paternalistic leader as a *benevolent dictator*, an approach where the leader "acts graciously but does so for the purpose of goal accomplishment." He adds that paternalistic leaders "are often described as 'fatherly' or 'motherly' toward their followers; regard the organization as a 'family'; make most of the key decisions; and reward loyalty and obedience while punishing noncompliance" (p. 81). This view contains truth but represents a Western bias against this widespread approach to leadership. Scholars researching and writing on paternalism in leadership today come mostly from outside the Western cultural context and present the paternalistic leader as leading with benevolence toward followers while maintaining a fatherly authoritarian approach derived from a mindset viewed as a healthy cultural fit within their society.

There is a small yet growing body of research around the concept of paternalistic leadership (Pellegrini & Scandura, 2008; Tang & Naumann, 2015). Though some see a "huge gap in the literature" (Jackson, 2016, p. 6) related to this topic, others (Chan, 2013) see this as an increasing field of study drawing "considerable attention" (Tang & Naumann, 2015, p. 291). A review of the literature shows that this attention has been taking place primarily since the year 2000 and therefore is a relatively new field of study in leadership.

Part of the reason for the lack of awareness of these studies in the Western world is that they come almost exclusively from outside of the Western context from countries like China, Turkey, and Pakistan where paternalistic leadership is viewed as acceptable and ideal within the culture. It is clear from this growing body of research that though paternalistic leadership is not viewed through a positive lens in the West that it is viewed positively in the rest of the world where collectivist societies operate more from a high power distance culture that is less egalitarian than the West and where respect and deference to authority is more culturally ingrained. Certainly, paternalistic leadership provides an improvement from the dangers of autocratic leadership, but it still suffers limitations due to its reliance on authoritarian rule coupled with benevolence. "Authoritarian leadership is conceptually similar to the theory of autocratic leadership" (Chan, 2013, p. 669). Chan, however, draws a distinction between the two when he states that "autocratic leadership was developed in the western context, while authoritarian leadership reflects the cultural characteristics of Confucianism, with family power, paternalistic control and submission to authority" (Chan, 2013, p. 669). Paternalistic leadership, even with its continued reliance on authoritarianism, clearly is distinct from autocratic leadership.

However, research on paternalistic leadership conducted in Western businesses reveals that "paternalistic leadership findings may generalize across cultures" (Tang & Naumann, 2015, p. 292) and that paternalistic leadership is the predominate mindset of leadership not only in the Eastern world but in the Western world as well (Laub, 2010).

Defining Paternalistic (Parental) Leadership: Authoritarian Power + Benevolence

Paternalistic (parental) leadership is a mindset through which the leader uses authoritarian power over followers with a benevolent approach to serve the collective group within the organization while creating a parent/child relationship between leaders and followers with an expectation of compliance, loyalty, and deference toward the leader. This definition emphasizes two key distinctives of paternalistic leadership: authoritarian use of power and benevolent behavior toward followers. Note the contrast with the definition of autocratic leadership that emphasizes authoritarian use of power over followers while exploiting them. In autocratic leadership, the leader is the focus and others are exploited for the benefit of the leader. In paternalistic leadership authoritarian power is used over followers but the leader provides benevolent behaviors through care, support, and protection to the worker and the worker's family. The focus of the paternalistic leader is the collective good while the autocratic leader's interest is to meet the needs and desires of himself or herself.

According to Aycan, Schyns, Sun, Felfe, and Saher (2013) paternalistic leadership is "a hierarchical superior-subordinate relationship, where the role of the superior is to create a family environment, and provide care, protection and guidance to subordinates in both the work and non-work domains, while the subordinates are expected to be loyal and deferent to the superior" (p. 962). Within this definition, five key dimensions of paternalistic leadership are identified:

1. *Creating a family environment in the workplace*—where the leader behaves like a senior family member
2. *Establishing close and personalized relationships with subordinates*
3. *Getting involved in employees' non-work lives*
4. *Expecting loyalty and deference from subordinates*—where loyalty is more important than performance
5. *Maintaining authority and status hierarchy*—subordinates are expected to respect the leaders' role and authority (p. 963)

One can clearly discern a transactional nature to paternalistic leadership. The kind authoritarian fatherly leader provides guidance, oversight, care, protection, and support to followers who are expected then to respond with loyalty and deference (Aycan et al., 2013; Tang & Naumann, 2015). In the literature on paternalistic leadership one will find both a two-factor model and a three-factor model to describe this mindset.

The two-factor model. The two-factor model includes the key constructs of authoritarianism and benevolence (Jackson, 2016; Tian & Sanchez, 2016; Zeynep, 2012). Authoritarian leadership "refers to a behavior that exerts absolute authority and demands unquestionable obedience" while benevolent leadership "refers to behavior that demonstrates individualized concern for personal or familial well-being beyond work relations" (Chan, 2013, p. 669). This benevolence, provided by the paternalistic leader, gives "care, protection and guidance" (Chan, 2013, p. 672) for followers as well as for their extended family members.

The three-factor model. Other scholars have posited a three-factor model adding the construct of *moral leadership* to the two factors of authoritarianism and benevolence (Chan, 2013; Cheng, Chou, Wu, Huang, & Farh, 2004; Dedahnaov, Lee, Rhee, & Yoon, 2016; Tang & Naumann, 2015). Moral leadership "refers to leadership behavior that demonstrates superior personal virtue, self-discipline and unselfishness" (Chan, 2013, p. 669). The addition of the construct of morality may be connected to considerations of Transformational Leadership (Chan, 2013) and the emphasis of that model on ethics and morality (Burns, 1978). The quality of unselfishness certainly reflects a key quality of the servant leadership model.

Coming from the Western viewpoint, influenced by egalitarian and individualistic values, one might struggle with the authoritarian nature of paternalistic leadership, but scholars writing from more collectivistic cultures view the melding of authoritarianism and benevolence as culturally beneficial. "Paternalism can be authoritative, meaning that although the leader exercises tight control, the underlying reason is to promote followers' welfare" (Tian & Sanchez, 2016, p. 236). In this way of thinking, the paternalistic leader serves the needs of the followers through authoritarian leadership behaviors. Tian and Sanchez reinforce this view when they state that "when employees perceive that their leader's challenging, authoritarian demands are accompanied by high levels of benevolent concern, employees assume that their leader's strictness is selfless and sincere" (Tian & Sanchez, 2016, p. 237).

Paternalistic leadership provides a healthier leadership mindset compared to autocratic leadership. It is the most common mindset of leadership throughout the world and is viewed by researchers from Eastern cultures as the best mindset to focus on the collective good while acknowledging a cultural acceptance of hierarchy and paternalistic care. However, a caution is raised from a review of research results on paternalistic leadership.

Research Studies on Paternalistic Leadership

Paternalistic leadership is an emerging new field of research study (Pellegrini & Scandura, 2008). Two key quantitative assessments have been developed for research, one by Cheng (Cheng, Chou, & Farh, 2000) and another by Aycan (2006). Both instruments have been used to study the effects of paternalistic leadership on follower behaviors such as creativity, employee voice, and information sharing. The results of these studies show contrasting results between the two key constructs of paternalistic leadership. The authoritarian construct tends to be negatively correlated to positive follower behaviors while the benevolent construct tends to be positively correlated. Therefore, the positive effects of the paternalistic leader's benevolence serve to moderate the negative effects of the leader's authoritarian approach. The two key constructs of the paternalistic leader model appear then to work in opposition to each other in terms of their effect on follower behaviors.

To illustrate this, consider these research study outcomes related to the authoritarianism and benevolence of paternalistic leaders and their effect on employee behavior. "The Benevolent Leadership (BL) component of paternalistic leadership has revealed a consistently positive main effect on a variety of employee outcomes, including identification and satisfaction with the leader, trust, organizational commitment, job performance and organizational citizenship behavior" (Tian & Sanchez, 2016, p. 237). However, "Evidence has demonstrated that a negative effect of authoritarian leadership is contradictory to the positive effect of benevolent and moral leadership on employee work behaviors" (Chan, 2013, p. 668). The strict controls placed on followers by paternalistic leaders undermine the follower's willingness to share information and speak openly to their leaders (Chan, 2013). Other research studies reinforce this oppositional effect. "Authoritarian leadership is negatively associated with employee voice … benevolent leadership is positively associated with employee voice" (Chan, 2013, p. 676). Research by Tang and Naumann (2015) found that "benevolent leadership and moral leadership increased subordinate OCB (Organizational Citizenship Behaviors) … in contrast, authoritarian leadership does not offer the same benefits needed to initiate reciprocal exchanges" (p. 301).

Though the interpretation of this contrasting result suggests that the two key constructs of paternalistic leadership are in opposition to each other, some scholars contend that it is the combination of the two that provides an overall positive effect within cultures compatible with this mindset. Tian and Sanchez (2016) state that "at least in China AL and BL are not only compatible, but in fact interact with each other in accordance with a leadership prototype that promotes employee innovative behavior and knowledge sharing" (p. 242). They go on to contend that "in today's Chinese organizations, a leadership style that employs solely authority or solely benevolence might not be as effective as one that employs authority and benevolence simultaneously" (p. 242).

Gallup's *State of the Global Workplace* (2017) speaks to the low level of worker engagement in India where only 13% of full-time workers report as being engaged in their work. The remaining workers report 65% not engaged and 22% actively disengaged (p. 195). The Gallup report attributes this low level of engagement, at least in part, to paternalistic leadership practices within that country. "Nudging the work culture out of its hierarchical construct won't be easy—it is a culture built on generations of patriarchal leadership structures. Family-owned businesses account for almost two-thirds of India's GDP and about half of its workforce" (p. 160). The Gallup report goes on to state that "hierarchical boss-employee relationships stifle innovation and productivity and discourage employee engagement. They reward obedience more than outcome" (p. 160). Admittedly, this analysis comes from a Western viewpoint, and it may be unfair to cast too much blame on paternalistic leadership in general. It may be that not enough paternalistic leaders in India are employing sufficient benevolence in their leadership to counterbalance the negative effects of paternalistic authoritarianism, but the low level of worker engagement in countries that tend culturally toward paternalistic leadership should provide a caution related to the use of this mindset of leadership.

Another important consideration is the changing face of employees across the world as new generations join the workforce. Gallup (2017) raises the issue of the growing influence of millennial workers who bring new expectations and needs into the workplace. Millennial workers are

> forecasted to account for 64% of all Indian workers by 2021, are more likely to be open to coaching and personal development, looking for a sense of purpose in the workplace and desiring ongoing conversations with their managers. But, this is not being provided. (p. 161)

Are younger workers, in all parts of the world, beginning to change expectations related to leadership? If so, is an ongoing reliance on hierarchical authoritarianism, even balanced by the nurture and care of a benevolent leader, sufficient to increase seriously low levels of worker engagement?

There is no doubt that paternalistic leadership provides a healthy alternative to the autocratic mindset of leadership. Current research reveals that paternalistic leadership positively correlates to factors such as employee voice, creativity, and information sharing. This is encouraging and worth noting, but will this approach to leadership create the higher levels of worker engagement needed for the next generation of workers? Can the paternalistic mindset move us to higher levels of organizational performance?

The Servant Leadership Mindset

Servant leadership is a mindset through which the leader uses power to serve the needs of followers over the leader's self-interest while creating an adult partnership relationship between leaders and followers that allows everyone to lead and serve. This definition expands on Laub's (1999) earlier definition of servant leadership, "an understanding and practice of leadership that puts the good of those led over the self-interest of the leader" (p. 83) by considering the unique relationship between the leader and follower; that of adult partnership.

The expanded definition offered here identifies how servant leaders view and use power contrasted to autocratic and paternalistic leaders. The servant leader uses power to serve followers over the leader's self-interest. The servant leader sees his or her central role as that of servant to those led. This is the servant leader's main focus. It is not the only focus, of course, since organizational goals are also critical for the servant leader, but the focus on the follower is central and foundational. Servant leaders believe that the best way to maximize organizational performance is to maximize individual employee contribution and performance. The more workers we have meaningfully connected to the mission of our organization, using their best skills and gifts to fully engage in their work, the healthier and more productive the organization will be.

This expanded definition also addresses the leader's view of and relationship to workers. Under the autocratic mindset, the workers are servants to the needs and desires of the leader. Under the paternalistic mindset, the workers are children and subjects to the benevolent authoritarianism of the leader. However, under the servant mindset, workers are viewed and related to as adult partners. Workers are empowered to fulfill their potential as people, as workers, and as leaders within the workplace.

They are not a means to an end; rather, they are the key end of the servant leader's attention, focus, and efforts. When workers are released from the servant or child roles and are empowered as adult partners to serve alongside the leaders, an incredible leveraged power is released as higher numbers of workers discover new ways to lead and to serve.

In Table 7.1 the definitions for the three leadership mindsets are provided to clearly show the different approach provided by each mindset. It should be noted that servant leadership does not emphasize the concept of benevolence, or taking care of the workers, which is a distinctive of the paternalistic approach. Servant leaders are concerned with empowering workers, not taking care of them as a parent takes care of a child. They are concerned with treating the worker as an adult partner who is gifted and capable to both lead and serve. Benevolence is the act of a positive paternalistic leader who cares for his or her followers like a kindly father cares for his children. The servant leader, however, creates a deeper expectation for workers requiring that they step up to a higher level of responsibility bringing their ideas, initiative, and committed effort to the work. Servant leaders desire to move beyond worker dependence and compliance to the more significant level of worker commitment and ownership.

Table 7.1 Definitions compared between autocratic, paternalistic, and servant leadership

Autocratic leadership	Parental/paternalistic leadership	Servant leadership
Autocratic leadership is a mindset through which the leader uses authoritarian power to control followers with an exploitative approach to serve the needs and desires of the leader at the expense of the well-being of the followers.	Parental/paternalistic leadership is a mindset through which the leader uses authoritarian power over followers with a benevolent approach to serve the collective group within the organization while creating a parent/child relationship between leaders and followers with an expectation of compliance, loyalty, and deference.	Servant leadership is a mindset through which the leader uses power to serve the needs of followers over the leader's self-interest while creating an adult partnership relationship between leaders and followers that allows everyone to both lead and serve.

In Table 7.2 the essential defining elements of the three mindsets are listed to highlight the key distinctions between each mindset. Autocratic leaders lead for self over others. They have a foundational worldview that is competitive and committed to winning. Self-interest is the driving force and others exist to serve the interests of the leader and the needs of the leader are foremost even over the needs of the organization. To illustrate, an adult student of this author, who serves in law enforcement, shared about a time when their city police department purchased three new fully equipped police cars. The cars were beautiful and had everything a patrol officer would need to do his or her job better. However, when the cars were assigned, the first one went to the Chief of Police while the other two were given to the highest-ranking patrol officers. The Chief, who already had the best and largest office, the highest salary, the most perks, and the most flexible work schedule, saw it as his right to take one of the new cars for his own use. The Chief, of course, did not do patrol work so his acquisition of one of the new cars did not benefit the organization. It did not provide better police service on the streets of the city. It merely provided

Table 7.2 A-P-S essential defining elements and view of power

Mindsets	Essential defining elements	View and use of power	View of and relationship to followers
Autocratic	Authoritarian power + exploitation Leading for self over Wothers Controlling followers	Power to serve the leader needs and to control followers	Followers are servants to the leader and a resource to exploit
Parental/ Paternalistic	Authoritarian power + benevolence Leading for the collective good/the organization parent-child relationship	Power to serve the leader and the needs of the organization	Followers are children to the parental, caring leader who requires compliance and deference
Servant	Empowerment + adult partnership Leading for others over self Followers as adult partners	Power to serve and empower others before self	Followers are adult partners who are challenged to lead and to serve

the Chief a chance to show that he was in charge and that he had the power and, in his mind, the right to take the car for himself. Autocratic leaders lead for self over others and they view their followers as resources to be controlled and exploited for the leader's own purposes.

Paternalistic leaders in contrast care about their followers and the organization they serve. As parental leaders they use their authority to lead their followers as a kindly father guides his children. Power remains in the able hands of the benevolent leader and workers in this relationship maintain a respectful fear of the leader. This leader-focused power combined with caring, benevolent behaviors leads to workers who are cared for and protected. The workers then respond with compliance, loyalty, and expected levels of performance. This transaction seems at first glance to be in the best interest of both the leader, who maintains control, and the workers, whose needs are provided, but it maintains a clear separation between leaders and followers and limits the potential for all to lead and all to serve.

Servant leaders care deeply about their workers as well, but they know the limitation that both authoritarianism and benevolence places on their followers. When leaders maintain control of power and decision making at the top of the organization, others do not have the opportunity to lead, envision, and create. When the benevolence of the parental leader is provided, a dependence on this benevolence is created limiting the development of the potential as leader of the worker. Servant leaders empower others to lead, which places on the worker a higher level of expectation and opportunity. When the servant leader views workers as adult partners they provide a respect and obligation to those workers. When workers accept this higher expectation and obligation placed on them they develop toward their full potential as leaders and servants.

Exploring the Paternalistic Leadership Culture and Communication: The Parent-Adult-Child (PAC) Model

Paternalistic leadership is the view the leader has of himself or herself as parent *over* those led and this view of leadership is not new. O'Toole (1995) observed that rule by a few wise and virtuous men has been the preferred mode since 400 B.C., the era of two influential near contemporaries, Plato in the West and Confucius in the East. Both believed that chaos is the enemy of efficiency and that it can be averted only by the strong leadership of an enlightened elite. (p. 185)

The kind of benevolent rule described here has the effect of producing a childlike response in the followers. Workers, under this mindset, readily accept that leaders know more, are wiser, and that the led must simply follow, even if it means abdicating their own responsibility to lead. This dynamic of leader as parent and worker as child requires a deeper exploration to determine what effect this relational role behavior may have on working relationships within the organization.

The PAC Model

Transactional analysis (TA) was developed by Berne (1961, 1964, 1972) and popularized by Harris (1969) to serve as "a unified system of individual and social psychiatry" (as cited in Northouse, 2013, p. 322) and refers to how people relate to each other and the roles they tend to play in transactions with others. Berne developed the concept of TA to explain the multiple ways people engage three key ego states, or roles, in their transactions. The three roles are parent, adult, and child. Berne (1961) tells us that "a Parental ego state is a set of feelings, attitudes and behavior patterns which resemble those of a parental figure" (p. 75). He goes on to explain that

> The Parent is typically exhibited in one of two forms. The *prejudicial* Parent is manifested as a set of seemingly arbitrary non-rational attitudes or parameters, usually prohibitive in nature … the *nurturing* Parent is often manifested as *sympathy for* another individual. (p. 76)

So, there are two types of parents within the TA scheme. The prejudicial, or negative, parent creates an atmosphere of mistrust and fear while the nurturing, or positive, parent emphasizes an atmosphere of care, support, and positive expectation. This system of TA goes beyond just providing a way to look at family dynamics but is also "a powerful tool in management and communications training and in organizational analysis" (Stewart & Joines, 1987, p. 3). The use of this three-role model is particularly helpful for exploring the dynamics of how paternalistic, or parental, leadership works within organizations to describe interactions and communication between leaders and workers (Fig. 7.3).

The leader as parent: the worker as child. When a leader acts out of the role of parent (father or mother) toward workers this tends to pull a childlike response from the followers. As we have seen, the parental leader can act as either a critical (negative) parent or a nurturing (positive) parent. The critical parent creates a negative atmosphere of suspicion and mistrust where workers must constantly prove themselves to their demanding leaders. These leaders view the workers as less than capable children who need strong guidance and control from the leader.

The nurturing parent, on the other hand, provides a place of care and support and views workers as capable children who continue to need the wisdom and experience of the leader. It is in this parent role where the benevolence of the paternalistic leadership model is most evident. This nurturing spirit helps the followers to trust more in the leader and to respect and appreciate the leader's support and care. The worker, responding as a nurtured child, finds the workplace to be safe and supportive, a place where they can excel in their work under the guiding hand of the parental leader. However, as positive as this sounds, there is a limitation that must be acknowledged. Under a

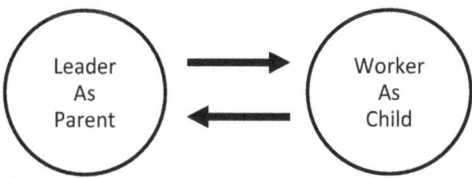

Fig. 7.3 PAC model (parent to child)

positive paternalistic leader, one who leads with both authoritarianism and benevolence, the follower remains dependent on the leader. This dependence works against the follower becoming a leader or developing his or her leadership capacities. Parental leadership can foster a positive workplace with satisfied workers but it perpetuates the sharp divide between leaders and followers in the workplace. A more open and expanded leadership culture where everyone is given the opportunity to both lead and serve is hindered within this mindset of leadership.

When workers act out of the child role this tends to encourage a stronger parental role from the leader and when leaders act out of a parental role this draws out more of a childlike response from the followers. This creates a self-perpetuating cycle such that when the parent-child dynamic is in play, each role reinforces and strengthens the other. Moving beyond this cycle requires a change of mindset from leader as parent and follower as child to a practice of leadership where both leaders and followers view and communicate with each other as adults. It is this view of followers as adult partners that distinguishes the servant leader mindset from other mindsets and provides the best foundation for a healthy, high performing organization.

> The answer to this dilemma is to foster adult roles for both leaders and followers that emphasize open, direct communication, partnership, receptive listening and mutual respect. When a leader operates in the role of Adult and relates to the worker in this way, the worker tends then to react in the role of Adult. This is the healthiest scenario—when people at all levels of the organization trust and respect one another and encourage active participation and leadership, the organization as a whole prospers. (Laub, 2005, p. 170)

The leader as adult: the worker as adult. When everyone in the organization views themselves and others as adult partners, it creates the healthiest organization where all people serve the interests of others above their own for the good of the organization. When Ricardo Semler, CEO of Brazil's Semco, was asked to describe the reason for the success of his organization, he stated, "It's all very simple, all we are doing is treating people like adults" (as cited in Showkeir & Showkeir, 2008, p. 44). Consider your own experience in the workplace. Since the paternalistic mindset of leading is so prevalent across the world, you likely have experienced being treated in a parental, patronizing way by leaders. How did this make you feel? If you were treated like this by a negative parental leader, you likely found yourself resisting by either pushing back against the leader or providing a low level of compliance to the leader's demands. If you were treated parentally by a positive parental leader, you may have found yourself grateful for the benevolence and authoritative direction given but also found that you were limited in opportunities to lead and fully use your gifts.

If you had a leader who treated you as an adult partner, you know the mutual respect you experienced in that relationship. The leader asked for your opinion and ideas. The leader allowed you to speak and provide opposing opinions. The leader gave you the opportunity to make important decisions, share your ideas, and own your own work. When leaders relate to followers as adults they create a different set of expectations about work and communication. They fully expect the workers to have valid ideas and they seek out this feedback. They truly listen showing deep respect for the worker and all they can contribute. The adult leader knows that their own experience is limited and that each worker has a perspective they need to learn from. So, they ask, and they listen. They agree, or they disagree. They act on the ideas of the workers or they do not, but they listen and value the input that workers, as adult partners, bring to the discussion.

The self-perpetuating cycle we discussed before comes into play here as well. As a parental leader will bring out a child response in followers, the adult leader will bring out an adult response from the followers and when this happens, adult conversations begin and each person, leader and worker, is reinforced in their view of themselves and each other as adult partners (Fig. 7.4).

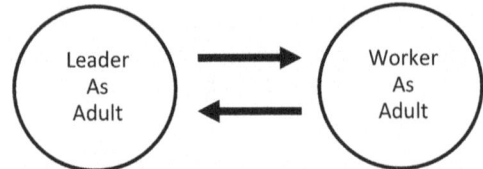

Fig. 7.4 PAC model (adult to adult)

Learning Adult Speak: Moving Beyond Paternalism

How do adults speak to each other? If leaders desire to come across as adult partners to their followers, how do they act and how do they communicate? They begin by communicating with an attitude of mutual respect. They begin by asking, in a spirit of appreciative inquiry, sincerely desiring to learn from their followers. Leaders make themselves vulnerable and open to the expertise of the follower. Leaders are also free to disagree and offer opposing ideas because the exchange is taking place in an atmosphere of mutual respect and accountability. Adults are free to speak their minds but they do so in a respectful way providing freedom for other adults to speak openly and honestly.

Showkeir and Showkeir (2008) provide seven descriptions of what adult-adult relationships create within organizations. They suggest that when leaders and followers take on an adult role that each individual

1. becomes the eyes and the voice of the business;
2. brings an independent point of view and is open to other's perspectives;
3. is expected to raise difficult issues;
4. extends a spirit of goodwill to the endeavor;
5. creates business literacy in others;
6. chooses accountability for the success of the whole business;
7. manages his or her own morale, motivation, and commitment. (pp. 70–73)

In other words, each individual, leader and follower, becomes responsible for leading and serving in the organization bringing their complete set of gifts, talents, and experience to the partnership. When leaders begin to view their followers differently and begin treating them and speaking to them as adult partners, it opens up opportunities for each person as they see that they are allowed and expected to speak as adults. "If organizations don't find a way to shift to an adult-adult culture, they will be ill equipped to survive in the highly technical, global, diverse, and changing-at-the-speed-of-light marketplace" (Showkeir & Showkeir, 2008, p. 25).

So, as a leader and as a follower, speak as an adult. Speak as if you have the right to speak; you do. Speak as if you are confident of what you are saying; you are. Speak directly about what you want and need, then, you will be understood. Speak without emotional childlike baggage or weapons; you don't need them anymore. Speak as an adult and the person you speak to will tend to respond as an adult. This cycle-breaking initiative may begin with the leader or the follower. Either way, it will produce a self-perpetuating cycle that develops an adult-adult culture, the healthiest culture of all.

When Thomas Jefferson, third president of the United States, was writing to Pierre S. Du Pont de Nemours, creator of the huge industry that bears his name, Jefferson wrote,

> I acknowledge myself strong in affection to our own form, yet both of us act and think from the same motive; we both consider the people as our children. And love them with parental affection. But you love them as infants whom you are afraid to trust without nurses, and I as adults whom I freely leave to self-government. (As cited in O'Toole, 1995, pp. 31–32)

The love of a parent is a beautiful and noble thing, whether the children receiving that love are infants, young children, or adult children. However, when our children become adults we don't love them less, but we treat them differently. We treat them as adults who are worthy of our respect and capable of offering leadership and valuable contribution in their own right. To fully engage our workers and maximize the performance of our organizations, we must give our workers full trust, power, and partnership.

Conclusion

The three mindsets of leadership provide helpful contrasts for more clearly defining servant leadership. Servant leadership is not benevolence or just treating workers in a kind, nurturing way. It resists creating a dependent relationship between leader and worker and seeks instead a mature, adult partnership relationship that expects more of each person and allows for each person's gifts to be fully realized and developed. Servant leaders use power but use it to empower their workers to become leaders and servants who share in the work with their leaders. In the next chapter we will apply these three mindsets to organizational culture development to identify distinct levels of organizational health as assessed by the OLA. This will reveal how these leadership mindsets serve to provide health or lack of health to the organization. Leadership matters but *how* we lead matters most. The mindset of leadership we adopt will determine our thoughts and actions of leadership creating teams and organizations that either flourish or languish. We move now beyond the servant leader to the servant organization.

References

Adams, G. B., & Balfour, D. (2009). *Unmasking administrative evil* (3rd ed.). Armonk and New York, NY: M.E. Sharpe, Inc.

Aycan, Z. (2006). Paternalism: Towards conceptual refinement and operationalization. In K. S. Yang, K. K. Hwang, & U. Kim (Eds.), *Scientific advances in indigenous psychologies: Empirical, philosophical, and cultural contribution* (pp. 445–466). London: Sage.

Aycan, Z., Schyns, B., Sun, J., Felfe, J., & Saher, N. (2013). Convergence and divergence of paternalistic leadership: A cross-cultural investigation of prototypes. *Journal of International Business Studies, 44*, 962–969.

Berne, E. (1961). *Transactional analysis in psychotherapy*. New York, NY: Grove Press.

Berne, E. (1964). *Games people play*. New York, NY: Ballantine.

Berne, E. (1972). *What do you say after you say hello?* New York, NY: Grove Press.

Burns, J. M. (1978). *Leadership*. New York, NY: Harper & Row Publishers.

Chan, S. C. H. (2013). Paternalistic leadership and employee voice: Does information sharing matter? *Human Relations, 67*(6), 667–693. https://doi.org/10.1177/0018726713503022

Cheng, B. S., Chou, L. F., & Farh, J. L. (2000). A triad model of paternalistic leadership: The constructs and measurement. *Indigenous Psychological Research in Chinese Societies, 14*, 3–64.

Cheng, B. S., Chou, L. F., Wu, T. Y., Huang, M. P., & Farh, J. L. (2004). Paternalistic leadership and subordinate responses: Establishing a leadership model in Chinese organizations. *Asian Journal of Social Psychology, 7*(1), 89–117.

Dedahnaov, A. T., Lee, D. H., Rhee, J., & Yoon, J. (2016). Entrepreneur's paternalistic leadership style and creativity. *Management Decision, 54*(9), 2310–2324. https://doi.org/10.1108/MD-11-2015-0537

Dweck, C. S. (2016). *Mindset: The new psychology of success* (2nd ed.). New York, NY: Ballantine Books.

Gallup. (2017). *State of the global workplace.* New York, NY: Gallup Press.

Harris, T. A. (1969). *I'm OK, you're OK: A practical guide to transactional analysis.* New York, NY: Harper & Row.

Hornstein, H. A. (1996). *Brutal bosses and their prey.* New York, NY: Riverhead Books.

Jackson, T. (2016). Paternalistic leadership: The missing link in cross-cultural leadership studies. *International Journal of Cross Cultural Management, 16*(1), 3–7. https://doi.org/10.1177/1470595816637701

Kellerman, B. (2004). *Bad leadership: What it is, how it happens, why it matters.* Boston, MA: Harvard Business School Press.

Laub, J. A. (1999). *Assessing the servant organization: Development of the servant organizational leadership assessment (SOLA) instrument.* Doctoral dissertation, Florida Atlantic University.

Laub, J. A. (2005). From paternalism to the servant organization: Expanding the Organizational Leadership Assessment (OLA) model. *International Journal of Servant-Leadership, 1*, 155–186.

Laub, J. A. (2010). The servant organization. In D. van Dierendonck & K. Patterson (Eds.), *Servant leadership: Developments in theory and research* (pp. 105–117). New York, NY: Palgrave Macmillan.

Northouse, P. G. (2013). *Leadership: Theory and practice* (6th ed.). Thousand Oaks, CA: Sage Publications Inc.

Northouse, P. G. (2016). *Leadership: Theory and practice* (7th ed.). Thousand Oaks, CA: Sage Publications Inc.

O'Donovan, C. & Anand, P. (2017, July 17, 7:14 pm). How Uber's hard-charging corporate culture left employees drained. Retrieved from https://www.buzzfeed.com/carolineodonovan/how-ubers-hard-charging-corporate-culture-left-employees?utm_term=.jbdPVMPR2#.jsbZNbZLA

O'Toole, J. (1995). *Leading change: Overcoming the ideology of comfort and the tyranny of custom.* Indianapolis, IN: Jossey-Bass.

Palmer, P. J. (1998). Leading from within. In L. C. Spears (Ed.), *Insights on leadership: Service, stewardship, spirit, and servant-leadership* (pp. 197–208). New York, NY: John Wiley & Sons.

Pellegrini, E. K., & Scandura, T. A. (2008). Paternalistic leadership: A review and agenda for future research. *Journal of Management, 34*(3), 566–593. https://doi.org/10.1177/0149206308316063

Schaef, A. W., & Fassel, A. (1988). *The addictive organization.* Sydney, Australia: Harper Publishers.

Showkeir, J., & Showkeir, M. (2008). *Authentic conversations: Moving from manipulation to truth and commitment.* San Francisco, CA: Berrett-Koehler Publishers, Inc.

Stewart, I., & Joines, V. (1987). *TA today: A new introduction to transactional analysis.* Chapel Hill, NC: Lifespace Publishing.

Tang, C., & Naumann, S. E. (2015). Paternalistic leadership, subordinate perceived leader-member exchange and organizational citizenship behavior. *Journal of Management & Organization, 21*(3), 291–306. https://doi.org/10.1017/jmo.2014.84

Tian, Q., & Sanchez, J. I. (2016). Does paternalistic leadership promote innovative behavior? The interaction between authoritarianism and benevolence. *Journal of Applied Social Psychology, 47*, 235–246. https://doi.org/10.1111/jasp.12431

Zeynep, H. O. (2012). Servant leadership and paternalistic leadership styles in the Turkish business context. *Leadership & Organization Development Journal, 33*(3), 300–316.

Zhu, D. H., & Chen, G. (2015). CEO narcissism and the impact of prior board experience on corporate strategy. *Administrative Science Quarterly, 60*(1), 31–65. https://doi.org/10.1177/0001839214554989

8

The Servant Organization: Levels of Organizational Health

What makes an organization healthy and able to sustain engaged and high-performing workers? This chapter takes the servant leadership concepts discussed previously and applies them to organizations creating a new reality, the servant organization. The implications of autocratic, paternalistic, or servant mindsets applied to organizations are explored to see how they create varying levels of organizational health. The Organizational Leadership Assessment (OLA) is presented, a tool through which leaders can assess the health of their own leadership and that of their organization. The organization as servant provides a practical model and vision for creating healthy high performing organizations.

The Organization as Servant: Greenleaf's Vision

Greenleaf's view of servant leadership extended beyond the relationship between leader and follower. He saw this concept impacting major institutions as well as the larger society. He (1977) states,

© The Author(s) 2018
J. Laub, *Leveraging the Power of Servant Leadership*, Palgrave Studies in Workplace Spirituality and Fulfillment, https://doi.org/10.1007/978-3-319-77143-4_8

This is my thesis: caring for persons, the more able and the less able serving each other, is the rock upon which a good society is built … if a better society is to be built, one that is more just and more loving, one that provides greater creative opportunity for its people, then the most open course is to raise both the capacity to serve and the very performance as servant of existing major institutions. (p. 49)

This is a powerful statement, one that acknowledges the simple act of people serving one another as the bedrock upon which a good society is built. To channel these acts of serving, organizations must become servant minded throughout their culture, values, attitudes, and behaviors. The truth is that our organizations can become places that bring us joy, empowerment, and purpose or they can be places that are joyless, disempowering, and directionless. The mindset of leadership we choose sets the stage for the organizational cultures we create.

What Makes an Organization Healthy?

The World Health Organization defines health as "a state of complete physical, mental and social well-being and not merely the absence of disease or infirmity" (World Health Organization, 1946). This definition is useful in addressing the question of what makes an organization healthy. It suggests that it is the presence of specific health factors that make a person, or an organization healthy, not merely the absence of negative factors such as disease or infirmity. A person may be healthy in terms of not having a disease but may be unhealthy due to poor eating or exercise habits. Like people, organizations can be healthy or unhealthy and the ability of the organization to reach full performance capability depends on possessing specific health factors throughout its leadership and organizational culture. When this author developed the Organizational Leadership Assessment (OLA) it was designed to assess the perception of the presence of servant leadership characteristics throughout the entire organization, not just for specific leaders (Laub, 1999). The belief was that servant mindedness must move beyond single leaders to become part of the overall organizational culture and that developing a servant mindset is the responsibility of everyone, leaders and followers, within the organization.

The OLA servant leadership model provides a list of positive health factors and disciplines that all leaders and organizations who desire to develop a servant mindset should pursue. According to the OLA servant leadership model, servant leaders:

1. Value People

    (a) By trusting and believing in people
    (b) By serving others' needs before their own
    (c) By receptive, non-judgmental listening

2. Develop People

    (a) By providing opportunities for learning and growth
    (b) By modeling appropriate behavior
    (c) By building up others through encouragement and affirmation

3. Build Community

    (a) By building strong personal relationships
    (b) By working collaboratively with others
    (c) By valuing the differences of others

4. Display Authenticity

    (a) By being open and accountable to others
    (b) By a willingness to learn from others
    (c) By maintaining integrity and trust

5. Provide Leadership

    (a) By envisioning the future
    (b) By taking initiative
    (c) By clarifying goals

6. Share Leadership

    (a) By facilitating a shared vision
    (b) By sharing power and releasing control
    (c) By sharing status and promoting others

It is the presence, or absence, of these disciplines or characteristics that makes an organization healthy or unhealthy and organizational health leads to organizational performance. When Collins (2001) conducted his *Good to Great* research on high performing companies, he and his team identified what he labeled Level 5 leadership, a leadership characterized by a paradoxical blend of "extreme personal humility with intense professional will" (p. 21). An example Collins shares of Level 5 leadership is Darwin E. Smith, an unassuming, mild-mannered lawyer who in 1971 took over a poor-performing paper company called Kimberly-Clark. Many, including Smith himself, thought that he was not the right man for the job, but he served for over two decades providing ferocious yet humble leadership that transformed the company into the "leading paper-based consumer products company in the world" (2001, p. 17). Collins describes Smith as carrying no airs of self-importance, no desire for celebrity or hero status, just a humble awkwardly shy persona coupled with a deep and abiding commitment to make his company succeed. In contrast to the self-effacing leadership of Smith at Kimberly-Clark, Scott Paper hired Al Dunlap as CEO. Dunlap was everything Smith was not, self-serving, arrogant, bragging, and self-promoting. *Business Week* reported that Dunlap received $100 million for the 603 days he was leader at Scott Paper ($165,000 per day) and his tenure became notorious for drastically cutting employees and sacrificing the future of the company for short-term profits (Collins, 2001).

Dunlap is an example of the autocratic leader, a leader committed to himself, who leads for self-serving gain over the interests of the organization and its employees. Smith, on the other hand, represents a more enlightened approach as did the other leaders of Collin's *Good to Great* companies. These leaders were described by those who worked with them as "quiet, humble, modest, reserved, shy, gracious, mild-mannered, self-effacing, understated" (2001, p. 27). There could not be a stronger contrast between two leaders than that of Darwin Smith and Al Dunlap. So, which of these leaders was most successful? Clearly, the employees benefited more under the selfless leadership of Darwin Smith but what about the organizations? Which of them found better, longer-lasting performance and success? Kimberly-Clark not only outperformed Scott Paper and Procter & Gamble, its two more famous competitors, but ended up owning Scott Paper. Yes, organizational health matters and the mindset of leadership brought to an organization will determine not only the satisfaction of its employees but the ultimate performance of the company.

There is one final note about Collin's research that bears mentioning in a book, like this one, on servant leadership. When Collin's research team found that the leaders of the highest performing organizations were leaders like Darwin Smith, they were surprised and debated what they should call this tough but humble way of leading. They considered titles like selfless executive or even servant leader, but they decided on the less descriptive title of Level 5 leader because several members of Collin's research team objected to the servant-oriented titles as sounding "weak or meek" (2001, p. 30) which they knew did not reflect the strength, power, and deep commitment these leaders displayed. Unfortunately, accepting the misconception of servant leadership as weak did not allow Collin's team to identify this leadership approach for what it is: servant leadership. Through Collin's research we are able to see a servant-minded approach to leadership as the driving mindset of higher performance.

The Six Levels of Organizational Health

The OLA servant leadership model, when assessed in organizations through the OLA instrument, has determined six levels of organizational health based on a continuum of the three key mindsets of leadership— autocratic, paternalistic/parental, and servant. For ease and conciseness, we will look at these levels in four basic categories:

1. Level 1–2: Toxic and Poor Health Organizations
2. Level 3: Negative Parental Organizations
3. Level 4: Positive Parental Organizations
4. Level 5–6: Servant-Minded Health Organizations

As we review each of the organizational health levels it is helpful to consider the percentage of organizations that fall within each of these health levels based on studies by Laub (2005) and Herman (2008). In Table 8.1 a summary of these two studies is presented with findings showing that an average of 31% of the organizations scored at the Autocratic (Toxic or Poor) health level, an average of 30% scored in the Negative Parental health level, 25% scored in the Positive Parental health level, and 14% scored in the Servant health level.

Table 8.1 Percentage of organizations falling into each A-P-S category

Organizational level	Laub study (2005) $n = 136$		Herman study (2008) $n = 440$		Organizational mindset (**A-P-S** model)
Organization[1]	7.35%	30.88%	6.59%	32.04%	Autocratic organizations **31% average**
Organization[2]	23.53%		25.45%		
Organization[3]	33.82%		25.90%		Parental (negative) organizations **30% average**
Organization[4]	23.53%		25.68%		Parental (positive) organizations **25% average**
Organization[5]	9.55%	11.76%	11.59%	16.36%	Servant organizations **14% average**
Organization[6]	2.21%		4.77%		

So, nearly one-third of organizations in these studies are autocratically led, exhibiting poor to toxic health. On the opposite extreme, 14% of organizations are servant led, revealing a healthy organizational culture. Though this is the lowest percentage of organizational culture type identified, it shows that servant-minded organizations exist and though few, they serve as models for how healthy organizations are led. Interestingly, the largest type of organization is the paternalistic (parental) organization with a total of 55% falling within this category. As we discussed in a previous chapter, the paternalistic mindset of leadership is the most practiced approach to leadership throughout the world (Jackson, 2016) and is prominent in Asia, Africa, and the Middle East. However, this research shows that the paternalistic mindset is also the most prominent in the Western world where these OLA studies were conducted.

Let's examine each of these organizational health levels in greater detail to see what they look like, how they are led, and what outcomes we might expect over time. It is important to note that these organizational health levels are not just theoretical. They describe how real organizations function in terms of their health as perceived by workers within the organizations. As the OLA research shows (presented in the next chapter) the level of organizational health correlates to key organizational health factors such as team effectiveness, employee trust in leaders, job satisfaction, employee safety, tenure, and absenteeism, revealing a positive connection between servant leadership and organizational health factors leading to higher performance.

Health Level 1–2: Toxic and Poor Health Organizations

Toxic and poor health organizations function under an autocratic (leader-first) mindset characterized by high fear, low trust, low risk taking, low creativity, and poor communication. It is the antithesis of a servant-minded organization and therefore reflects the opposite of the 6 disciplines and 18 descriptors from the OLA servant leadership model. The high levels of fear present in these organizations combined with low levels of trust create an environment where workers are unwilling to take risks to exhibit creativity in their jobs. Instead, they do the minimum necessary to stay below the radar in order to protect themselves from a harsh and abusive workplace. Communication is poor and unidirectional with demands sent down to workers from top leaders with minimal feedback requested from the workforce. Workers are afraid to speak their minds, to ask questions, or to seek clarity on tasks resulting in the risk of poor productivity and poor product and task quality.

As Table 8.1 reveals, these organizations account for 31% of organizations and the leadership behaviors within these organizations can be considered as self-focused, narcissistic, or even addictive. This is an unhealthy environment that far too many workers are subjected to and this accounts for the high level of workers who report as *actively disengaged* from their work and workplace. The Gallup report *State of the Global Workplace* (2017) indicates that the highest level of engaged employees is at 33% in the United States while that percentage of engaged workers drops down to 10% for Western Europe. The tragedy of lost potential and productivity from these disengaged workers should provide a reality check for all organizational leaders. We are allowing negative and even harmful workplace cultures to continue in order to satisfy short-term gains or the ego needs of autocratic leaders. The toxic leader does not care about the workers, but only sees them as means to an end, an end that meets the immediate and self-focused needs of the leader. Consider this description of a toxic/poor health organization and how workers experience this organizational culture.

Description of Level 1–2: Toxic/Poor Health Organization

The Workers: *Motivation, morale, attitude and commitment, listening, relationships versus tasks*

Most workers do not feel valued or believed in here. They often feel *used* and do not feel that they have the opportunity of being developed either personally or professionally. Workers are rarely listened to and only when they speak in line with the values and priorities of the leaders. Their ideas are rarely sought and almost never used. Most decisions are made at the top levels of the organization. Relationships are not encouraged and the tasks of the organization come before people. Diversity is not valued or appreciated.

The Leadership: *Power, decision making, goals, and direction*

Leadership is autocratic in style and is imposed from the top levels of the organization. Power is held at the highest positions only and is used to force compliance with the leader's wishes. Workers do not feel empowered to create change. Goals are often unclear and the overall direction of the organization is confused.

The Team: *Community, collaboration, and team learning*

This is a highly individualistic and competitive environment. Almost no collaboration exists. Teams are sometimes utilized but often are put in competition with each other in order to motivate performance.

The Culture: *Authenticity, integrity, accountability, creativity, trust, service, communication*

This is an environment often characterized by lack of honesty and integrity among its workers, supervisors, and senior leaders. It is an environment where risks are seldom taken, failure is often punished, and creativity is discouraged. There is a very low level of trust and trustworthiness along with a high level of uncertainty and fear. Leaders do not trust the workers and the workers view the leaders as untrustworthy. People lack motivation to serve the organization because they do not feel that it is *their* organization or *their* goals. This is an environment that is characterized by closed communication.

The Outlook: *Type of workers attracted, action needed*

This is an autocratic organization, which will find it very difficult to find, develop, and maintain healthy productive workers. Change is needed but very difficult to achieve. The outlook is not positive for this organization. Serious measures must be instituted in order for this organization to establish the necessary improvements to move towards positive organizational health. (Laub, 2005, p. 182)

From this description we see an unhealthy organization that will find it extremely difficult to sustain success over time. The fear permeating the workplace stifles the creative worker and limits new ideas and solutions. Workers are not engaged, but are actively working against the organization and its success. Individual workers may do their jobs out of a strong sense of personal responsibility but they are not committed to the organization or its leaders. This is an unhealthy and sometimes dangerous place for workers. We can do better.

Health Level 3: Negative Parental Organizations

The next highest percentage of organizations within OLA studies are Negative Parental at (30%). Parental (or paternalistic) organizations account for a full 55% of organizations which should stimulate interest in this mostly unexamined mindset of leadership. A parental leader mindset is when the leader views himself or herself as being in a *parental* role while the followers are viewed in a *child* role. There are both negative and positive expressions of this parental mindset (health levels 3 and 4). The negative parental mindset is characterized by a critical spirit toward followers connected to a tendency for negative reinforcement (punishment)-oriented tactics. Leaders with a negative parental mindset are not primarily self-focused, as found in an autocratic (leader-first) mindset. Instead, they are focused first on the needs and goals of the organization over, and sometimes to the expense of, the needs of the workers. They bring a sense of parental care to their leadership role, but their demeanor, language, and actions exhibit attitudes of mistrust and suspicion which serves to instill fear and uncertainty in the followers. Consider this description of a negative parental organization and its effects on the workers, the team, and the culture of the organization.

Description of Level 3: Negative Parental Health Organization

The Workers: *Motivation, morale, attitude and commitment, listening, relationships versus tasks*

Most workers sense they are valued more for what they can contribute than for who they are. When they receive training in this organization it is primarily to increase their performance and their value to the company not to develop personally. Workers are sometimes listened to but only when they speak in line with the values and priorities of the leaders. Their ideas are sometimes sought but seldom used, while the *important* decisions remain at the top levels of the organization. Relationships tend to be functional and the organizational tasks almost always come first. Conformity is expected while individual expression is discouraged.

The Leadership: *Power, decision making, goals, and direction*

Leadership is negatively paternalistic in style and is focused at the top levels of the organization. Power is delegated for specific tasks and for specific positions within the organization. Workers provide some decision making when it is appropriate to their position. Goals are sometimes unclear and the overall direction of the organization is often confused.

The Team: *Community, collaboration, and team learning*

This is mostly an individualistic environment. Some level of cooperative work exists, but little true collaboration. Teams are utilized but often are characterized by an unproductive competitive spirit.

The Culture: *Authenticity, integrity, accountability, creativity, trust, service, communication*

Workers are unsure of where they stand and how open they can be with one another, and especially with those in leadership over them. This is an environment where limited risks are taken, failure is not allowed, and creativity is encouraged only when it fits within the organization's existing guidelines. There is a minimal to moderate level of trust and trustworthiness along with an underlying uncertainty and fear. People feel that they must prove themselves and that they are only as good as their last performance. People are sometimes motivated to serve the organization but are not sure that the organization is committed to them. This is an environment that is characterized by a guarded, cautious openness.

The Outlook: *Type of workers attracted, action needed*

This is a negatively paternalistic organization. The compliant worker will find this a safe place to settle in. The best and most creative workers will look elsewhere. Change here is long term and incremental and improvement is desired but difficult to achieve. The outlook for this organization is uncertain. Decisions need to be made to move toward more healthy organizational life.

In times of organizational stress there will be a tendency to move backward toward a more autocratic organizational environment. (Laub, 2005, p. 183)

Health Level 4: Positive Parental Organizations

The third highest percentage of organizations within OLA studies are Positive Parental at (25%). Positive parental (or paternalistic) leaders are still focused primarily on the organization's needs and goals, but bring a positive, nurturing approach to their followers. They truly care about their workers and they work to create positive, family-oriented workplaces. However, the workers are still a means to an end for the leader and not an end in themselves. Workers are viewed as *children* and the leaders hold to the role and responsibility of *parents*, creating a significant limitation. What can be wrong with a nurturing, caring leader who is benevolent toward his or her followers? The key limitation under this mindset is that leaders are not developed, adult partnership with followers is not encouraged, and a clear separation is drawn between the role of leader and that of follower. This mindset creates a good, positive workplace environment that experiences increased performance but this organization or team will not be able to move beyond the capacities of those in leadership positions. Positive parental mindset leaders are nurturing and emphasize positive reinforcement (rewards) tactics. Some level of fear and uncertainty exists but now the fear is mixed with respect and appreciation from the followers. The biggest downside of this mindset is its tendency to create dependency of followers on leaders and this limits the potential of these followers to display their own creative leadership and become partners in the work of the organization. Consider this description of a Level 4 Positive Parental Health Organization describing its workers, teams, leadership, culture, and outlook.

Description of Level 4: Positive Parental Health Organization

The Workers: *Motivation, morale, attitude and commitment, listening, relationships versus tasks*
   Many workers sense they are valued while others are uncertain. People receive training in this organization in order to equip them to fulfill company goals. Workers are listened to but usually when they speak in line

with the values and priorities of the leaders. Their ideas are often sought and sometimes used, but the *important* decisions remain at the top levels of the organization. Relationships are valued as they benefit company goals but organizational tasks often come first. There is a tension between the expectation of conformity and encouragement of diversity.

The Leadership: *Power, decision making, goals, and direction*

Leadership is positively paternalistic in style and mostly comes from the top levels of the organization. Power is delegated for specific tasks and for specific positions within the organization. Workers are encouraged to share ideas for improving the organization. Goals are mostly clear though the overall direction of the organization is sometimes confused.

The Team: *Community, collaboration, and team learning*

Some level of cooperative work exists, and some true collaboration. Teams are utilized but often compete against one another for scarce resources.

The Culture: *Authenticity, integrity, accountability, creativity, trust, service, communication*

Workers are sometimes unsure of where they stand and how open they can be with one another and especially with those in leadership over them. This is an environment where some risks can be taken but failure is sometimes feared. Creativity is encouraged as long as it doesn't move the organization too much beyond the status quo. There is a moderate level of trust and trustworthiness along with occasional uncertainty and fear. People feel trusted but know that that trust can be lost easily. People are motivated to serve the organization because it is their job to do so and they are committed to doing good work. This is an environment characterized by openness between select groups of people.

The Outlook: *Type of workers attracted, action needed*

This is a positively paternalistic organization that will attract good motivated workers but may find that the "best and brightest" will seek professional challenges elsewhere. Change here is ongoing but often forced by outside circumstances. Improvement is desired but difficult to maintain over time. The outlook for this organization is positive. Decisions need to be made to move toward a more healthy organizational life. This organization is in a good position to move towards optimal health in the future. (Laub, 2005, p. 184)

Health Level 5–6: Servant-Minded Healthy Organizations

The lowest percentage of organizations from the OLA studies is the servant-minded organizations at 14%. These are organizations where the workforce agrees that the disciplines of servant leadership, as measured by the OLA model, are present throughout the organization. These healthy characteristics are observed in the leader's behavior as well as in the behavior of all throughout the organization including top leaders, managers/supervisors, and the workforce. When this health level is achieved a servant organization exists and the potential for empowered employees and high performance is significantly increased. Servant-minded leaders view their followers as adult partners focusing first on the needs of the followers believing that, if the followers succeed, the organization will succeed. The workers serve not as a means to an end, but as an end in themselves. They are true partners in creating the future of the organization and are encouraged to lead and fulfill their potential as both followers and leaders. Servant-minded organizations value people and develop people, build community, provide and share leadership, and display authenticity. It is a place of radical openness and honesty where expectations for performance are high and all workers develop their skills, leadership, and unique contribution to the organization. Consider this description of a level 5–6 organization and contrast it with the descriptions provided previously of the other organizational health levels.

Description of Level 5–6: Servant-Minded Healthy Organization

The Workers: *Motivation, morale, attitude and commitment, listening, relationships versus tasks*

Workers are valued here, for who they are as well as for what they contribute to the organization. They are believed in and are encouraged to develop to their full potential as workers and as individuals. Leaders and workers listen receptively to one another and are involved together in some of the *important* decisions of the organization. Relationships are strong and healthy and diversity is valued and celebrated.

The Leadership: *Power, decision making, goals, and direction*
People are encouraged to provide leadership at all levels of the organization. Power and leadership are shared so that workers are empowered to contribute to important decisions, including the direction that the organization is taking. Appropriate action is taken, goals are clear, and vision is shared throughout the organization.

The Team: *Community, collaboration, and team learning*
A high level of community characterizes this positive work environment. People work together well in teams and prefer collaborative work over competition against one another.

The Culture: *Authenticity, integrity, accountability, creativity, trust, service, communication*
This is an environment characterized by the authenticity of its workers, supervisors, and senior leaders. People are open and accountable to others. They operate with honesty and integrity. This is a *people first* environment where risks are encouraged, failure can be learned from, and creativity is encouraged and rewarded. People are trusted and are trustworthy throughout the organization. Fear is not used as a motivation. People are motivated to serve the interests of each other before their own self-interest and are open to learning from each other. This is an environment characterized by open and effective communication.

The Outlook: *Type of workers attracted, action needed*
This is a servant-oriented organization, which will continue to attract some of the best and most motivated workers who can welcome positive change and continuous improvement. It is a place where energy and motivation are continually renewed to provide for the challenges of the future. The outlook is very positive. Ongoing attention should be given to building on existing strengths and continuing to learn and develop toward an optimally healthy organization. (Laub, 2005, p. 182)

Assessing the Accuracy of These Organizational Health Level Descriptions

The accuracy of the descriptions provided for each organizational health level was tested having adult students, after completing the OLA on their organizations and receiving the descriptions matching their score, assess the accuracy of the description on a scale of 1 as *very inaccurate* to 6 as *very accurate*. The results of this study, displayed in Table 8.2, concluded that the organizational health level descriptions are accurate and useful for describing the various organizational health levels within the OLA report. In addition, the face validity of these descriptions was confirmed by this author over the past 18 years working with all types of organizations.

These organizational health levels allow us to apply the meaning of the autocratic, paternalistic (parental), and servant mindsets to organizations and provide for them a pathway to develop a healthier organizational level and a stronger, more positive mindset of leadership. When leaders can see how workers within their organization are truly experiencing the organization, they can work to create a better, more engaged place to work. When this happens, worker satisfaction and engagement increases, resulting in higher organizational performance.

Table 8.2 Results of research on the accuracy of the OLA organizational health level descriptions

Organizational level	Entire description	Workers section	Leaders section	Team section	Culture section	Outlook section
1	5.30	5.20	5.60	5.60	5.00	5.50
2	4.88	5.00	5.09	4.47	4.75	5.09
3	4.87	4.91	4.98	4.70	5.13	4.96
4	5.06	4.75	5.25	4.58	4.97	5.34
5	5.31	5.38	5.23	5.38	5.23	5.38
6	5.67	5.67	6.00	5.33	6.00	6.00
Total	5.18	5.15	5.35	5.01	5.18	5.37

Laub (2005, p. 168)

Summary of Six Organizational Health Level Descriptions (Table 8.3)

Improving Organizational Health

The good news is that organizations can change. They can improve and grow, but it takes intentional, focused effort to alter the underlying mindsets that guide our leadership behavior and create our organizational cultures. One way to begin improvement is to use the six disciplines of the OLA model to address key questions related to each of these six disciplines. The chart below provides a set of questions to consider along with key actions to begin to change the mindset of your organization.

Ideas for Improvement Worksheet (Table 8.4)

Conclusion

To take up Greenleaf's challenge to "raise both the capacity to serve and the very performance as servant of existing major institutions" (1977, p. 49) we have presented, in this chapter, a description of the servant organization and how it contrasts to descriptions of other leadership mindsets applied to organizations. In this way, servant leadership is viewed not just as a way individual leaders lead, but as a foundation of an organization's culture and its behaviors. Through this, servant leadership becomes the responsibility of each person in the organization to build and maintain a healthy organizational culture. Will the servant-minded organization result in higher performance? Our next chapter reviews 18 years of servant leadership research using the Organizational Leadership Assessment (OLA) to address this question.

Table 8.3 Brief descriptions of the six OLA organizational health levels

Servant leadership	Organization[6] Optimal Health	Workers experience this organization as a servant-minded organization characterized by authenticity, the valuing and developing of people, the building of community, and the providing and sharing of positive leadership. These characteristics are evident throughout the entire organization. People are trusted and are trustworthy throughout the organization. They are motivated to serve the interests of each other before their own self-interest and are open to learning from each other. Leaders and workers view each other as partners working in a spirit of collaboration.
	Organization[5] Excellent Health	Workers experience this organization as a servant-oriented organization characterized by authenticity, the valuing and developing of people, the building of community and the providing and sharing of positive leadership. These characteristics are evident throughout much of the organization. People are trusted and are trustworthy. They are motivated to serve the interests of each other before their own self-interest and are open to learning from each other. Leaders and workers view each other as partners working in a spirit of collaboration.
Paternalistic leadership	Organization[4] Moderate health	Workers experience this organization as a positively paternalistic (parental-led) organization characterized by a moderate level of trust and trustworthiness along with occasional uncertainty and fear. Creativity is encouraged as long as it doesn't move the organization too far beyond the status quo. Risks can be taken, but failure is sometimes feared. Goals are mostly clear, though the overall direction of the organization is sometimes confused. Leaders often take the role of nurturing parent while workers assume the role of the cared-for child.
	Organization[3] Limited health	Workers experience this organization as a negatively paternalistic (parental-led) organization characterized by minimal to moderate levels of trust and trustworthiness along with an underlying uncertainty and fear. People feel that they must prove themselves and that they are only as good as their last performance. Workers are sometimes listened to but only when they speak in line with the values and priorities of the leaders. Conformity is expected while individual expression is discouraged. Leaders often take the role of critical parent while workers assume the role of the cautious child.

(continued)

Table 8.3 (continued)

| Autocratic leadership | Organization[2] | Poor health | Workers experience this organization as an autocratic-led organization characterized by low levels of trust and trustworthiness and high levels of uncertainty and fear. People lack motivation to serve the organization because they do not feel that it is *their* organization or *their* goals. Leadership is autocratic in style and is imposed from the top levels of the organization. It is an environment where risks are seldom taken, failure is often punished, and creativity is discouraged. Most workers do not feel valued and often feel *used* by those in leadership. Change is needed but is very difficult to achieve. |
| | Organization[1] | Toxic health | Workers experience this organization as a dangerous place to work … a place characterized by dishonesty and a deep lack of integrity among its workers and leaders. Workers are devalued, *used*, and sometimes *abused*. Positive leadership is missing at all levels and power is used in ways that are harmful to workers and the mission of the organization. There is almost no trust and an extremely high level of fear. This organization will find it nearly impossible to locate, develop, and maintain healthy workers who can assist in producing positive organizational change. (Laub, 2005, p. 180) |

Table 8.4 Ideas for improvement worksheet

Discipline	Questions to consider	Actions to consider
Provide leadership	Do we have a clearly stated vision? Do our workers know where we are headed in the future?	Implement a vision and strategic planning process including people throughout the organization.
	Does everyone understand their role in pursuing the strategic plan of the organization? Are the key goals clear?	Review job descriptions and definition to clarify roles and responsibilities.
	Do people have the direction they need to do their jobs successfully?	Ask people what they need to understand and perform their jobs and provide this to them.
	Are people (leaders and workers) held accountable for reaching work goals?	Insure that goals are clear, progress is monitored, and there is a time for review to measure results and learning.
	Are people at all levels encouraged to lead … to take risks, even if they may fail?	Offer ways for people to increase their voice in the organization—to take leadership to create positive change.
	Do leaders take appropriate action when it is needed?	Identify areas where indecisiveness has been chronic and push for clear decisions to be made to move forward.
Build community	Do people experience strong, positive relationships at work? How is this encouraged?	Develop ways for people to communicate, share about themselves, and build stronger relationships.
	Are people encouraged to work with each other in a collaborative partnership or to compete with each other for scarce resources?	Identify where policies and procedures tend to encourage unproductive competition—create expectations for people to work together.
	Is diversity and difference honored and encouraged as a strength in your organization or is conformity a higher value than individual uniqueness?	Create an intentional way to celebrate diversity and differences and promote how these are honored and encouraged.
	Are people encouraged to work effectively in teams?	Provide training in teamwork and collaboration. Find ways to publicly support partnership and supportive work relationships.
	Are the leaders seen as working with workers or as working separately from them?	Create ways for the leaders and workers to interact and work together on projects.

(continued)

Table 8.4 (continued)

Discipline	Questions to consider	Actions to consider
Value people	Are people listened to? Do they feel that they are heard? Is non-judgmental listening a skill of your leadership?	Build listening skills. Ask your workers if they feel they are listened to and heard.
	Do workers see leaders as serving the worker's interests first ahead of the interests of the leaders?	Work to create an atmosphere of servanthood—serving the needs of each other ahead of each person's self-interest.
	Do people trust each other in your organization? Do the leaders trust the workers? Do the workers trust the leaders?	Build trust. Speak the truth, even when it is hard to do. Honor your commitments. Be trustworthy. Expect honesty.
	Do we accept and respect people making it clear that they are valued for who they are in addition to their performance? Do they know that they are appreciated?	Expect responsible behavior and high work performance, but, separate from that, communicate that others are valued and respected. Share appreciation openly and frequently.
	Do we find ways to show care and compassion to people especially when they are going through difficult times?	While maintaining consistent and fair policies, find ways to assist people going through a hard time. Model kindness and care.
Display authenticity	Are leaders trustworthy? Do people believe them when they speak and believe that the leader's actions are consistent with their words?	Commit to total and complete integrity. Speak the truth. Don't tone it down to protect yourself.
	Are ethics and integrity of the highest level … or are people cutting corners on the truth in dealing with each other?	Consider areas where more openness is called for and provide ways for ethical issues to be reviewed by others.
	Is your organization a place where open discussion and the sharing of ideas is encouraged and rewarded, even if what is shared could be perceived as being negative?	Create forums for open discussion on issues and the collecting of ideas. Reward and recognize good ideas and work to implement those that can really make a difference.
	Are people willing to learn from others? Are leaders open to learning from those beneath them in the organization?	Find ways to share new learning and changes you have made due to input from others. Model learning and openness.
	Are leaders willing to admit personal limitations and mistakes? Do they model honesty and self-reflection?	Admit it—don't be afraid to identify an error. Ask for forgiveness. Work to make it right. Look within first before assessing others.

Develop people	Do people receive ongoing opportunities for personal and professional development? Do you foster a learning environment in your organization?	See training as an investment more than a cost. Encourage individual learning plans where people can develop their own plans supported by you and the organization.
	Do leaders model the behavior they desire to see from their workers? Or, is there a separate standard of behavior for leaders and workers?	Do what you expect others to do. Model what you want to see from others.
	Is encouragement and affirmation a natural and common way of assessing each other's work? Do we "catch people doing things right"?—Or, do we tend to be more critical and negative in our assessment of performance?	Create a culture of affirmation. Catch people doing it right and point it out. Assess honestly the work performance of yourself and others, but don't get biased to the negative.
	Is conflict viewed as an opportunity for each person to learn and grow? Or, does it tend to lead to blaming and finger-pointing?	Model a learning attitude. View conflict as an inevitable part of working together with people who are different. Seek to positively manage conflict not to avoid it.
Share leadership	Have people throughout the organization been a part of creating the future of the organization by speaking to the vision and direction?	Create forums and processes whereby people can speak to the direction the organization is going. Expect people to have ideas and to care about the larger organizational issues.
	Does each person have the opportunity of making important decisions and are they encouraged to take more responsibility as appropriate?	Evaluate where decisions are made. Consider ways for decisions to be made closer to the client or customer. Provide training on how to take responsibility in new areas.
	Do we make specific efforts to share power, status, and privilege throughout the organization or are these opportunities only provided to the leaders?	Review how separate the leaders are from the managers and the workers. Consider ways to share power, status, and privilege to encourage others to be leaders
	Do leader use persuasion and positive relationship to influence others instead of coercion or force?	Review how things get done through other people. Seek to influence true cooperation rather than forcing mere compliance.
	Are leaders humble, resisting promoting themselves?	Put others first. Find visible ways to model this.

References

Collins, J. (2001). *Good to great: Why some companies make the leap … and others don't.* New York, NY: HarperCollins Publishers.

Gallup. (2017). *The state of the global workplace.* New York, NY: Gallup Press.

Greenleaf, R. K. (1977). *Servant leadership: A journey into the nature of legitimate power and greatness.* Mahwah, NJ: Paulist Press.

Herman, R. (2008). *Servant leadership: A model for organizations desiring a workplace spirituality culture.* Doctoral dissertation, Capella University.

Jackson, T. (2016). Paternalistic leadership: The missing link in cross-cultural leadership studies. *International Journal of Cross Cultural Management, 16*(1), 3–7. https://doi.org/10.1177/1470595816637701

Laub, J. A. (1999). *Assessing the servant organization: Development of the servant organizational leadership (SOLA) instrument.* Unpublished doctoral dissertation, Florida Atlantic University.

Laub, J. A. (2005). From paternalism to the servant organization: Expanding the organizational leadership assessment (OLA) model. *International Journal of Servant-Leadership, 1*, 155–186.

World Health Organization. (1946). Constitution. Retrieved from http://www.who.int/about/mission/en/

9

Servant Leadership Research Review: Eighteen Years of OLA Research

There is a growing, ever-stronger research base to support the value and usefulness of servant leadership in the workplace. This chapter will explore just a part of the total servant leadership research conducted over the past 18 years with a focus on research completed using the OLA servant leadership model and the Organizational Leadership Assessment (OLA) instrument. This research provides evidence that servant leadership goes well beyond being a good and moral way to lead, but also produces outcomes that are good for employees, for leaders, and for the bottom line of our organizations.

In 1995, Huselid and Becker used US Department of Labor data and surveys with over 1500 companies from multiple industries to consider whether participative leadership practices, like those within the servant leadership model, had a positive effect on increased productivity, employee retention, and improved financial performance. They found that not only did these practices correlate positively with each of these categories but "each standard deviation in the level of participative practices increased a company's market value between $35,000 and $78,000 per employee" (as cited in Blanchard, Blanchard, & Zigarmi, 2007, p. 272).

The Magellan Executive Resources research project utilized the same metrics that Collins used in his well-known *Good to Great* study (2001) to evaluate 11 publicly traded companies "most frequently mentioned in

© The Author(s) 2018
J. Laub, *Leveraging the Power of Servant Leadership*, Palgrave Studies in Workplace Spirituality and Fulfillment, https://doi.org/10.1007/978-3-319-77143-4_9

the literature as implementing the principles of Servant Leadership" (Sipe & Frick, 2009, p. 199). These organizations were the Toro Company, Southwest Airlines, Starbucks, AFLAC, Men's Wearhouse, Synovus Financial, Herman Miller, Service Masters, Marriott International, FedEx, and Medtronic. The Magellan project compared these servant leadership companies with the 11 *Good to Great* companies studied by Collins comparing financial performance (percentage of pre-tax profit returns) between the two lists of companies from 1994 to 2004. The study found that in this ten-year period when the S&P (500 largest) companies grew by 10.8% and Collins' *Good to Great* companies grew by 17.5%, the servant-led companies grew by an amazing 24.2% (Sipe & Frick, 2009, p. 200).

In 2013, Zigarmi, Roberts, Houson, Witt, and Diehl conducted a study on the impact of self-focused versus other-focused leaders. The study assessed 740 people from different business roles from multiple industries to complete a set of statistically validated subscales to see if the leader's focus on self or others made a difference in employee attitudes and performance. A summary of the key findings shows that:

- Individuals who feel connected with their leader will also have a higher intention to stay and act in ways that support the organization.
- People with "other-oriented" leaders and a sense of connection with their colleagues and leader will have higher positive associations about their job.
- People with a more positive outlook about their job will also have higher intentions in regard to all five employee work intentions.
- Leader self-concern correlates to negative work effect.
- Employees with a greater connection with their colleagues are more likely to voluntarily give more effort to their jobs and to help others at work.
- Employees with managers demonstrating high other orientation had higher intentions to help at work while employees with highly self-concerned managers were less likely to intend to remain with their organization in the future (Zigarmi, Peyton Roberts, Houson, Witt, & Diehl, 2013, p. 5).

This study specifically addressed servant leadership—identified as other-focused leaders—and showed a consistently positive correlation between this mindset of leading and positive worker intentions, tenure, and performance.

In September, 2016, at the Third International Servant Leadership Research Roundtable held in Bifröst, Iceland, a presentation was given on the influence of servant leadership on organizational performance. The study addressed the question, does employee well-being lead to revenue and earnings growth? The study looked at 54 business units within a retail chain in France utilizing a multilevel structural equation modeling approach. There were two key findings from this study. First was that employees who work for servant leaders experience a higher level of holistic well-being, and, second, that business units with servant leaders get better sales and earnings growth (Giolito, Liden, & Van Dierendonck, 2016). For this study, the servant leadership model from Liden, Wayne, Zhao, and Henderson (2008) was used, including conceptual skills, putting subordinates first, helping them grow and succeed, empowering employees, creating value for the community, and behaving ethically.

These four studies represent a growing set of research results that speak to the potential for seeing servant leadership as a way of leading that not only improves the organizational climate for employees but also positively affects the bottom-line performance of the organization.

Laub (1999) created the first research-based assessment tool to measure the perception of servant leadership within organizations. Over the past 18 years a series of studies were conducted using the Organizational Leadership Assessment (OLA) to explore the effect servant leadership has on the health of an organization. The development of this tool, a summary of the variety of studies completed, and a summary of the findings are included to show a growing research base for servant leadership.

The Development of the OLA

The Organizational Leadership Assessment (OLA) was developed to quantitatively measure the perceptions of people as to the level of servant leadership present in their group or organization. How could we get to the truth of what is happening in an organization in terms of how well, or to what level, the organization is displaying servant leadership characteristics? It became clear that to simply ask leaders to rate themselves or to assess what is happening in their organization was not the best way to get an accurate picture. It was decided to pursue an organizational assessment rather than an individual leader assessment. The OLA was designed to seek feedback from top leaders, managers/supervisors, and the workforce on a common list of servant leadership criteria. In this way responses are collected from everyone in the organization to determine how perceptions differ between position or role levels. It was found that these perceptions differed in a consistent and meaningful way and that this perception gap was important information to provide to leaders and their organizations. As might be expected, top leaders viewed the organization, and their own leadership, more positively than did the managers or the workforce. Also, managers typically viewed the organization more positively than did the workforce. This consistent perception gap, seen in almost all organizations, led to the decision to focus on the workforce response as the most accurate view of how well the organization and its leaders were living out the characteristics of servant leadership. The workforce is almost always the most populous position level and it is the workforce that directly experiences the effects of leadership practice and the culture of the organization. So, when reporting to organizations their OLA results, the workforce response is used to determine the overall level of organizational health.

The OLA became the first organizational assessment tool developed to measure servant leadership in organizations and it attracted the attention of researchers who desired to quantitatively measure servant leadership. To date more than 85 studies have been completed using the OLA, most of them dissertation studies. Efforts were made early on to bring the OLA to organizations of all types to allow them to get an accurate picture of what is truly going on in their organizations. How can we know if organizations espouse servant leadership, but may not actually live it out? Who, within the organization, has the best perspective on this? The OLA takes the position that everyone in the organization should speak to this—top leaders, managers/supervisors, and workforce—through a research-based assessment but that the workforce has the most accurate perspective on the organization's level of health.

The first step in the development of the instrument was to identify how servant leadership should be described; so a three-part Delphi survey was conducted with 14 experts in the field of servant leadership.

> The experts were chosen based upon the fact that they had written on servant-leadership or had taught at the university level on the subject. Fourteen of the original 25 experts who were asked to participate completed all three parts of the Delphi. These participants included: Larry Spears, The Greenleaf Center for Servant-Leadership; Jim Kouzes, Learning Systems, Inc, The Tom Peters Group; Ann McGee-Cooper and Duane Trammell, Ann McGee-Cooper & Associates (note: these two worked together on a single response for each part of the survey and were therefore counted as one respondent); Dr. Bill Millard, Life Discovery and Indiana Wesleyan University; Lea Williams, Bennett College; Dr. Joe Roberts, Suncoast Church of Christ; Jack Lowe, Jr., TD Industries; Dr. Pam Walker, Cerritos College; Grace Barnes, Azusa Pacific University; Ann Liprie-Spence, McMurray University; Deborah Campbell, Servant-leadership Community of West Ohio; Dr. Ted Ward, Trinity Evangelical Divinity School and Michigan State University; Bishop Bennett Sims, The Institute for Servant-leadership. (Laub, 2005, p. 158)

The results of this Delphi process resulted in consensus around 60 characteristics of the servant leader and from this the OLA servant leadership model was formed and the OLA was created. The OLA is a 60-item assessment that utilizes a 5-point Likert scale and can be completed in an average of 15 minutes. Respondents are asked to indicate which position level (top leader, manager/supervisor, or workforce) they represent. A 6-item job satisfaction scale was added to the 60 items of the OLA to allow for a comparison to the OLA servant leadership constructs. The addition of this scale has encouraged many researchers to consider this relationship in their studies. In the original study, this author found "a high positive correlation between the OLA score (servant leadership) and the level of job satisfaction. A significant ($p < 0.01$) positive correlation of 0.53 was found between the OLA score and the job satisfaction score" (Laub, 2010, pp. 111–112).

The six items of the OLA Job Satisfaction Scale are:

- I am working at a high level of productivity.
- I feel good about my contribution to the organization.
- My job is important to the success of this organization.
- I enjoy working in this organization.
- I am able to be creative in my job.
- I am able to use my best gifts and abilities in my job. (Laub, 1999, p. 73)

To facilitate use of the OLA instrument, access was created whereby all respondents can complete the instrument online and all data can be easily collected and transferred to the researcher in a format ready for data analysis. This ease of implementation and data collection helped to make the OLA a desirable and usable instrument for conducting servant leadership research.

Testing the OLA Instrument (Psychometrics)

Construct validity for the OLA was determined by the expert panel through the Delphi process just described. Reliability through multiple studies was found to be very high with the OLA obtaining a reliability

Table 9.1 Reliability testing of the OLA

	Laub (1999) $n = 828$	Horsman (2001) $n = 540$	Ledbetter (2003) $n = 138$	Miears (2004) $n = 165$ Ed. Version
Entire OLA	0.98	0.99	0.98	0.99
Values people	0.91	0.92	0.89	0.92
Develops people	0.90	0.94	0.88	0.94
Builds community	0.90	0.91	0.89	0.92
Displays authenticity	0.93	0.95	0.90	0.93
Provides leadership	0.91	0.92	0.91	0.93
Shares leadership	0.93	0.95	0.88	0.94

score of 0.9802 using the Cronbach-Alpha coefficient. Additional studies supported this original finding as revealed in Table 9.1.

Item analysis revealed that all items have a strong correlation with the instrument as a whole with the lowest item-to-item correlation at 0.41 and the highest at 0.77 (Laub, 1999). Ledbetter conducted a test-retest showing "the means and standard deviations between the Test and the Retest for this study remain constant. The correlation between the Test and Retest were significant and the findings indicate that the validity of the OLA remains consistent over time" (Ledbetter, 2003, p. 88). Both the test and the retest were significant at $p < 0.01$.

Summary of Research Findings from the OLA

The OLA has been used in over 85 research studies, most of which are doctoral dissertation studies and most with organizations in the United States. However, it has also been used for research in Brazil (Miguel, 2009), Bolivia (Chavez, 2012), Iran (Azadfada, Besmi, & Doroudian, 2014), Saudi Arabia (Al-Yousef, 2012), Jordan (Salameh, 2011), Turkey (Cerit, 2009), and Canada (Black, 2010). Currently the OLA instrument is available in English, Spanish, Portuguese, Arabic, French, German, Icelandic, and Dutch.

Studies in Different Organizational Settings

The OLA has been used for research studies in many types of organizations as displayed in Table 9.2. Though most studies have been conducted in education or higher education organizations studies have also been conducted in religious organizations, law enforcement, healthcare, manufacturing, military and healthcare.

Studies on Different Themes or Topics

Several themes or topics have been studied using the OLA as identified in Table 9.3. By far the topic most studied is that of the relationship of servant leadership to employee job satisfaction. Other topics such as team

Table 9.2 OLA studies in different types of organizations

Type of organization	Study completed
Higher education	Thompson (2002), Stamba (2003), Drury (2004), Iken (2005), Van Tassell (2006), Meredith (2007), Beaver (2008), Hannigan (2008), Adamson (2009), McDougle (2009), Miguel (2009), Jacobs (2011), Palmer (2011), Chavez (2012), Padron (2012), Nyamboli (2014)
Law enforcement	Ledbetter (2003), Freeman (2011)
Healthcare	Freitas (2003), Krebs (2005), Bradshaw (2007), Amadeo (2008), Wyllie (2009)
Education	Herbst (2003), Freitas (2003), Lambert (2004), Miears (2004), Anderson (2005), Ross (2006), Anderson (2006), Witter (2007), Svoboda (2008), Metzcar (2008), Cerit (2009), Black (2010), Salameh (2011), Babb (2012), McKenzie (2012), Shears (2012), Mortan (2013), Van Worth (2015)
Religious (Christian) organizations	Anderson (2005), Arfsten (2006), Ross (2006), McCann (2006), Witter (2007), Kong (2007), Beaver (2007), Inbarasu (2008), McNeff (2012), Harless (2015)
Religious (Islamic) organizations	Salie (2008)
Manufacturing/ industry	Rauch (2007)
Nonprofit organizations	McCann (2006), Goodwin (2011)
High tech organizations	Johnson (2008)
Call center	Chu (2008)
Residential treatment	Bradshaw (2007)
US Military	Kegler (2007)
Sports teams	Azadfada, Besmi & Doroudian (2014)
Credit union	Ghormley (2009)
Distribution center	Hodoh (2016)
Pharmaceutical organization	Krebs (2005)

effectiveness, spirit in organizations, organization and leader trust, and student performance have allowed researchers to look at the relationship between servant leadership and these key organizational health factors.

Servant leadership has been found to correlate positively to employee job satisfaction, team effectiveness, student achievement on standardized

Table 9.3 OLA studies on different themes/topics

Theme/topic	Study completed
Women leaders	Braye (2000)
Spirit in organizations	Horsman (2001), Beazly (2002), Herman (2008)
Team effectiveness	Irving (2005)
Organizational safety	Krebs (2005)
Organizational succession	Cater (2006)
Organizational commitment	Drury (2004)
Social enterprise	Klamon (2006)
Cultural studies	Molnar (2007)
Emotional intelligence	Johnson (2008)
Job satisfaction	Laub (1999), Thompson (2002), Hebert (2003), Drury (2004), Miears (2004), Irving (2005), Anderson (2005), Van Tassell (2006), Klamon (2006), Kong (2007), Svoboda (2008), Chu (2008), Johnson (2008), Amadeo (2008), Inbarasu (2008), Salie (2008), Cerit (2009), Wyllie (2009), Goodwin (2011), Al-Yousef (2012), McKenzie (2012), Wilson (2013), Mortan (2013), Azadfada, Besmi & Doroudian (2014)
Organization and leader trust	Joseph and Winston (2005)
Employee absenteeism and attrition	Rauch (2007)
Volunteer participation and satisfaction	Ghormley (2009), Harless (2015)
Student performance	Herbst (2003), Lambert (2004), Shears (2012), Babb (2012)
Student satisfaction	Padron (2012)
School climate	Black (2010)
Employee productivity	Hodoh (2016)
Core self-evaluation	Tischier, Giambatista, KeKeage, and McCormick (2016)
OLA and the LMX theory	Freitas (2003)
Female athlete satisfaction (Iran)	Azadfada, Besmi & Doroudian (2014)
Teacher effectiveness	Metzcar (2008), Jacobs (2011)

(*continued*)

Table 9.3 (continued)

Theme/topic	Study completed
Teacher job satisfaction	McKenzie (2012), Shears (2012)
Perception match between administrators and workforce	McDougle (2009)
Millennials and effective leadership	Nordbye (2012)
Board leadership	Denning (2016)
Leader-member exchange (LMX)	Freitas (2003)

tests, organizational climate, trust in leaders, and the organization and employee productivity. Servant leadership negatively correlates to employee attrition and absenteeism meaning that the higher servant leadership is perceived to be in the organization the longer employees remain in their jobs and the less days they are absent from their work. Here is a summary of the key OLA research findings to date.

Servant Leadership and Job Satisfaction

Twenty-five studies have been conducted with the OLA on job satisfaction of employees in general, culturally diverse employees, and teachers and athletes from multiple types of organizations. The results are consistent. Servant leadership is positively correlated to job satisfaction in all types of organizations. In the original study a significant ($p < 0.01$) positive correlation of 0.653 was found (Laub, 1999, p. v).

Most of these studies were done using the embedded 6-item OLA job satisfaction scale but others found similar results using the *Minnesota Satisfaction Questionnaire* (MSQ). "The Pearson correlation revealed that the total OLA scores and the MSQ score were significantly related, $r(114) = +0.704, p < 0.01$, two tails" (Thompson, 2002, p. 72). Thompson went on to validate the OLA job satisfaction scale providing support for multiple studies on the topic of job satisfaction.

Servant leadership relates positively to job satisfaction among employees. When leaders build an organizational culture that values and develops people, provides and shares leadership, builds community, and displays authenticity employees are more satisfied with their work and their role within the organization. This is a significant finding for encouraging servant leadership practice in our organizations. We want workers who are satisfied and engaged in their work and with each other. We want workers who come to their work with a sense of belonging, passion, and challenge, workers who find their jobs satisfying and their organizations as satisfying places to work.

Servant Leadership and Team Effectiveness

Servant leadership practice has shown a positive relationship with the effectiveness of team function in organizations (Irving, 2005; Irving & Longbotham, 2007). In these studies, the OLA was used along with the *Team Effectiveness Questionnaire* (Larson & LaFasto, 1989) to determine if this relationship does, in fact, exist. "A statistically significant and positive correlation was found for each of the variables associated with servant leadership and job satisfaction when analyzed in reference to team effectiveness" (Irving, 2005, p. iii).

In addition, "the Pearson r for the relationship between servant leadership at the organizational level ... and team effectiveness at the team level ... was 0.522. The p value for the Pearson r finding was 0.000 indicating that the finding was statistically significant. Additionally; when controlling for the effects of position, gender and level of education; the findings were similar ($r = 0.527$, $p = 0.000$)" (p. 57). Increased servant leadership behavior in organizations correlates positively to team effectiveness. Based on these findings, Irving (2005) suggests that a mandate exists for leaders to pay attention to the level of servant leadership within their organization. The far-reaching implications of teams being more effective and productive are critical to overall organization success.

Servant Leadership and Student Achievement

Studies conducted in secondary schools in the United States have sought to see if the level of servant leadership practiced by school leaders, teachers and staff relates to student performance on standardized tests. The indication from these studies reveals that it does. Three studies were conducted (Herbst, 2003; Lambert, 2004; Shears, 2012) on this topic. Lambert (2004) found that the "analysis of the data revealed a significant relationship between servant leadership of secondary school principals and gains in student achievement" (p. v).

Herbst (2003) studied 24 high schools in Broward County, Florida, looking specifically at the relationship between the OLA score (servant leadership) and "the *Florida Comprehensive Assessment Test* (FCAT) test scores in writing, reading, mathematics" among others scores. It was found that "in schools where greater degrees of servant leadership is being practiced students are achieving at a higher rate than in schools where lower degrees of servant leadership were found" (p. 100).

If servant leadership creates an environment within our schools to encourage higher student performance, shouldn't this be looked at more closely in terms of education reform? We pay attention to how teachers interact with students, and we should, but we also should be helping to build servant leadership cultures within our school organizations, from the principal down through all levels of the school along with the administrative offices that oversee school systems.

Servant Leadership and Employee Sustainability (Attrition and Absenteeism)

Some may assume that servant leadership is only appropriate for people-oriented organizations like education, religious groups, or community service work, but a very interesting study conducted by Rauch (2007) shows that servant leadership can make a difference in other types of organizations as well. Rauch studied 28 manufacturing (automotive parts) locations from the same company located in the Midwestern, United States. This study involved 3896 respondents with a meaningful 88.9% response rate. The research question was, "To what extent are established manufacturing performance measures correlated with the presence of servant leadership?" (p. 63).

Two key performance measures that relate to employee sustainability are absenteeism and attrition. On absenteeism, it was found that "as servant leadership increases, absenteeism rates generally decline. For example, locations with an OLA score of 2.5 had absenteeism rates of 3% to 10%, while locations with an OLA score of 4 had absenteeism rates of only 2% to 4%" (p. 82). On the topic of employee attrition, it was found that the highest attrition rates occurred at locations with lower OLA scores (p. 84). Also, it was revealed that those organizations with the highest OLA scores had attrition rates below the industry average while those organizations with the lowest OLA scores had rates above the industry average.

When the absenteeism and attrition scores were compared to the OLA organizational health levels it was found that absenteeism decreases 41% for each increase in organizational health level and attrition decreases 22% for each increase in organizational health level. One of the key health factors in any organization is its ability to sustain workers: to retain them (low attrition) and to have them consistently present at work (low absenteeism). The presence of servant leadership has an inverse relationship to both of these organizational heath factors, suggesting that a servant-minded organization is better at retaining good workers and keeping those workers present and engaged on a daily basis.

Servant Leadership and Employee Safety

Might servant-led organizations create safer places for people to work? Krebs (2005) conducted a study to address "whether the existence of servant-leadership in an organization influences individuals' propensity to *actively care* for safety" (p. 94), thereby promoting beliefs and actions to engage in safe behaviors in the workplace. The results indicated that "a significant, positive relationship was found between servant-leadership and actively caring" (p. 95) and further this study indicates that servant-leadership can be considered one of many safety indicators present in a given work environment and that its effects on safety are both direct and indirect. Thus, this research supports the notion that organizations may benefit from a safety perspective by utilizing servant-leadership as an espoused corporate leadership model. Organizations that include servant-leadership in its corporate and management practices would then not only be able to increase actively caring perceptions and behaviors, but may also be able to decrease accidents and near misses. (p. 114)

Rauch (2007) in contrast did not find that the recordable accident rate varied with changes in servant leadership and no relationship between the OLA score and Accident Severity rates were found. More research needs to be done in this important area of employee safety.

Servant Leadership and Trust

Trust is crucial for healthy organizations to function well: trust in both the organization and the leaders. Joseph and Winston (2005) conducted a study using the OLA and the *Organizational Trust Inventory* (OTI) to see if there is a relationship between servant leadership and trust. They utilized Nyhan and Marlowe's definition of trust as "the level of confidence that one individual has in another's competence and his or her willingness to act in a fair, ethical and predictable manner" (pp. 6–7). This powerful combination of competency and consistency allows workers to feel confident in doing their work knowing that their leaders can be trusted to do what is best. The study found that the "perception of servant leadership correlated positively with both leader trust and organizational trust. The study also found that organizations perceived as servant-led exhibited higher levels of both leader trust and organizational trust than organizations perceived as non-servant" (p. 6). Servant leadership behaviors build employee trust in leaders and in organizations.

Servant Leadership and School Climate

Black (2010) used the OLA along with the *Organizational Climate Description Questionnaire-Revised* (OCDQ-RE) to reveal a significant positive correlation between servant leadership and school climate within Catholic elementary schools in Canada. Black states that "previous research supports the concept that a positive school climate influences student achievement. In a culture of faith-centered education, Catholic school leaders can influence the school's climate and student achievement by adopting the theory of servant leadership to guide their behavior" (pp. 461–462).

Lambert (2004) looked at the issue of servant leadership, student learning, and school climate in secondary schools in Florida school districts in the United States finding "a significant relationship between servant leadership ... and gains in student achievement. An even stronger relationship was shown to exist between servant leadership and school climate. Further, when controlling for socioeconomic status, school climate correlated strongly with student achievement in lower socioeconomic schools" (p. v). Servant leadership positively impacts school climate which then supports and encourages student achievement.

Servant Leadership and Employee Core Self-Evaluation

A 2016 study by Tischler, Giambatista, McKeage, and McCormick looked at servant leadership and the concept of core self-evaluation which is defined as "a self-concept measure with four components of self-esteem, generalized self-efficacy, (internal) locus of control and (low) neuroticism or emotional stability" (p. 3). The authors suggest that identifying a relationship between servant leadership and core self-evaluation is critical because this would "confirm that servant leadership affects important changes in employees as people" (p. 1) and this is one of the central tenets of the servant leadership concept. In servant leadership the focus is on the followers and the belief is that if followers grow and become stronger people and more positive workers then the organization will benefit. In fact, it is this focus on the follower first that provides one of the best distinctions between servant leadership and Transformational Leadership (Patterson, Russell, & Stone, 2004).

The 2016 study of three different organizations by Tischler et al. found that "servant leadership predicts both core self-evaluation and job satisfaction" (p. 1). This predictive relationship supports the contention that servant leadership helps to produce positive changes within individuals. This study also confirms the many studies that have shown a strong and positive relationship between servant leadership and job satisfaction. Also, studies by Judge and Bono found that core self-evaluation is positively correlated to job performance (Judge & Bono, 2001).

For this study, the OLA was used with the *Core Self-Evaluation Scale* (CSES) and the researchers conducted a regression analysis to test whether servant leadership predicts core self-evaluation. It was found that "across three firms, servant leadership was positively correlated with job satisfaction ($r = 0.80$, $p < 0.001$) and core self-evaluation ($r = 0.50$, $p < 0.001$)" (Tischler et al., 2016, p. 11).

Servant Leadership and Employee Productivity Scores

Hodoh (2016) conducted a study in three for-profit distribution centers of a national supply chain company to see if a relationship exists between servant leadership and individual worker productivity. The OLA was used along with the *Total Productivity Model* (TPM) scale. "Results from the regression analysis revealed a statistically significant relationship between participants individual productivity scores and overall servant leadership behavior ($R = 0.628$, $R^2 = 0.395$, $F(1131) = 85.486$. $p < 0.001$)" (p. v). Hodoh concludes that team productivity is positively and significantly affected by servant leadership within the work environment. When workers report being valued by their leaders, team productivity increases.

Research Summary

What are we discovering from this body of research, and what do we still need to learn? We are finding out that the presence of servant leadership characteristics within organizations correlates positively with key organizational health factors, such as

- Employee job satisfaction
- Trust in leaders and organizations
- Organizational safety
- Team effectiveness
- Student achievement scores

We are also discovering that the presence of servant leadership correlates negatively to employee absenteeism and attrition. The more servant leadership characteristics are perceived in the organization, the less our employees are absent from the job and the less they tend to leave the organization. This is critical for organizational performance due to the high cost of making up for lost employee production due to absences and retraining for newly filled positions. If we can keep our employees longer, have them present on the job more, keep them safer, provide a more satisfying work experience, build trust between employees and their leaders, and provide for stronger performance, we have an obligation to do so. If we can help our followers to be more satisfied with their jobs and more engaged in their work, we can build a healthier culture that results in higher performance.

Conclusion

Servant leadership makes a positive difference in leader behavior, follower response, and organizational health. The hope is that research will continue and grow to provide more insight into how servant leadership works and how it connects to various organizational health factors. As this body of research grows we will have an increasingly stronger business case to support the use of servant leadership in our organizations. In our next chapter, we will consider the critical issue of organizational structure and how different structures serve to enhance or hinder servant leadership practice.

References

Adamson, L. (2009). *Servant leadership in a community college: A multivariate analysis of employees' perceptions.* Doctoral dissertation, Walden University.

Al-Yousef, B. A. (2012). *Servant-leadership perception and job satisfaction among Saudi food and drug authority employees: A correlational study.* Master thesis, King Saud bin Abdulaziz University.

Amadeo, C. (2008). *A correlational study of servant leadership and registered nurse job satisfaction in acute health-care settings.* Doctoral dissertation, University of Phoenix.

Anderson, J. D. (2006). *Servant leadership in public schools: A case study.* Doctoral dissertation, University of Missouri.

Anderson, K. P. (2005). *A correlational analysis of servant leadership and job satisfaction in a religious educational organization.* Doctoral dissertation, University of Phoenix.

Arfsten, D. J. (2006). *Servant leadership: A quantitative study of the perceptions of employees of a Christian-based, for-profit organization.* Doctoral dissertation, Colorado State University.

Azadfada, S., Besmi, M., & Doroudian, A. A. (2014). The relationship between servant leadership and athlete satisfaction. *International Journal of Basic Sciences & Applied Research, 3,* 528–537.

Babb, C. A. (2012). *An analysis of the relationship between organizational servant leadership and student achievement in middle level schools.* Doctoral dissertation, Widener University.

Beaver, S. (2008). *Second fiddle? An interpretive study of followers of servant leaders.* Doctoral dissertation, Iowa State University.

Beaver, T. (2007). *Servant leadership in religious congregations: The effect on donations.* Doctoral dissertation, Indiana Wesleyan University.

Beazly, D. (2002). *Spiritual orientation of a leader and perceived servant leadership behavior: A correlational study.* Doctoral dissertation, Walden University.

Black, G. L. (2010). Correlational analysis of servant leadership and school climate. *Catholic Education, 13,* 437–466.

Blanchard, K., Blanchard, S., & Zigarmi, D. (2007). Servant leadership. In The Founding Associates and Consulting Partners of the Ken Blanchard Companies (Ed.), *Leading at a higher level: Blanchard on leadership and creating high performing organizations* (pp. 249–276). Upper Saddle River, NJ: Prentice Hall.

Bradshaw, M. (2007). *Organizational leadership and its relationship to outcomes in residential treatment*. Doctoral dissertation, Indiana Wesleyan University.

Braye, R. H. (2000). *Servant-leadership: Belief and practice in women-led business*. Doctoral dissertation, Walden University.

Cater, J. J. (2006). *Stepping out of the shadow: The leadership qualities of successors in family business*. Doctoral dissertation, Louisiana State University.

Cerit, Y. (2009). The effects of servant leadership behaviors of school principals on teacher's job satisfaction. *Educational Management Administration & Leadership, 37,* 600–623.

Chavez, E. G. (2012). *Servant leadership in Bolivia: a phenomenological study of long-term effects of a founding servant leader on two educational organizations*. Doctoral dissertation, Regent University.

Chu, H. (2008). *Employee perception of servant leadership and job satisfaction in a call center: A correlational study*. D.M thesis, University of Phoenix.

Denning, R. B. (2016). *Servant-leader boards: A quantitative study of for-profit firms in the United States*. Doctoral dissertation, Piedmont International University.

Drury, S. (2004). *Employee perceptions of servant leadership: Comparisons by level and with job satisfaction and organizational commitment*. Doctoral dissertation, Regent University.

Freeman, R. (2011). *An examination of the CompStat management model on organizational health and job satisfaction*. Doctoral dissertation, Walden University.

Freitas, W. M. (2003). *Servant leadership characteristics in a health care organization, and the relationship with leader-member exchange*. Master thesis, University of Nebraska.

Ghormley, J. C. (2009). *A correlational analysis: Servant leadership and participation by volunteer leaders of credit unions*. Doctoral dissertation, University of Phoenix.

Giolito, V., Liden, R. C., & Van Dierendonck, D. (2016, September). *The influence of servant leadership on objective performance and employee holistic well-being*. A presentation made to the 3rd Global Servant Leadership Research Roundtable, Bifröst University, Iceland.

Goodwin, O. K. (2011). *Committed to serve: A descriptive study of the growing presence of servant leadership within a nonprofit organization.* Doctoral dissertation, Capella University.

Hannigan, J. (2008). *Leadership in higher education: An investigation of servant leadership as a predictor of college performance.* Doctoral dissertation, Capella University.

Harless, J. T. (2015). *Leading volunteers: Understanding correlations between servant leadership practices and volunteer satisfaction within a non-denominational church.* Doctoral dissertation, Piedmont International University.

Hebert, S. C. (2003). *The relationship of perceived servant leadership and job satisfaction from the follower's perspective.* Doctoral dissertation, Capella University.

Herbst, J. D. (2003). *Organizational servant leadership and its relationship to secondary school effectiveness.* Doctoral dissertation, Florida Atlantic University.

Herman, R. (2008). *Servant leadership: A model for organizations desiring a workplace spirituality culture.* Doctoral dissertation, Capella University.

Hodoh, S. D. (2016). *Servant leadership: An effective leadership model for achieving optimal productivity.* Doctoral dissertation, Grand Canyon University.

Horsman, J. H. (2001). *Perspectives of servant-leadership and spirit in organizations.* Doctoral dissertation, Gonzaga University.

Iken, S. L. (2005). *Servant leadership in higher education: Exploring perceptions of educators and staff employed in a University setting.* Doctoral dissertation, University of North Dakota.

Inbarasu, J. (2008). *Influence of servant-leadership practice on job satisfaction: A correlational study in a lutheran organization.* Doctoral dissertation, University of Phoenix.

Irving, J. A. (2005). *Servant leadership and the effectiveness of teams.* Doctoral dissertation, Regent University.

Irving, J. A., & Longbotham, G. J. (2007). Team effectiveness and six essential servant leadership themes: A regression model based on items in the organizational leadership assessment. *International Journal of Management Studies, 2,* 98–113.

Jacobs, K. (2011). *Assessing the relationship between servant leadership and effective teaching in a Private University setting.* Doctoral dissertation, Northcentral University.

Johnson, R. (2008). *An exploratory study of servant leadership, emotional intelligence and job satisfaction among high-tech employees.* Doctoral dissertation, University of Phoenix.

Joseph, E. E., & Winston, B. E. (2005). A correlation of servant leadership, leader trust and organizational trust. *Leadership & Organizational Development Journal, 26*, 6–22.

Judge, T. A., & Bono, J. E. (2001). Relationship of core self-evaluation traits self-esteem, generalized self-efficacy, locus of control, and emotional stability with job satisfaction and job performance: A meta-analysis. *Journal of Applied Psychology, 86*, 80–92.

Kegler, M. A. (2007). *Star Gazers or servant leaders? An examination of the belief and practice of servant leadership in the U.S. military and a comparison to business leaders.* Doctoral dissertation, Capella University.

Klamon, V. (2006). *Exploring social enterprise organizational climate and culture.* Doctoral dissertation, Gonzaga University.

Kong, P. (2007). *A study of the Church staff organization's servant leadership tendency and job satisfaction of the pastor and of another ministerial staff person in Southern Baptist convention Church.* Doctoral dissertation, Southwestern Baptist Theological Seminary.

Krebs, K. D. (2005). *Can servant-leaders be safety indicators? Development and test of a model linking servant-leadership to occupational safety.* Doctoral dissertation, DePaul University.

Lambert, W. E. (2004). *Servant leadership qualities of principals, organizational climate and student achievement: A correlational study.* Doctoral dissertation, Nova Southeastern University.

Larson, C. E., & Lafasto, F. M. J. (1989). *Team work: What must go right, what can go wrong.* Newbury Park, CA: SAGE Publications.

Laub, J. A. (1999). *Assessing the servant organization: Development of the Servant Organizational Leadership (SOLA) Assessment.* Doctoral dissertation, Florida Atlantic University.

Laub, J. A. (2005). From paternalism to the servant organization: Expanding the organizational leadership assessment (OLA) model. *International Journal of Servant-Leadership, 1*, 155–186.

Laub, J. A. (2010). The servant organization. In D. van Dierendonck & K. Patterson (Eds.), *Servant leadership: Developments in theory and research* (pp. 105–117). Basingstoke: Palgrave Macmillan.

Ledbetter, D. S. (2003). *Law enforcement leaders and servant leadership: A reliability study of the Organizational Leadership Assessment (OLA) model.* Doctoral dissertation, Regent University.

Liden, R. C., Wayne, S. J., Zhao, H., & Henderson, D. (2008). Servant leadership: Development of a multidimensional measure and multi-level assessment. *Leadership Quarterly, 19*, 161–177.

McCann, R. J. (2006). *Servant-leadership in a catholic charities agency: A case study.* Doctoral dissertation, Gonzaga University.

McDougle, L. R. (2009). *Servant leadership in higher education: An analysis of the perceptions of higher education employees regarding servant leadership practices at varying types of institutions.* Doctoral dissertation, University of Texas.

McKenzie, R. A. (2012). *A correlational study of servant leadership and teacher job satisfaction in a public education institution.* Doctoral dissertation, University of Phoenix.

McNeff, M. E. (2012). *Servant leadership training and development in selected evangelical churches.* Thesis, Bethel University.

Meredith, S. C. (2007). *Servant leadership from the student officer perspective in Phi Theta Kappa.* Doctoral dissertation, Capella University.

Metzcar, A. M. (2008). *Servant leadership and effective classroom teaching.* Doctoral dissertation, Indiana Wesleyan University.

Miears, L. D. (2004). *Servant leadership and job satisfaction: A correlational study in Texas education agency region X public schools.* Doctoral dissertation, Texas A&M University.

Miguel, J. I. (2009). *Organizational leadership: A study of the perceptions of servant leadership practices and beliefs, and its implications for a private Christian institution of higher education in Brazil.* Doctoral dissertations, Andrews University.

Molnar, D. (2007). *Serving the World: A cross-cultural study of national culture dimensions and servant leadership.* Doctoral dissertation, Capella University.

Mortan, M. M. (2013). *Servant leadership in Mississippi private Christian School: A correlational study of servant leadership and job satisfaction.* Doctoral dissertation, Mississippi College.

Nordbye, V. C. (2012). *The impact of servant leadership within a US national campus ministry: An examination of effective leadership among millennials.* D. Min. thesis, Bethel University.

Nyamboli, R. N. K. (2014). *Perceptions of organizational servant leadership and doctoral student satisfaction with e-learning.* Doctoral dissertation, Grand Canyon University.

Padron, J. (2012). *Higher education leadership: Servant leadership and the effects on student satisfaction.* Doctoral dissertation, Argosy University.

Palmer, M. D. (2011). *Faculty perceptions of organizational leadership at Christian Colleges and Universities with missions of servant leadership.* Doctoral dissertation, Dallas Baptist University.

Patterson, K., Russell, R. F., & Stone, A. G. (2004). Transformational versus servant leadership: A difference in leader focus. *Leadership & Organizational Development Journal, 25*, 349–361.

Rauch, K. (2007). *Servant leadership and team effectiveness: A study of industrial manufacturing correlation.* Doctoral dissertation, Indiana Wesleyan University.

Ross, D. B. (2006). *Perceptions of the evidence of a servant leadership culture among educators in the P-12 School system in the North American division of seventh-day Adventists.* Doctoral dissertation, Andrews University.

Salameh, K. M. (2011). Servant leadership practices among School Principles in educational directorates in Jordan. *International Journal of Business and Social Science, 3*, 138–145.

Salie, A. (2008). *Servant-minded leadership and work satisfaction in Islamic organizations: A correlational mixed study.* Doctoral dissertation, University of Phoenix.

Shears, M. M. (2012). *A study of elementary School administrators' implementation of servant leadership and elementary School teachers' job satisfaction.* Doctoral dissertation, Mississippi College.

Sipe, J. W., & Frick, D. M. (2009). *Seven pillars of servant leadership: Practicing the wisdom of leading by serving.* New York, NY: Paulist Press.

Stamba, L. M. (2003). *Servant leadership practices and beliefs, job satisfaction, and the organizational leadership assessment.* Doctoral dissertation, Central Michigan University.

Svoboda, S. (2008). *A correlational study of servant leadership and elementary principal job satisfaction in Ohio public school districts.* Doctoral dissertation, North Central University.

Thompson, R. S. (2002). *The perception of servant leadership characteristics and job satisfaction in a Church-related College.* Doctoral dissertation, Indiana State University.

Tischler, L., Giambatista, R., McCormick, D., & McKeage, R. (2016). Servant leadership and its relationships with core self-evaluation and job satisfaction. *Journal of Values-Based Leadership, 9*, 1–20.

Van Tassell, M. (2006). *Called to serve: Servant-leadership perceptions at a Franciscan sponsored University correlated with job satisfaction.* Doctoral dissertation, Capella University.

Van Worth, S. (2015). *Exploring the leadership practices of principals of Blue Ribbon Schools.* Doctoral dissertation, Grand Canyon University.

Wilson, D. F. (2013). *Servant leadership and job satisfaction in a multicultural hospitality organization: A quantitative, non-experimental descriptive study.* Doctoral dissertation, Grand Canyon University.

Witter, S. R. (2007). *An analysis of the leadership practices of the Churches of the Plymouth Brethren movement in the United States.* Doctoral dissertation, Capella University.

Wyllie, J. E. (2009). *Servant leadership and job satisfaction among long-term care employees.* Doctoral dissertation, Saint Joseph's College.

Zigarmi, D., Peyton Roberts, T., Houson, D., Witt, D., & Diehl, J. (2013). Leader values and employee work intentions: The impact of "self-focused" versus "other-focused" leaders. *Perspectives—Employee Work Passion, 5,* 1–8.

10

Considering Servant Organizational Structures

Can servant leadership function effectively in all organizational structures or might some structures work to enhance the effectiveness of a servant mindset? Could a servant leadership mindset help to support and even create new types of organizational forms that can take us beyond the limitations of authority-based hierarchy? In this chapter, we will explore various organizational structures to consider possible answers to these questions. The foundational work of Mintzberg (1989) will create a starting point for considering the variety of organizational structures available. The more recent work of Frederic Laloux (2014) will be examined to see how his model of Green and Teal organizations might relate to the servant leadership approach. Issues of self-managing teams, high-trust organizations, and building leadership cultures are considered to explore whether there is an optimal organizational structure for servant-led organizations.

New Wine in Old Wineskins

What would happen if a leader decided to adopt a new servant mindset and then began to act on this new mindset. Workers would be valued, trusted, and asked for their opinion and ideas. They would be

© The Author(s) 2018   **233**
J. Laub, *Leveraging the Power of Servant Leadership*, Palgrave Studies in Workplace
Spirituality and Fulfillment, https://doi.org/10.1007/978-3-319-77143-4_10

empowered to act and make decisions within their area of expertise and competence. Teams would move from teams *with* a leader to teams *of* leaders. People throughout the organization would be treated as adult partners and expected to speak out and engage fully in the work and vision of the organization. Honesty and transparency would be the expectation at all levels and leadership would be a dispersed commodity that all employees would be allowed and expected to exercise. Would you expect this new level of empowerment and openness to work well within current organizational structures? Or, might these structures work against the full implementation of this new way of leadership thinking?

When Jesus was challenged as to why he and his disciples were following a new set of rules related to fasting and prayer, he shared a powerful metaphor. He said, "no one puts new wine into old wineskins. For the wine would burst the wineskins, and the wine and the skins would both be lost. New wine calls for new wineskins" (Mark 2:22, New Living Translation). Yes, new ideas call for new frameworks to hold the ideas allowing them to fully develop and flourish. Old structures, if they do not fit the new mindset well, will end up hindering and damaging the potential of this newer way of thinking and leading.

New fermenting wine is a helpful metaphor related to the servant mindset. Like new fermenting wine, servant leadership is an idea in ferment. Like a chemical reaction, servant leadership is alive and growing with new potential and possibility. New wine calls for new wineskins. One does not take newly fermenting wine and place it into an old stretched-out wineskin. The old wineskin will not safely contain the new wine and ultimately both will be lost. We must consider the optimal forms, structures, or organizational models to hold this new fermenting leadership concept. To be sure, servant leadership, when viewed as a mindset, will bring value to any organizational structure, but we are wise to consider new structures that serve to enhance these new leadership ideas and to contain and maintain them effectively.

Mintzberg's Five Organizational Types

Mintzberg's (1989) list of five organizational types is a good place to begin. To Mintzberg, the organizational structure must fit the strategy of the organization, the environmental forces it must deal with, and the life cycle position of the organization. The five organizational types are:

1. The machine (bureaucracy) organization
2. The divisional (diversified) organization
3. The professional organization
4. The innovative organization
5. The entrepreneurial organization

In considering different structures for different needs, think of the structure appropriate for a new tech startup compared to what is necessary for that same organization once it achieves market success. Can the same structure that provided a climate for innovation by a relatively small group of highly creative people provide what is needed for a larger, more complex organization requiring more stability?

The Machine (Bureaucracy) Organization

The machine organization strives for standardization and is guided by a myriad of rules, procedures, regulations, and guidelines. Decision making is centralized and work is divided by functions and specialties. The organization strives for efficiency and productivity and is careful to measure everything to achieve the highest possible performance level. Relationships are formalized and job functions are clearly defined. Leadership is shaped by a hierarchy that places one key leader at the top of the decision-making grid. Authority is top-down and power to act is granted according to a person's relative position in the hierarchy. Strategic planning is formally structured and is the responsibility of those at the top levels of the organization.

The Divisional (Diversified) Organization

Due to multiple products lines, a central headquarters may oversee separate autonomous divisions that have been granted power to develop their own business specialty under the guidance of the central office. This provides a decentralized decision-making structure where each of the organizational divisions may operate as separate centralized entities which may end up in conflict over resources allocated from central headquarters. This is a structure that fits large organizations with product or market diversification requiring focus and commitment for each specific part of the larger organization.

The Professional Organization

The professional organization, like the machine and divisional organization, is bureaucratic in approach. The difference is in the level of professional training and expertise of those who make up the organization's workforce. High levels of professional education and specialty focus require more decentralized levels of decision making. These professional knowledge workers have a high level of autonomy and power granted to act within their particular areas of expertise. Rules and regulations are abundant due to the professional nature of their work (i.e. law, higher education, healthcare). Power is dispersed and professional employees are granted high levels of freedom to act as long as productivity is insured.

The Innovative Organization

For organizations to innovate and create new directions, traditional reliance on centralized power and bureaucracy must give way to freer organizational forms. This structure, like the professional organization, relies on people with unique talents and expertise to drive creative teams who focus on projects and products to move the organization forward. Cross-functional teams are commonly employed and rules are minimized to allow for new thinking and new ways to address problems and opportunities. Flexibility is promoted though authority can be ambiguous since power is more dispersed within this organizational structure.

The Entrepreneurial Organization

The entrepreneurial organization provides the simplest and flattest of organizational forms. This structure is high on flexibility, freedom, and speed while low on standards, systems, and controls. Decision-making power is located at the top of the organization usually in a single-leader or small leadership team who guides the organization forward. This organizational type is common in new startup organizations that are seeking to establish new products for the marketplace. It shares several characteristics with the innovative organization but may see the need to create a more structured organization as it becomes established and successful.

What we see in Mintzberg's five organizational types are structures built from the organization's key purpose fitted to its organizational strategy and life stage. New organizations tend toward the entrepreneurial structure while older more established organizations tend toward the machine or professional type of organization. Once organizations are established and the hierarchy entrenched there may be a need to seek a more diversified or innovative structure to provide the flexibility, freedom, and informal processes lost by the growing bureaucracy natural to all developing organizations.

If one adopts a servant leadership mindset and then seeks to create an organizational structure to best fit that mindset, what might that structure look like? If new wine requires new wineskins, what is the best structure to contain the new and fermenting ideas of servant leadership?

Flipping the Pyramid

One approach to considering new organizational structures for servant leadership involves flipping the normal hierarchical pyramid on its head. A common organization chart is designed to show levels of decision-making authority with top leaders at the top, managers in the middle, and the workforce at the bottom. The implication is that the one (or a few) leaders at the top of the organization hold the power while workers at the bottom implement the work. A large gap exists between the conceptualizing work of top leaders and the implementing function of workers. Managers, or supervisors, operate between the two to insure that the work gets done according to the desire of the leaders. Decisions are made by top leaders and then funneled down to managers/supervisors who are expected to implement these decisions through the workforce. It seems to be a clear and effective way to get things done, but there are implications of this model that we should consider. One concern is clarity of communication. When decisions made at the top of the organization (often, literally on the top floors) begin to filter down to those who implement the decisions, the clarity of the reasons for and the desired outcomes of the decisions can easily be lost. Communication is notoriously unclear in organizations. Top leaders assume that a well-worded document or a directive shared in a management team meeting will be accurately communicated down the line, but there are multiple ways miscommunication can, and will, occur. Communication is not only faulty coming down the pyramid, but it is also problematic moving up from workers to managers to top leaders. Often workers are expected to work without the necessary resources provided or clarifying questions are not addressed because the structure does not allow these questions to be asked. When top leaders are the strategic thinkers and the workers are the doers, there is often no channel for workers and leaders to connect around strategic questions needed to clarity the tasks workers are expected to complete.

Another issue with this model is the focus of authority at the top of the structure. When decisions are far removed from the actual work being done it is not uncommon for multiple layers of control checkpoints to be instituted to help guarantee the quality of work performed. Approvals must be obtained for any changes and the approvals must move up and down the hierarchy with the risk of becoming stalled at any of the approval points along the way. The end result is inefficiency and stalled workflow.

Due to these and other problems some have suggested that the standard hierarchical pyramid needs to be flipped over so that the workers are now viewed at the *top* of the organizational pyramid and top leaders are at the bottom. The implication is that top leaders should support the work of the managers who then support the work of the workforce who actually do the work and deal directly with customers.

This dramatic shift in organizational structure and flow is questioned by the belief that top leaders should set the vision for the organization and determine the key strategic direction. So, based on this questionable belief, some suggest that the hierarchal top-down pyramid should remain in place for establishing direction and *then* the pyramid is flipped to provide the support model needed for implementation. Blanchard is one proponent of this model of using both the standard *top-down* pyramid and the flipped *support-up* pyramid (Blanchard & Hodges, 2005). He suggests that top leaders are responsible for providing the vision and direction for the organization so the top-down pyramids works well for this part of the process. However, once the vision has been established and sent down to managers and the workforce, then the pyramid is flipped and leaders serve in a support role toward managers and followers. Though this adjustment provides an improvement over the top-down, authority model, it raises questions as to whether this goes far enough to establish a culture of servant-minded adult partnership between workers, managers, and top leaders. Should workers share in the responsibility of shaping the future direction of the organization? If they are included at this step in a more meaningful way, might they own the vision and direction more, resulting in a stronger commitment to pursue and implement the vision? Ultimately, is the flipped pyramid structure a strong enough "wineskin" to hold the leveraged power of servant leadership?

Organizational Structures for OLA Organizational Health Levels

The four organizational health levels, based on the OLA servant leadership model, call for specific structures built from a basic form of three organizational position levels as displayed in (Fig. 10.1). The three position levels are top leaders, managers/supervisors, and workforce. Almost all organizations utilize at least these three basic positional levels to distinguish one level of employee from the others. However, the roles of the leaders can and will change based on the health level of the organization and this change has a dramatic effect on all within the organization and the potential for building a healthy high performing organization.

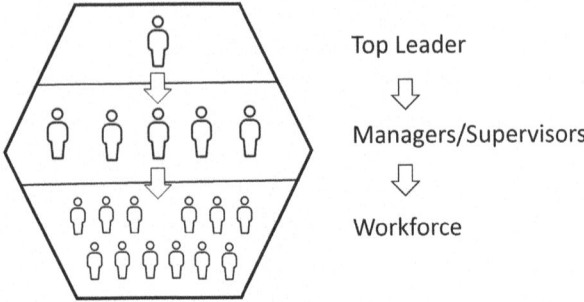

Fig. 10.1 Organizational structure (basic)

Level 1–2: Toxic and Poor Health Organization Structure

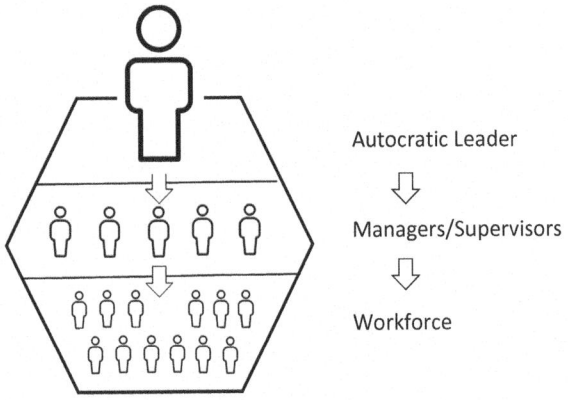

Fig. 10.2 Organizational structure (autocratic)

Toxic and poor health organizations operate in a top-down structure with the main focus being on the single top leader. He or she holds centralized power for vision creation and decision-making directives are sent down to managers/supervisors to implement through the workers.

The concern is that this unchecked power will lead to the abuse of that power and the organization will find itself limited to the ideas and initiatives of a single leader, a leader who demands that he or she be the focus of the organization's attention. "The minute a leader allows himself to become the primary reality people worry about, rather than reality being the primary reality, you have a recipe for mediocrity, or worse" (Dweck, 2016, p. 124). The worse referred to here is the abuse of workers and the misdirection of effort from the company's mission to serve the leader's ego. The strong belief that fosters this kind of mindset and structure is that of the heroic leader, the leader who will solve all of our problems and rescue us from all dangers. The heroic leader concept is appealing since it depends on finding the right leader while absolving all others (board members, company leaders and managers, workers) from responsibility for the success of the organization. All of the concerns and negative dynamics concerning top-down organizations are present in this structure with the added complication of the focus on a self-absorbed leader who is leading for self over others.

Level 3: Negative Parental Organization Structure

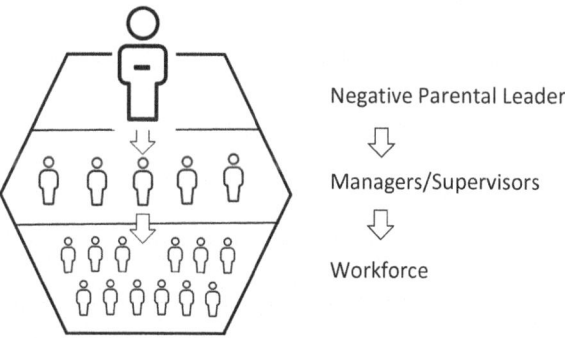

Fig. 10.3   Organizational structure (negative parental)

Negative parental organizations also operate in a top-down structure though the mindset of the leader has now moved from self to the needs of the organization. The focus remains on the leader at the top of the structure, but now the leader sees himself or herself in the role of parent to those below. The mindset of this leader believes that managers and workers cannot be trusted and must be controlled and led with direction from above to insure the organization's success. Negative parental leaders present a default response of suspicion toward others and emphasize control and negative accountability. People must continually prove themselves to this leader who views others as children needing strong and controlling leadership to insure that they focus on doing the right things.

Level 4: Positive Parental Organization Structure

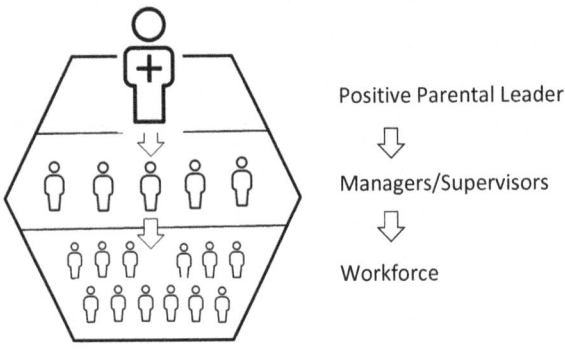

Positive Parental Leader

⇩

Managers/Supervisors

⇩

Workforce

Fig. 10.4 Organizational structure (positive parental)

Positive parental organizations maintain a top-down structure, but the leader takes on the role of the nurturing, benevolent parent who focuses first on the good of the organization seeking to develop others to fulfill the leader's vision. The positive leader as parent provides a caring, supportive environment but the direction and vision continue to come from the top of the organization. Workers are treated as children who need direction and care but should be treated in a benevolent and supportive manner. Workers sense that this is a positive place to work since the fear present in the toxic or negative parental organization is now replaced by a respectful fear that maintains the primacy of the role of the top leader to provide the direction the organization needs.

Level 5–6: Servant-Minded Healthy Organization Structure

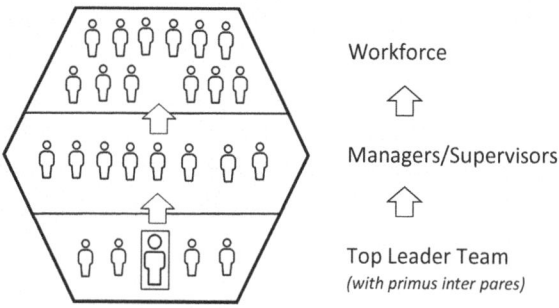

Fig. 10.5   Organizational structure (servant)

Like the flipped pyramid, the servant-minded healthy organization structure provides a support-up model versus an authority-down model. Top leaders are placed at the bottom of the model to show the support they provide to the managers/supervisors who then support the workers. This not only provides a support model, including a team of leaders versus a single leader, but also promotes a concept introduced by Greenleaf (1977) called *primus inter pares* meaning *first among equals*. This structure calls for a team of leaders rather than a single-leader approach while recognizing that one key leader initiates first and guides the team forward.

Greenleaf presented two organizational principles. The first principle is "the hierarchical principle that places one person in charge as the lone chief atop a pyramidal structure" (Greenleaf, 1977, p. 61). The second principle, taken from Roman times, is this idea of a team of leaders with one who serves as first among equals. Greenleaf addressed a number of key flaws he saw in the hierarchical model where one leader holds positional power over all others in the organization. He viewed this structure as being "abnormal and corrupting" (Greenleaf, 1977, p. 63) since no leaders are perfect and complete in themselves and when power is held by a single person there is a stronger likelihood of corruption. Followers simply do not talk the same way with their bosses as they do with fellow workers so communication from workers to top leaders is non-existent or severely limited. When the leader's thoughts are not challenged there can develop an "image of omniscience" (p. 63) in the leader that further removes him or her from those who follow. As a result, leaders find themselves incredibly lonely in their insular role of top leader. Leaders can only know what others tell them and no one feels free to tell them the whole unvarnished truth. Interestingly, the single-leader structure tends, in Greenleaf's view, toward a "burden of indecisiveness" (p. 64). Since accountability is limited for top leaders, a tendency toward indecisiveness may become stronger than the leader's desire for closure.

Another limiting factor is that this model creates too few leaders. As the top of the organizational pyramid comes to its peak there is limited space for leaders. When the single leader departs, it creates a significant time of insecurity and interruption for the organization. Who will lead now? Who will make critical decisions? This succession problem is heightened by the centralization of power that the hierarchical principle places on the single leader and the organization. The amassing of power in one position not only leads to multiple problems for the organization but also creates a debilitating effect on the leader. "In the end, the chief becomes a performer, not a natural person, and essential creative powers diminish" (Greenleaf, 1977, p. 65).

The alternative is to create a team of leaders who share the power, influence, creativity, and responsibilities of the enterprise while identifying a leader among leaders to serve as primus inter pares who will be the point person for the group. Imagine the difference between having a team with a single leader and having a team of leaders. This model is not required for servant leadership to be successfully implemented within an organization, but it does support servant leadership disciplines while decreasing the negative tendencies of a single-leader hierarchical structure. According to Greenleaf, "it is important that the primus constantly test and prove … leadership among a group of able peers. This principle

Table 10.1 Comparison of a single-leader versus *primus* model

Issues with a single-leader model	Benefits of a *primus* model
Centralized power with a tendency toward corruption	Shared power with accountability beyond a single leader
Limited to the skill and experience of the single leader	Open to the influence from many different leaders with varied skills and experience
Leads to isolation and loneliness of the leader	Supports a community approach to leading and serving
Allows leadership opportunity for too few leaders	Provides opportunities for more leaders to lead and serve
Creates a major interruption to the organization when the single leader leaves	Minimizes the disruption when one leader leaves since others leaders are already leading
Can lead to indecisiveness when a single leader is uncertain how and when to act	Creates accountability for action for all leaders on the team
Limited to what one leader can provide	Open to what multiple leaders can provide

is more difficult to find in practice, but it does exist in important places— with conspicuous success" (Greenleaf, 1977, p. 61). As we consider all this structure provides in contrast to the limitations of the single-leader model we see the benefits available to the servant-minded organization. Table 10.1 provides a list of concerns or issues that exist within a single-leader hierarchical structure contrasted to the benefits gained from a primus inter pares structure.

The first among equals model clearly has benefits for leaders and the organization, but a mindshift is needed to make this truly effective. If a leader sets up a leadership team, which is not uncommon in organizations, but views that team within a team-with-a-leader mindset this can be just another way to structure a top-down organization that is autocratic or parental in leadership. What is needed is a mindshift from a team-with-a-leader approach to a team-*of*-leaders.

The team-with-a-leader is simply a microcosm of the hierarchical organizational model that provides a single leader over a group of team members. These members may be top leaders in the organization (i.e. VPs, division heads, department leaders) but if the team functions with a team-with-a-leader approach it is still subject to the limitations of the single-leader model. The single leader still holds the power, makes the decisions, and determines the direction while holding the team members accountable. However, under this model, mutual accountability is not provided.

The team-of-leaders approach is the proper mindset to make the primus inter pares concept work as designed. With this model, everyone on the team is expected to lead, not just *down* the organization through their specific divisions or departments, but to lead *with* each other, in full partnership, for the good of the organization. So, what is the unique role of the primus inter pares, the leader who is designated first among equals? The primus has the key role of bringing the leadership team together. He or she provides guidance to the team, but does not serve as the lone leader. Responsibility and accountability are shared and true partnership is established. A community of leaders is created to model the disciplines of servant leadership at the very top of the organization. People are valued and developed, community is built, authenticity is practiced, and leadership is provided and shared. When a company practices its values and a servant mindset at the highest levels, the organization is in a strong position to create a servant-minded culture. As top leaders learn how to function in a team-of-leaders approach they are apt to duplicate these teams throughout their departments and divisions and will encourage leadership to emerge from all levels of the organization. By emphasizing a team-of-leaders approach a leadership expectation culture is created where each person sees himself or herself as a leader, a change agent, a person who can use their power to make a positive difference. This then serves to transform the leader's approach to and use of power. Laloux (2014) suggests this about the leader's relationship to power.

The relationship to power could be transformed in quite fundamental ways. When trust replaces fear, will a hierarchical pyramid still provide the best structure? Will we need all the rules and policies, detailed budgets, targets, and roadmaps that give leaders today a sense of control? Perhaps there are much simpler ways to run organizations when the fears of the ego are out of the way. (p. 50)

Servant Organizations: Green or Teal?

Frederic Laloux developed a typology of organizational structures based on the work of Wilber and Wade on developmental stages of consciousness. Laloux's (2014) concern about organizations is that they "are more often than not playfields for unfulfilling pursuits of our egos, inhospitable to the deeper yearnings of our souls" (p. 4). Yes, organizations can be places of flourishing or they can be places that serve to deplete the soul and energy of their people. Laloux states that "the hierarchical pyramid feels outdated but what other structure could replace it?" (p. 4), and then adds that "if we are to overcome the daunting problems of our times, we will need new types of organizations—more purposeful businesses, more soulful schools, more productive non-profits" (p. 8). According to Laloux, there are five types of organizations, each identified by a unique color.

The first is the Red organization which relies upon a top leader who exercises autocratic and complete power over his or her people. Fear is the clear motivator of action and this kind of organization works best in chaotic situations. The guiding metaphor for this type of organization is the wolf pack and an example of it in action is a street gang. The Amber organization is structured with a formal hierarchical pyramid with the power of the organization focused on the top leaders of the organization. This is a command and control structure that pursues stable processes and consistency over time. The guiding metaphor is of an army; therefore, one of the key examples of this structure in practice is the military. The Orange organization is focused on achievement and winning over the competition. Innovation is highly valued and processes are guided by a management-by-objectives approach. Roles are clearly delineated and some freedom is given to managers to determine the best way to achieve the goals first established by the top leaders. The guiding metaphor here is the machine and the living example is most corporations in the world today. These three organizational types, though ubiquitous, are not complementary with newer ways of leading. To address this, Laloux presents two more organizational types: Green and Teal.

The Green organization also functions with a top-down pyramid structure, but seeks to build a family culture to encourage empowerment and motivation for its workers. These culture-driven organizations like Southwest Airlines, the Container Store, and Starbucks seek to develop a culture of performance based on positive values that all in the organization rally around. Teams are emphasized and the guiding metaphor is the family. It is in this organizational structure that Laloux places the concept of servant leadership since this way of leading has been so often identified with organizations that operate within the Green organizational structure. However, the question should be raised as to whether this structure is the most ideal for servant leadership to flourish. Might the family orientation of the Green organization better fit the Positive Parental mindset of leadership? Laloux quotes a CEO who sees himself as a servant leader, but thinks of himself more within a Teal organization structure. He states, "if I'm your boss and you are reporting to me, does the metaphor imply that I'm a father and you are a child? Green (organization) insists on caring, serving leadership, but from a Teal perspective, I don't want to be a father to anybody in the organization, not even a caring-serving father" (Laloux, 2014, p. 56). This CEO understands that the Green organization calls out more of a positive parental mindset while the servant leadership mindset with its emphasis on creating adult partnership and mutual accountability fits better within the Teal organization.

The Teal organization is the first of Laloux's organizational types to break up the hierarchical pyramid structure so foundational to all other types. There are three major breakthroughs that the Teal organization introduces. The first breakthrough is self-management where people and teams within the organization manage their own work without the need for a controlling hierarchy. This is probably the most radical departure from previous organizational types since it is based on a high trust and shared accountability structure. Power is no longer concentrated at the top of the organization but is now dispersed throughout the organization giving everyone the power to act and the opportunity to lead. Laloux sees the self-management concept as "the first major breakthrough of Teal Organizations: transcending the age-old problem of power inequality through structures and practices where no one holds power over anyone else, and yet paradoxically, the organization as a whole, ends up being considerably more powerful" (Laloux, 2014, p. 62). The second breakthrough of the Teal organization is the focus on wholeness. Teal organizations recognize that people are multifaceted and made up of minds, emotions, spiritual longings, and relational needs. Employees are encouraged in Teal organizations to bring their whole self to the workplace to find a place that encourages the flourishing of the complete person including all parts of their lives. The third breakthrough of the Teal organization is evolutionary purpose. These organizations do not find their purpose and meaning through the vision of a single powerful leader, but rather have a deep purpose of their own that all people within the organization are encouraged to discover as they play their unique part in guiding the organization forward. Teal organizations see themselves as always emerging and becoming as everyone participates in defining and clarifying the organization's vision and purpose. These three breakthroughs—self-management, wholeness, and evolutionary purpose—are the hallmarks that distinguish the Teal organization from the Red (impulsive), the Amber (conformist), the Orange (achievement), and the Green (pluralistic) types of organizations.

How are these three breakthroughs practiced by real organizations? Laloux researched 12 organizations that practice successfully within a Teal organization structure. Table 10.2 presents just a few of the contrasts in practice between Teal organizations and Orange (achievement) organizations drawn from Laloux's research.

It is clear that the practices of a Teal organization are radically different than those of an Orange (achievement) organization. To get a sense of the types of organizations that serve as models for this study, below are the 12 companies that successfully practiced the beliefs of the Teal organization. They include both national and global companies from five different countries employing from 90 to 40,000 employees.

1. **AES:** Energy sector—Global—40,000 employees—for profit—based in the United States
2. **BSO/Origen:** IT consulting—Global—10,000 employees—for profit—based in the Netherlands
3. **Buurtzorg:** Healthcare—Netherlands—7000 employees—non-profit
4. **ESBZ:** School (grades 7–12)—Germany—1500 students, staff, and parents—non-profit
5. **FAVI:** Metal manufacturing—France—500 employees—for profit

Table 10.2 Comparison of Orange versus Teal organizations

Orange organization practices	Teal organization practices
Hierarchical pyramid	Self-managing teams, with coaches as needed
Job titles and job descriptions	No job titles, fluid adjustable job descriptions
Important decisions are made by top leadership	Important decisions made by anyone as long as they use the "advice process"
Performance appraisals are focused on individual performance and is conducted by the hierarchical superior	Performance appraisals are focused on team performance and are conducted by peers
Conflict is often avoided but can be addressed by supervisors or those who are specially trained in conflict management	Conflict is addressed on an ongoing basis with regular time and forums committed to that purpose. Everyone is trained in conflict management
Projects are managed by project management experts implementing formal processes designed to gain control of outcomes	There are no project managers but teams self-manage their own projects with minimum plans for budgets
Many staff functions provided by a central office (HR, IT, finance, purchasing, quality control, risk management)	These functions are performed by the teams or special voluntary task forces set up specifically for the function. Staff serve in an advisory role
Salaries are set based on predetermined employee levels overseen by superiors. Tends toward large salary differences between top and lower employee levels	Salaries are self-set with peer calibration for base pay. No bonuses, but equal profit sharing. Smaller salary differences between top and lower employee levels.
Offices assigned with clear status markers to indicate position levels	Offices are self-decorated, warm, open to children and pets. No status markers.
Information is handed out from the top on a need-to-know basis	Information including company financials and compensation is made available to all. Total transparency.

Adapted and summarized from (Laloux, 2014, pp. 327–331)

6. **Heiligenfeld:** Mental health hospitals—Germany—600 employees—for profit
7. **Holacracy:** Organizational operating model
8. **Morning Star:** Food processing—United States—400–2400 employees—for profit
9. **Patagonia:** Apparel—United States—1350 employees—for profit
10. **RHD:** Human services—United States—4000 employees—non-profit
11. **Sounds True:** Media—United States—90 employees and 20 dogs—for profit
12. **Sun Hydraulics:** Hydraulics components—Global—900 employees—for profit—based in the United States (Laloux, 2014, pp. 57–59)

This list provides a diverse set of companies in terms of location, type of industry, and size and includes both non-profit and for-profit companies. Each company decided to structure according to the key concepts of the Teal organization and each has found success in doing so. The point to be made here is not to say that servant leadership can only flourish within a Teal organization. A servant leader mindset can work within any type of organizational structure. However, this study does suggest that there are other successful ways organizations can function and the servant leader has different structures to utilize and is not limited to an Orange (achievement) or even Green (family) type of organizational structure. It may be that the Teal organization provides the best framework for fully utilizing a servant leader mindset.

Dennis Bakke was the CEO of AES, one of the companies identified as a Teal organization. Bakke developed *the advice process* that became a common method for decision making within a decentralized Teal organization. The advice process creates a framework within which anyone in the organization can lead and make important, consequential decisions. Bakke states that "the decision maker—who is almost always not an official leader—seeks advice from leaders and from peers" (Bakke, 2005, p. 97). Before decisions are made the decision maker must seek the advice of anyone who is affected by the decision or may have important information related to the decision. The decision maker will begin by seeking advice from his or her own team, but then considers other teams that may be affected and consults with them as well. If the decision is such that it will have an effect on the organization as a whole, top leaders, including the board, will be consulted. Those consulted do not make the decision but offer advice to the decision maker and that person is empowered to make the decision, but only after they have worked through the advice process. Bakke suggests that there are five clear benefits to this process:

1. It draws the people whose advice is sought into the question at hand.
2. Asking for advice is an act of humility.
3. Making decisions is on-the-job education.
4. Chances of reaching the best decision are greater than under conventional top-down approaches.
5. The process is just plain fun for the decision maker (Bakke, 2005, pp. 98–99).

Fun (or joy) at work is not frivolous. It is a way of getting all employees actively engaged in the workplace and the advice process allows for people at all levels to gain control over their work, their goals, and the decisions that most affect them.

Servant leaders can function within multiple organizational structures, but there are structures that serve to enhance the servant leader to truly empower his or her workers and build a true team-of-leaders and a leadership culture where everyone is engaged, everyone leads, and everyone makes decisions that further the organization. There is a risk, of course, in moving away from the traditional hierarchy because there is always a risk when leaders give up control, but when we begin to change our mindset and realize that control is an illusion and that it is more strategic to free others to lead, we can begin to see the immense benefits of leading with a servant leader mindset. As Collins shared,

> all companies have a culture, some companies have discipline, but few companies have a *culture of discipline*. When you have disciplined people, you don't need hierarchy. When you have disciplined thought, you don't need bureaucracy. When you have disciplined action you don't need excessive controls. When you combine a culture of discipline with an ethic of entrepreneurship, you get the magical alchemy of great performance. (Collins, 2001, p. 13)

Servant leadership sets the stage for achieving great performance. It is about maximizing the potential of all people in the organization to make their best contribution to move the company forward while enhancing the growth and potential of each employee. As servant leaders we agree with Laloux when he states that "as human beings, we are not problems waiting to be solved, but potential waiting to unfold" (Laloux, 2014, p. 46).

Conclusion

The mindset of servant leadership pulls us toward particular organizational structures, those that encourage all within the organization to lead while creating an open, transparent, and empowering environment. Though servant leadership can function within any organizational structure it will be hindered by forms that require a strict separation between leaders and followers and those that expect high levels of leader control over followers. Organizational forms need to facilitate the leveraging of servant leadership power so that all in the organization can be empowered to lead. It is to this leveraging of servant leader power that we now draw our attention.

Icon in Figs. 10.1, 10.2, 10.3, 10.4 and 10.5 made by iconnice from www.flaticon.com.

References

Bakke, D. W. (2005). *Joy at work: A revolutionary approach to fun on the job*. Seattle, WA: PVG.

Blanchard, K., & Hodges, P. (2005). *Lead like Jesus: Lessons from the greatest leadership role model of all time*. Nashville, TN: W Publishing Group.

Collins, J. (2001). *Good to great: Why some companies make the leap … and others don't*. New York, NY: HarperCollins Publishers.

Dweck, C. S. (2016). *Mindset: The new psychology of success* (2nd ed.). New York, NY: Ballantine Books.

Greenleaf, R. K. (1977). *Servant leadership: A journey into the nature of legitimate power and greatness*. New York, NY: Paulist Press.

Laloux, F. (2014). *Reinventing organizations: A guide to creating organizations inspired by the next stage of human consciousness*. Brussels: Nelson Parker.

Mintzberg, H. (1989). *Mintzberg on management: Inside our strange world of organizations*. New York, NY: The Free Press.

11

Leveraging Servant Leadership Power

Power is defined as the ability a person has to act in a given situation. It is essential that leaders understand how power is necessary and is to be used for effective leadership. Unfortunately, servant leaders are so fearful of the abuse of power that they have often viewed power in totally negative terms. One result of this is that these leaders refuse to admit that they have leadership power and therefore must use that power to benefit others while also fulfilling the mission and vision of the organization. In this chapter, various theories of power will be presented and contrasted to create a practical and unique view of the leveraged power of servant leadership.

What Is Power and Why Must Servant Leaders Accept and Use It?

As servant leaders, how are we to understand the role of power in our attempts to create change? A thought experiment may be helpful here. Please review the lists in Table 11.1 and consider the contrast between those listed in Group A and those listed in Group B. Which of them (Group A or B) possesses, or possessed, the most power?

© The Author(s) 2018
J. Laub, *Leveraging the Power of Servant Leadership*, Palgrave Studies in Workplace
Spirituality and Fulfillment, https://doi.org/10.1007/978-3-319-77143-4_11

Table 11.1 Leader comparison chart

Group A	Group B
Mother Teresa	Adolf Hitler
Gandhi	The British Empire
A local church pastor	The CEO of a multinational company
The mayor of a mid-sized town	A state senator
The complete list of US registered voters	The president of the United States
An unknown housewife and mother	A famous actress
You	Others

What may become clear as you work through these contrasts is that power can be viewed through different lenses. Power may be seen through the lens of leadership position or through the platform of personal leadership influence. Power may be viewed as displayed within an organization or it can be something that individuals may possess within themselves. Power can also be judged by its outcome as we contrast the effects of the work of Mother Teresa with the work of Adolf Hitler, for instance, or the success of Gandhi's efforts against the might of the British Empire. We can also view power through the lens of feeling disempowered as some may have viewed *Others* as having more power than *You*. Power is essential to leadership, and understanding what it is and how it works is necessary to use it to create positive change and enhance human flourishing.

Defining Power: Three Approaches

Let's consider different ways that leadership writers have defined the term *power*. There are three main approaches; first, a coercive type of influence that one has over another to force compliance; second, an ability to influence others positively or negatively; or, third, power as the ability to act or make something happen.

Power as coercive influence. Most assume, like Rost (1993), that power is somehow coercive by nature. Rost states that leadership "is not coercive, meaning that it is not based on authority, power or dictatorial actions" (p. 107) suggesting that, in his view, power is directly related to coercion. Rost also shares a definition from Jacobs that "power is defined … as the capacity to deprive another needed satisfactions or benefits, or to inflict 'costs' on him for noncompliance with an influence attempt" (Rost, 1993, p. 131). Dahl's definition of power clearly fits within this power-over approach. He states that a leader has power when "A has power over B to the extent that he can get B to do something that B would otherwise not do" (as cited in Mintzberg, 1983, p. 5). This is a view of power where it is seen as foundationally negative bringing a corrosive effect on the targets of power as well as the wielders of power. Lord Action's famous phrase "power corrupts, and absolute power corrupts absolutely" fits well within this coercive understanding of power.

Power as positive or negative influence. Others see power as influence over others that may be negatively or positively displayed. Antonakis et al. (2004) believe that "power refers to the means leaders have to potentially influence others" and that "the ability to lead others requires that one has power" (p. 5). Lussier and Achua (2001) agree, stating that "power is the leader's potential influence over followers" (p. 340). Mintzberg (1983) defines power within the context of organizational leadership stating that "power is defined as ... the capacity to effect (or affect) organizational outcomes" (p. 4). He then goes on to explain that the French word for power, *pouvior*, serves as both the noun *power* and the verb *to be able* instructing us that "to have power is to be able to get desired things done, to effect outcomes" (p. 4). This suggestion leads us to a third, and preferred, way of defining power.

Power as the ability to act. Clawson (2003) states that "power is the ability to make something happen ... when you make a change in something, you are exerting power in that thing" (p. 35). Power viewed in this way is not power *over* someone to punish or reward or to exert a level of influence. Power is simply the ability to act in a given situation. Kanter (as cited in Mintzberg, 1983) captures this foundational way of viewing power as "the ability to *do*" (p. 4). If one can act in a given situation, then one has power within that given situation. This act of power does not require a position of authority or the permission of another, but rather the personal belief and ability one possesses to take action to create some kind of change, for self or for others. It is precisely this type of power that servant leaders are called to accept and exercise for the good of others. Power seen as the ability to act must also consider how that power is exercised. If the leader has power by nature of the authority granted by an organizational or political position, then that positional leader may act toward the benefit of others or act to withhold benefit from others. The leader may act in either way. The servant leader, by definition, will choose to act in a way that promotes the good of those led over the self-interest of the leader. Therefore, power exists and the servant leader must use that power to benefit those he or she leads and the organization they serve.

Sources and Types of Power

There are two sources of power—positional and personal (Lussier and Achua, 2001). Positional power is that granted to leaders through their position or role within an organization. This power comes from authority granted to the leader since it belongs to them solely due to their current position level and is removed once their position changes. Positional power relates most to the first three of French and Raven's five types of power (as cited in Johnson, 2016):

1. Legitimate power—authority received due to a leadership position or role
2. Coercive power—the ability to punish others or withhold something of value
3. Reward power—the ability to give something of value to others

Legitimate power refers to the authority granted to a positional leader due to their role within an organization or group. This authority is granted with the full expectation that the leader will use it to benefit the organization. This puts the servant leader in a challenging tension since they are expected to focus on the success of the enterprise while their mindset tells them to focus on the well-being of those led. The servant leader, of course, must fulfill the duties of their job and leadership role and use the authority granted for the good of the organization. The servant leader, however, fully believes that the best path toward the good of the organization runs through a commitment to focus on the good of the workers. Within this tension, the servant leader must find a way to use legitimate power while maintaining a servant-minded view of their leadership role.

Coercive power is alive and well in our organizations today as evidenced by Greene's book, *The 48 Laws of Power*, in which he presents a Machiavellian and autocratic view of leadership power. He begins the preface of his book with this quote:

> The feeling of having no power over people and events is generally unbearable to us—when we feel helpless we feel miserable. No one wants less power; everyone wants more. In the world today, however, it is dangerous to seem too power hungry, to be overt with your power moves. We have to seem fair and decent. So we need to be subtle—congenial yet cunning, democratic yet devious. (Greene, 1998, p. xvii)

Note the Machiavellian manner of looking at power as the inevitable desire of each leader along with the need to keep up appearances that might suggest the opposite. A sample of just a few of the *48 Laws* from Greene's nationally best-selling book provides a flavor of this view of power.

Law 2: Never Put Too Much Trust in Friends, Learn How to Use Enemies (be wary of friends—they will betray you more quickly).

Law 3: Conceal Your Intentions (keep people off-balance and in the dark by never revealing the purpose behind your actions).

Law 7: Get Others to do the Work for You, But Always Take the Credit (use the wisdom, knowledge, and legwork of other people to further your own cause).

Law 8: Make Other People Come to You—Use Bait If Necessary (when you force the other person to act, you are the one in control).

Law 11: Learn To Keep People Dependent on You (make people depend on you for their happiness and prosperity and you have nothing to fear). Never teach them enough so that they can do without you.

Law 12: Use Selective Honesty and Generosity to Disarm Your Victim (once your selective honesty opens a hole in their armor, you can deceive and manipulate them at will) (Greene, 1998, pp. ix–x).

There is little subtlety in Greene's view of coercive power as a means to success for leaders who work from an autocratic (self-power) mindset. This view of power operates within many organizations today and is one key cause for low levels of employee engagement.

Reward power relates more to a paternalistic or parental mindset of leadership that, within its negative view, will withhold reward (negative reinforcement) while, in its positive view, will provide it (positive reinforcement). The leader is the one with the power to dispense or deny rewards and has the ability to use these external incentives to meet the needs of the leader or the organization.

In contrast to positional power, personal power is granted to a leader by the followers and is based on the behavior of the leader and how that leader relates to the followers. This level of power and influence most connects to the final two types of power from French and Raven's list (as cited in Johnson, 2016):

4. Expert power—power derived from a leader's skill and knowledge
5. Referent power—power derived from a leader's personal charisma and the ability to relate positively to followers

Greenleaf framed this topic of power within three types: coercive power, manipulative power, and persuasion as power. He believed that "coercive power exists because certain people are granted (or assume) sanctions to impose their will on others … to exploit or bring pressure to bear on others" (as cited in Spears, 1998, p. 83). Manipulative power, in contrast, "rests more on plausible rationalizations than on the threat of sanctions or on pressure. People are manipulated when they are guided by plausible rationalizations into beliefs or actions that they do not fully understand" (p. 84). Greenleaf found both of these forms of power unacceptable for the servant leader and instead promoted a form of power based on persuasion that encourages an open, honest, and mutual exchange of influence between leader and follower within a partnership relationship. Within this type of power he believed that "both leader and follower respect the autonomy and integrity of the other and each allows and encourages the other to find his or her own intuitive confirmation of the rightness of the belief or action" (p. 85).

When those espousing a servant leadership view respond negatively to the concept of power they are reacting to power of a coercive or manipulative kind. De Pree's book (1997), *Leading Without Power*, is an example of this reaction. These leaders see the abuse of power and the harm done to others from autocratic leaders who seek to impose their will as they use legitimate power to force or manipulate others to bend to their will. It should be clear that the servant leader will seek to move beyond coercive or reward power to a servant-minded power and will even move beyond a power based on expertise or personal charisma. The servant leader seeks a different kind of power, a servant power based on adult partnership and mutual obligation.

Servant Power

When a leader chooses to serve others first a new and unique kind of power is released. This servant power certainly includes the process of persuasion as Greenleaf suggested since the leader will use persuasion to influence rather than coercion or manipulation. The servant leader will be authentic in presenting all relevant facts and options to followers while seeking mutual understanding and agreement, if agreement can be obtained. The leader will resist forcing their will on followers to gain a short-term advantage or to win at the expense of the well-being of others. Consider a time when you had someone who believed in you before you had provided a reason to believe. Someone, a parent, teacher, coach, or friend, decided to trust in you and believe the best of you and your potential. What did this servant act do for you? For those who experience this, a power is released opening up new ways of seeing ourselves and new ways of acting in the world. We begin to see potential we never saw before. We begin to believe in ourself and our growing abilities. We believe because someone believed in us first. This power of personal belief is created by a leader who decides to value you and serve you ahead of their own self-interest. When a servant leader views you as not just a follower or an employee, but as a valued partner, what does this do to your own view of your work and potential contribution? When I am a partner, I co-own the enterprise; I am committed at a higher level to the outcomes agreed upon and I am willing to engage more, serve more, work more, and love more.

Carl Jung stated that "where love rules, there is no will to power; and where power predominates, there love is lacking" (as cited in Hagberg,

1994, p. iii). With servant power we can possess both power and love together.

To the oft, and recently, quoted phrase from Lord Acton "power corrupts and absolute power corrupts absolutely," Crouch (2013) responds with a different perspective, "love transfigures power. Absolute love transfigures absolute power" (p. 48). Crouch's idea is that power should be seen as a gift, a creative force rather than a coercive one. Power, according to Crouch (2013), "is the ability to make something of the world" (p. 4), providing people with the ability to advance either human flourishing or human languishing. Power, like leadership, can be used for good or for evil. It is not inherently prone to evil but can create an amazing potential for leading positive change. Nouwen (1989) states,

> what makes the temptation of power so seemingly irresistible? Maybe it is that power offers an easy substitute for the hard task of love. It seems easier to be God than to love God, easier to control people than to love people. (p. 77)

Power, guided by love, becomes a tool for building a better world and higher performing organizations. Power, guided by self-interest, can quite literally create hell on earth. The choice as to how we as leaders use our power begins with our choice of leadership mindset.

Positioning the Fulcrum to Move the World

The purpose of leadership is to create movement, to move the world. In Chap. 1 we were introduced to Archimedes and the concept of the lever. This metaphor can help us understand the key role of various mindsets in leveraging power to create leadership movement. As we apply the metaphor of the lever we must consider three distinct mindsets of leadership that serve as fulcrums for leveraging leadership power. Archimedes described how the lever works to maximize the use of power or force to move an object. Where the fulcrum is placed beneath the lever relative to the weight to be moved determines how much power is required to move the object. The heavier the weight the closer to the object the fulcrum must be placed. The further away the fulcrum is placed from the object the more force is required to create the movement desired. As we apply this metaphor to servant leadership we propose that the servant mindset is in the best position to leverage the power of leaders to create the most effective movement.

The Autocratic Leadership Mindset

With an autocratic (leader first) mindset the force needed to move the weight is roughly equal to the weight to be moved. Archimedes established this in his law of the lever from his text *Equilibrium of Planes* explaining how the lever does its work. The law of the lever states that "to balance a pair of unequal weights, the weights must be placed at distances from the fulcrum that are in inverse proportion to their magnitudes" (as cited in Hirshfeld, 2009, p. 79). This leads to the diagram (see Fig. 11.1) showing that when the fulcrum is placed as shown the force being applied must be equal to the weight to be moved. This illustrates how power is used through an autocratic mindset. Autocratic leadership is about the leader first. It is a self-focused leadership (*auto* = self, *cratic* = power) that puts the leader's interests and desires first and views the workers as servants to the leader. This mindset requires a high level of force to be applied by the leader (think of Atlas holding the world on his mighty shoulders) in order to create leadership movement. Not many leaders can maintain this kind of power based on their personal characteristics, charisma, and their power to punish and reward. This is the leadership of the strong,

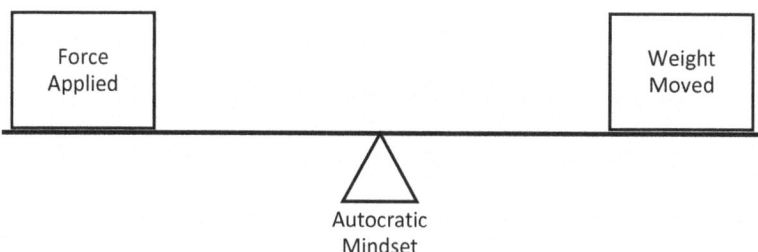

Fig. 11.1 Lever diagram for autocratic leadership

heroic leader who stands alone as the driving force of an organization's success. The image of the autocratic leader is often what people have in mind when they call for *strong* leadership to solve the seemingly impossible problems we face. We long for leaders who will fight our battles for us and who will move the world through the power of their individual genius and personal strength. To be sure, autocratic leadership works, but it carries a heavy price since it is guaranteed to create resistance against the leader's force by workers who exist, in this mindset, to serve the leader.

Some see autocratic power as the strongest, most effective type of power because it places all power into the hands of the single leader at the top of the organization. The leadership of film director Francis Ford Coppola is provided as an example from the documentary *Hearts of Darkness: A Filmmaker's Apocalypse.*

'A film director is kind of one of the last truly dictatorial posts left in a world getting more and more democratic.' He had the power since he wrote, directed, produced and paid for the film. But how much power did Coppola actually have? In the documentary, we see actor Dennis Hopper flatly refusing to play a scene as written. Coppola begs, pleads, reasons, and finally gives in and does it Hopper's way. When production falls a week behind schedule, Coppola is forced to telephone Marlon Brando in Tahiti, asking him to come a week later than planned to the shooting location. Brando tells Coppola he's booked then, so he'll just pocket the million bucks he's been advanced. After Coppola has groveled to his satisfaction, Brando finally arrives on location (when he pleases) and proceeds to show everybody who the *real* dictator is. In subsequent scenes, 'dictator' Coppola finds himself dependent on the technical skill of his cameraman, the artistic judgment of nearly everyone in the company, and the whims of his host, the Philippine government. Even with the enormous powers—unparalleled in our democratic age—at Coppola's disposal, the gofers and gaffers in his employ insist on doing things *their* way. In the hour-long documentary, we never see him give an order that is obeyed directly. Imagine, then, being a leader who really is powerless—say, the CEO of General Motors. (O'Toole, 1995, pp. 131–132)

The truth is that it takes an incredible amount of personal leadership power to force people to do anything and that kind of force rarely has the effect we anticipate. When workers worldwide are reporting low engagement levels in their work it is clear that worker engagement cannot be forced. Worker creativity cannot be manipulated. Worker commitment cannot be gained through coercive power. Only compliance, a much weaker level of engagement, can be obtained through an autocratic use of leadership power.

The Paternalistic (Parental) Leadership Mindset

The paternalistic (parental) mindset views the leader's role as that of parent and the worker's role as that of children. These roles exist mostly unacknowledged by both leaders and followers, but the dynamics are observable and powerful. The parental mindset can be either negative or positive, but the end result, in terms of power, is the same; power is focused on the leader's ability to influence the follower as a parent seeks to direct and guide a child. These resulting roles relegate workers to a dependency that keeps them from being developed as leaders and limits the organization from benefiting from the leadership potential of all. We often hear about organizations that are seen as a family where people are nurtured and cared for by their benevolent (or less-than-benevolent) leaders. Figure 11.2 shows that in keeping with the law of the lever, the fulcrum has moved closer to the weight to be moved and therefore the force required has decreased. This certainly is an improvement on the autocratic mindset, but still not an optimal leveraging of leadership power. Too much is dependent on the parental leader and the most we

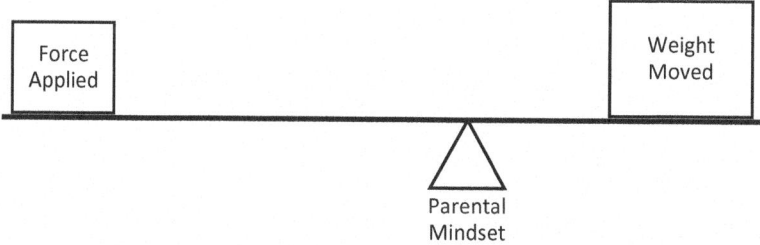

Fig. 11.2 Lever diagram for parental leadership

can hope for from our followers is faithful compliance. So, the job may get done, the hands and feet of the workers are well employed, but the deep commitment that comes from shared leadership is not realized. Parental leadership, though an improvement on the autocratic approach, limits the potential of leadership power and of organizations to perform at optimal levels. This mindset is the most prevalent in organization's today, throughout the world, and yet not well understood.

The Servant Leadership Mindset

The servant (other-focused) mindset is uniquely positioned to maximize the contribution of each and every person in the group. Through this mindset, leadership is dispersed between positional leaders and followers and the emphasis of everyone in the organization is to focus their efforts toward the benefit of others. This mindset creates an outward view rather than an inward view (The Arbinger Institute, 2016) allowing each person, regardless of position, to be empowered to assume responsibility, partnership, and ownership of organizational goals and outcomes. As seen in Fig. 11.3, the fulcrum is positioned, in this mindset, at the optimal location relative to the weight to be moved. This position allows for the greatest leveraging of force applied to create successful movement. The servant mindset leverages power to create the maximum effect.

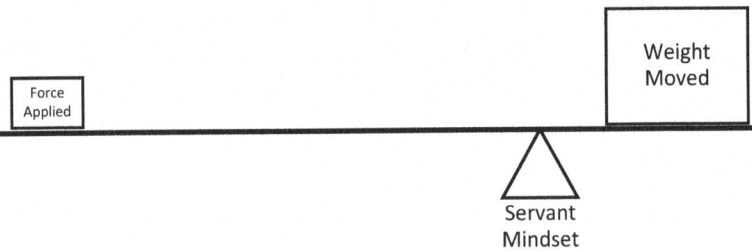

Fig. 11.3 Lever diagram for servant leadership

Servant leaders do not need to emulate Atlas or other heroic leaders in order to lead. They can use less overt power to achieve amazing movement and change. This should be encouraging news to those of us (the vast majority of potential leaders) who do not possess an elite set of impressive traits that would cause others to submit to our leadership. Through this kind of leadership mindset, all of us can take on the responsibility to lead, to effect change and to move the world. As Martin Luther King, Jr., shared, "everybody can be great ... because anybody can serve. You don't have to have a college degree to serve. You don't have to make your subject and verb agree to serve. You only need a heart full of grace. A soul generated by love" (King et al., 1998). Yes, anyone can serve and, as King suggests, anyone then can lead and lead with more effectiveness and more power.

The practice of leadership is often filled with uncertainty, chaos, and unresolved issues. The leader works with ever-changing situations, markets, and environments while dealing with the most uncontrollable factor of all—people. Therefore, the leader must be able to effectively handle high levels of ambiguity at any given time while keeping the team moving in the right direction. Leadership is both a science and an art and the wise leader will always seek the longer view, keeping today's decisions and actions in perspective in light of the vision of the group. The purpose of leadership is to move the world and our metaphor of Archimedes' lever suggests that our ability to lead, to move situations and people, and our power to act and make a lasting difference is not determined ultimately by our personal charisma or strength but by our mindset of leadership. Mindset comes first. The lever board of our leadership must be placed firmly yet accurately on a solid base, a well-positioned fulcrum, that will maximize our use of leadership power while producing the greatest and most meaningful results. To paraphrase Archimedes, give us a lever long enough and a place to stand *and* a fulcrum placed in the optimal spot, and we will move the world.

Practical Issues of Servant Power Used from a Positional Leadership Role

When a leader seeks to function from a servant mindset and also serves as a positional leader with legitimate assigned authority to act in the best interests of the organization, how does the servant leader deal with this tension? As a positional leader the servant-minded leader is expected to put the needs of the organization first while as a servant leader the needs of the followers come first. When these two fall into conflict, how is the servant leader to act? This is not just a theoretical question, but a practical one that causes some to decide that the leader must be servant-minded at times and autocratically minded at other times. This unfortunately makes servant leadership a situationally applied style rather than an underlying mindset that applies in all situations at all times.

Can Servant Power Function Together with Legitimate Power?

Some see servant leadership as illegitimate since it is assumed that the servant leader cannot use the legitimate power granted as an organizational leader and still maintain focus on the needs of the followers. It is assumed, and rightly so, that there will be conflicts between what is good for a worker and what is good for the team or for the overall organization. For instance, what is the servant leader to do when a worker is underperforming and negatively affecting the team's performance? First, the servant leader will seek to function out of a servant mindset just as any leader is expected to lead consistently out of their personal and leadership values. So, the servant leader will always value others, develop others, build community, provide leadership, share leadership, and display authenticity. All six disciplines need to be considered and displayed consistently out of a servant-minded leadership. Here is how the thinking of the servant leader might progress through the scenario of dealing with an underperforming worker:

1. I value this worker—I will believe in them and I will trust them. I believe they have incredible potential but for some reason, right now, that potential is not being realized within their current role.

2. I want to help this worker develop—what might be causing this low performance? It could be a number of things including a poor job fit, or a need for training and job clarity. Should I, as leader, provide something to this worker to help them to perform better? How can I best provide this?

3. I want to build community within the team—this worker's low performance is affecting the team's performance and morale. If other team members do not see me holding this worker accountable it will have a negative effect on the team. How can I support this individual worker while also serving the needs of the team? I must work within this tension.

4. I need to provide clear and effective leadership in this situation—I can't push off the decision and fail to act. I must provide vision and direction to the team and to this worker. I need to be fair but decisive and I need to consider the effect of this worker's poor performance on the future success of the team and the organization.

5. I must share leadership with others—I will talk over the worker's poor performance with them directly to discover their view of the situation. I will seek their input as well as the input of others to insure that I am making a decision that is in the best interest of the worker, the team, and the organization.

6. I must display and encourage authenticity—I will be honest and transparent in how I deal with the worker and the team. I will acknowledge the poor performance and make clear what is expected. I will hold the worker accountable and will be truthful in all of my communications.

Once I have reviewed this situation through this servant leadership mindset grid, I will consider the decision options available to me.

• I can terminate the poor-performing employee if it is determined that he or she is not a good fit for the job or the organization, and cannot (or will not) improve through training and job adjustment. I will continue to serve this employee by offering job transition training and opportunities and a fair severance package if appropriate. I also will be honest about why the termination decision has been made so that the employee can learn from the situation.

- I can keep the employee in the job, placing him or her on a job improvement plan that includes job adjustments, job definition, and focused training. Expectations will be made clear with written deadlines and accountability points. The employee will be part of the process of putting together and owning this plan.

Situations like these are never clean and neat and always involve difficult variables and deep emotions that make it difficult to hypothesize. Using a servant mindset does not guarantee that the employee will agree or appreciate the effort or will call our actions servant-oriented. They may see our actions as self-serving and not in their best interest at all. As servant leaders, we do our best to operate consistently out of a servant mindset realizing that our efforts ultimately may not be understood or appreciated. Leadership is hard. The point, here, is that the servant leader must make difficult, uncomfortable decisions as a part of granted positional authority but he or she must always do this through the grid of a servant mindset. A leader does not set aside a servant mindset and become autocratic (self-serving) in order to make hard decisions that followers may not understand, like, or agree with. Servant power can function alongside legitimate power and authority and it is done by maintaining a servant mindset at all times as a way of understanding the role of the leader, leadership, and those being led.

If Servant Leadership *Appears* Weak to Some, Then Is Its Power Negated?

Servant power is not negated just because it may appear to some as a weaker way to lead. Servant leadership is not weak, but possesses a leveraged type of power that actually creates a higher level of power effect for leaders and organizations. Grant (2016) presents what he calls the Sarick Effect which involves communicating from an apparent position of powerlessness. He contends that when we communicate our own flaws and approach others from a humble position they become less defensive and resistant to our ideas. People shift from being self-defensive to problem solving with us. By appearing to come from a weaker position, we actually increase our power to influence others. When someone leads with an approach that suggests that they do not have all the answers or that they have much to learn and are willing to let others teach them, an amazing dynamic occurs. People are drawn toward that leader rather than pushed away. Grant found that "being forthright about faults alters how audiences evaluate us" (p. 71). When I am open enough to present my own faults and those of my ideas, others are more apt to become an ally. In this way my weakness becomes my strength. Grant (2016) identified four benefits of leading with our limitations:

1. Leading with weakness disarms the audience.
2. Leading with limitations makes you look smart.
3. Being upfront about the downsides of your ideas makes you appear more trustworthy.
4. Being upfront about flaws leaves an audience with a more favorable assessment of your idea (pp. 69–73).

Can you see why unique benefits come from leading with limitations? Audiences are used to being sold to, but they are disarmed by someone who admits to faults and limitations. When you do, you actually appear smart and confident and able to present not only the good side of your idea but also the flaws. Also, people consider you more trustworthy if you are willing to admit faults without being forced to do so and research shows that an approach from weakness leaves people more positive about you and your ideas (Grant, 2016, p. 73).

Schein (2013) in his book, *Humble Inquiry: The Gentle Art of Asking Instead of Telling*, makes the point that "we all live in a culture of Tell and find it difficult to ask" (p. 8) The value of asking, rather than telling, especially when done in a humble way, communicates a weakness that becomes a strength. Schein shares it this way.

> Asking temporarily empowers the other person in the conversation and temporarily makes me vulnerable. It implies that the other person knows something that I need to or want to know. It draws the other person into the situation and into the driver's seat; it enables the other person to help or hurt me and, thereby opens the door to building a relationship. (p. 9)

This is a powerful concept. When I humbly and authentically ask others for an opinion, for information or to help me in some way, I approach them from a position of apparent weakness. In so doing, I empower them to take the lead. They are empowered through this exchange and my influence with them increases. I do this not by being weak, but by a willingness to *appear* weak in order to allow them the opportunity to be strong. The distinction is important. We are right to claim that servant leadership is not weak while agreeing that it can often *appear* weak and through that appearing turn into an increased level of power. Even Napoleon Bonaparte, never accused of being a servant leader, found an immediate connection to the soldiers serving under him because he was not afraid to ask for their opinions. He honestly revealed that he did not know everything but welcomed having those under him teach him what they knew and this created a loyalty and bond that could never have developed through the use of coercive power (Roberts, 2014).

So, the appearance of weakness can be a strength and the appearance of strength can be a weakness. Consider research conducted by political scientist Ivan Arreguin-Toft and reported by Gladwell (2009) on every war fought in the last 200 years between strong and weak armies. The conflicts studied only included those where the stronger army was at least ten times as powerful as the weaker army. If you assume that these much stronger armies won most of the time you would be right, but the strong armies won only 71.5% of the time. The smaller, weaker armies won a surprising 28.5% of the time. However, when Arreguin-Toft looked deeper he found that when the weaker armies acknowledged their weaker status and adopted bold, unexpected, and unconventional strategies, the weaker armies won a staggering 63.6% of the time (Gladwell, 2009, para. 4–5). The weaker army refused to fight by the rules set by the stronger army. New strategies based on speed, boldness, or engaging the enemy on a preferred battlefield often led to unexpected success. One can think of the American Revolution forces pitted against the stronger British army as a good example. As opposed to the common, accepted wisdom, the spoils do not always go to the strong. They sometimes go to the smart and the unconventional, to those who recognize that power is something that can be leveraged such that those who are weaker can succeed over those who appear to possess greater strength.

"For when I am weak, then I am strong." (2 Corinthians 12:10)

Why Servant Leaders Must Use Power: Leveraged Power

The servant leader will agree with Martin Luther King, Jr., who stated "I am not interested in power for power's sake, but I'm interested in power that is moral, that is right and that is good" (King et al., 1998). Before Albert Einstein (and other quantum thinkers) came on the scene in the early 1900s the world was satisfied with the formula $E = mv^2$; Energy = mass × velocity (squared). Consider two vehicles of 4000 pounds of mass each colliding at a velocity of 60 miles per hour. The energy produced by this collision is immense and measurable. This formula, $E = mv^2$ might represent leadership from the autocratic or parental mindsets. Organizations, led through these mindsets, have the ability to act, to meet their goals, and to become good companies. Most organizations fall in this category. Good, but not great. They are missing their full potential by limiting the effect of potential power. The energy they produce is sufficient to keep the organization moving forward, but cannot move them to the next level of exceptional performance. That kind of quantum leap will require a new formula … a totally new way of thinking about how organizations are led. Enter Albert Einstein and a new theory of relativity producing a different formula—$E = mc^2$. What changed in this formula? Just one small letter. Now we are looking at energy equaling mass times *the speed of light* (squared). Within the last half of the twentieth century this formula has led to the creation of space flight, new and devastating weapons, increased energy production, and innovations that were unthinkable prior to this new understanding of power. This new formula can represent the mindset of servant-minded leadership, with a potentially exponential increase in leadership power and effectiveness.

Healthy servant-minded organizations are powerful organizations that have found a way to tap into the awesome energy of a servant-oriented culture unleashing the incredible capacity within each individual and team. Leveraging our power through a servant mindset can unleash power that cannot be created through outdated leadership approaches. However, servant leadership is not the easy path, nor the safe path, but provides the best opportunity to maximize our leadership power, our ability to act to move the world.

Conclusion

How do mindsets change? If we desire to move from an autocratic or paternalistic mindset to a servant mindset what process might we use? This kind of change involves more than sitting through a training program, listening to a special speaker, or reading a book. No, an intentional process of critical thinking is required to challenge our underlying assumptions and consider, then practice, new ways of thinking and acting. We now move to a consideration of foundational and developmental mindshifts that can prepare us to build the kind of servant mindset to enable us to lead through a leveraged kind of power to move the world through our leadership.

References

Antonakis, J., Cianciolo, A. T., & Sternberg, R. J. (Eds.). (2004). *The nature of leadership.* Thousand Oaks, CA: Sage Publications.

Clawson, J. G. (2003). *Level three leadership: Getting below the surface* (2nd ed.). Upper Saddle River, NJ: Pearson Education, Inc.

Crouch, A. (2013). *Playing god: Redeeming the gift of power.* Downers Grove, IL: InterVarsity Press.

De Pree, M. (1997). *Leading without power: Finding hope in serving community.* San Francisco, CA: Jossey-Bass, Inc.

Gladwell, M. (2009, May 11). How David beats goliath. *The New Yorker.* Retrieved from https://www.newyorker.com/magazine/2009/05/11/how-david-beats-goliath

Grant, A. (2016). *Originals: How non-conformists move the world.* New York, NY: Penguin Books.

Greene, R. (1998). *The 48 laws of power.* New York, NY: The Penguin Group.

Hagberg, J. O. (1994). *Real power: Stages of personal power in organizations.* Salem, WI: Sheffield Publishing Company.

Hirshfeld, A. (2009). *Eureka man: The life and legacy of Archimedes.* New York, NY: Walker Publishing Company, Inc.

Johnson, C. (2016). *Organizational ethics: A practical approach* (3rd ed.). Los Angeles, CA: Sage Publications.

King, M. L., Carson, C., & Holloran, P. (1998). *A knock at midnight: Inspiration from the great sermons of Reverend Martin Luther King, Jr.* New York, NY: Intellectual Properties Management in association with Warner Books.

Lussier, R. N., & Achua, C. F. (2001). *Leadership: Theory, application, skill development.* Cincinnati, OH: South-Western College Publishing.

Mintzberg, H. (1983). *Power in and around organizations.* Englewood Cliffs, NJ: Prentice-Hall, Inc.

Nouwen, H. J. M. (1989). *In the name of Jesus: Reflections on Christian leadership.* New York, NY: Crossroad Publishing Company.

O'Toole, J. (1995). *Leading change: Overcoming the ideology of comfort and the tyranny of custom.* San Francisco, CA: Jossey-Bass Publishers.

Roberts, A. (2014). *Napoleon: A life.* New York, NY: Penguin Books.

Rost, J. C. (1993). *Leadership for the twenty-first century.* Westport, CT: Praeger.

Schein, E. H. (2013). *Humble inquiry: The gentle art of asking instead of telling.* San Francisco, CA: Berrett-Koehler Publishers.

Spears, L. C. (Ed.). (1998). *The power of servant-leadership: Essays by Robert K. Greenleaf.* San Francisco, CA: Berrett-Koehler Publishers.

The Arbinger Institute. (2016). *The outward mindset: Seeing beyond ourselves.* Oakland, CA: Berrett-Koehler Publishers, Inc.

12

Mindshifting: The Critical Thinking Leader

How does a leader shift their underlying assumptions about leadership? How might someone transform their thinking from an autocratic or paternalistic view toward a servant-minded view? Leadership mindshifts must take into consideration the leader's view of himself or herself, the leader's view of the led, and the leader's view of the true purpose of leadership. In this chapter, models of critical thinking will be applied to the practical challenge of addressing and changing our mental models to leverage and increase our servant leadership power.

When Greenleaf developed his philosophy of servant leadership and put it into writing back in 1970 he may have had in mind an incident that occurred in his high school days in Terre Haute, Indiana. The principal of his high school, Orville Conner, was an older, awkward man who possessed an odd manner of walking causing students to call him old step-and-a-half. Mr. Conner did not relate well to students and they saw him as distant and harsh. As often happens in such situations, a pattern developed where both principal and students avoided contact, accepted the tense relationship, and adopted it as unfortunate yet normal. That is, until Jerry Fitzgerald challenged this attitude and mindset. Here is how Greenleaf himself describes the situation.

© The Author(s) 2018
J. Laub, *Leveraging the Power of Servant Leadership*, Palgrave Studies in Workplace Spirituality and Fulfillment, https://doi.org/10.1007/978-3-319-77143-4_12

At a Hi-Y meeting Jerry brought up the subject of our attitude toward Mr. Conner. He said, in effect, 'Our negative feelings toward this old man are going to cast a shadow on our memories of this place. What do you say that we decide to like him and show it?' There was some discussion of this and the group bought it … the first thing we did was to decide that we would dedicate the next year's yearbook … to him and that in other tangible ways we would show our good feeling for him. The effect of this was spectacular. The old man changed in attitude and appearance. Perhaps it was our attitude, but he seemed to mellow. There was often a smile on his face. It was a good year. (As cited in Frick, 2004, p. 58)

What Greenleaf describes is a group mindset, an attitude based on a set of shared assumptions. The students concluded, based on good evidence, that Mr. Conner was a negative old man, that he would not change, that the students were not responsible for the way he acted, and that the situation was beyond their power to change but Jerry Fitzgerald challenged this mindset. He acknowledged the problem but suggested that maybe, just maybe, the students could initiate a change in *their* attitude and this, of course, is what happened. The students acted as leaders to create a mindset change that saw themselves not as victims but as people with the power to act. After this experience and after completing college, Greenleaf went on to a long career with AT&T serving as head of management research. He retired in 1964 and six years later produced what he called his little essay (Greenleaf, 1970). Until his death in 1990, he challenged prevalent and ingrained assumptions on leadership, recommending new ways for leaders to think and act. He challenged mindsets, settled ways of thinking that were assumed to be true, but upon reflection were found to be insufficient or even false.

As seen throughout this book, three distinct mindsets of leadership—autocratic, paternalistic, and servant—have always existed. It is the choice of all leaders as to which paradigm they will adopt. Becoming aware of the existence of these mindsets is the first necessary step in the process. In this chapter, we explore a pathway to develop a new servant leadership mindset. Before moving on to this pathway, we begin with an explanation of a process of critical thinking to identify, challenge, and then reshape our underlying assumptions. A foundational choice of focus between others or self is considered as the beginning point of this mindset choice. We then review three foundational mindsets that prepare a leader to enter into a true servant mindset:

1. A growth versus fixed mindset
2. A giver versus taker mindset
3. A Theory Y versus Theory X mindset

With these three foundational mindsets in play we then explore four specific servant leadership mindset choices that lead to six servant leadership disciplines or behaviors. These actions will then encourage preferred performance outcomes for the leader and the organization. The *Mindset Pathways Model* will guide us through this process and is displayed in full at the conclusion of the chapter. Our goal is to create a pathway for any leader who desires to create a servant leadership mindset to move from where they are to where they desire to be. Mindsets are not static and fixed. They can be changed based on our ability and willingness to think critically, challenge our own belief systems, and explore our underlying assumptions.

The Critical Thinking Leader: Understanding Mindsets

A mindset is a collection of assumptions about how the world works. It is a way of seeing that defines our reality and largely determines how we think and act. Some have called these mindsets mental models (Senge 1990), paradigms (Barker, 1993), or worldviews (Sire, 2009). Our leadership understanding and practice is determined by the way we see ourselves, how we view others, and how we understand the world around us. Mindsets involve the concept of perspective and point of view. They are powerful frameworks made up of assumptions and attitudes that determine ultimately how we view the world and how we act in the world. Mindsets allow us to see and they also keep us from seeing. Mindsets appear to *be* reality, but actually they reflect a reality, our own reality, one that can and should be challenged by new learning and new experiences. Mindsets appear to be the way that things are and we therefore accept them as given. We don't tend to question them because they seem so natural, so obvious. They serve as reflections of reality, not reality itself.

This becomes clear when we consider differences of culture. For instance, people of one culture (Culture A) will find it completely natural to look another person in the eyes and speak to them in direct, declarative statements. This is viewed within Culture A as a good and natural manner of communicating that conveys confidence, trust, and responsible action. People from another culture (Culture B) will find it completely natural to look down when talking to someone, especially if they are speaking to someone with authority or someone deserving of high respect. This act of deference is viewed in Culture B as a good and effective manner of communicating that conveys respect, esteem, and responsible social behavior. Our cultural view determines ways of thinking about good and effective communication. Our culture also places values on specific behaviors that tell us what behaviors are good and right in given situations. These cultural differences reflect strong, ingrained mindsets that seem to define reality even if that reality creates limitations in effectiveness.

Brookfield (1987) states that critical thinking "involves calling into question the assumptions underlying our customary, habitual ways of thinking and acting and then being ready to think and act differently on the basis of this critical questioning" (p. 1). He provides three steps for becoming critical thinking leaders.

Step 1: Identify your underlying assumptions
Step 2: Challenge your assumptions
Step 3: Consider and test alternatives ways of thinking and acting

He first challenges us to identify our underlying assumptions. This is easier said than done since assumptions like these seem so natural to us that we don't even know they exist. However, leaders can do this by finding people who will speak truth into their lives. They also can conduct assessments in their organization to determine how people are experiencing their leadership. All leaders have blind spots so they must be intentional in seeking data and then reflecting deeply on the results to identify what unknown assumptions might be driving their leadership actions. Once assumptions are identified they can then be questioned and challenged. If leaders assume that their workers are undisciplined and lazy and if not controlled will take advantage of the organization, their resulting behavior will be suspicion and control oriented resulting in poor communication, fear, and lack of positive energy in the workplace. Challenging these assumptions, by choosing to see their workers as capable and motivated will serve to change the leader's behavior toward them. Once leader's assumptions have been reviewed and challenged, they can consider alternate ways of thinking and acting toward those they lead. If they choose to trust their workers and believe in their potential, they will delegate more, control less, and relate more positively to them. It all begins with a willingness to identify and challenge our underlying assumptions about leadership, ourselves, and those we lead and then experiment with different ways of thinking and acting to create new foundational assumptions to serve our leadership, and those we lead, better. The first foundational mindset we need to consider is whether we tend to be more focused on self or on others. This is the first step on the mindset pathway and is critical to moving toward a servant leader mindset.

The Foundational Mindset Focus (Others vs. Self)

Leaders sometimes share that their people are the organization's most important asset but this claim, and the assumptions underlying it, need to be reconsidered. Leaders can believe that if they provide competitive salaries and special perks to employees then they are taking care of their people, but when a leader puts the organization and the leader's vision first before the well-being of the workers they are living out a foundational focus toward self over others. Once this focus is set, people become a means to an end and abuse does not follow far behind. Consider this story from the shake-up that erupted at Uber in 2017.

Uber's Attempts to Change Their Culture

In February of 2017, Susan Fowler, a former engineer at Uber, went public with allegations of sexism and sexual harassment, creating a shock wave through the company that resulted in two investigations led by former Attorney General Eric Holder and the resignation of the president and founder, Travis Kalanick. Chief human resource officer, Liane Hornsey, who came to Uber one month before Fowler's accusations, was charged to lead the culture change efforts in response to Holder's recommendations. Uber had created a culture of fear variously described by employees as "abusive, belittling, mean, aggressive, high-pressure, combative, all consuming" where "work becomes a blood sport" (as cited in O'Donovan & Anand, 2017, para. 24). Changes instituted by Hornsey involved small efforts like serving free dinner at an earlier time so that people would not feel pressure to stay late, to corporate wide changes like reworking the 14 corporate values of the company. Hornsey stated that executives at Uber "know that we need to put our people first and know that this is an existential issue for us" (as cited in O'Donovan & Anand, 2017, para. 65). Executives had been "shaken" and "shocked" at the upheaval within the organization and therefore were open in a new way to these changes. Only time will tell if a huge organization of 15,000 employees can make the changes necessary to see people not as objects to be used, but as partners to be served. Hornsey shares,

> 'I have talked to people … who felt overworked, who felt concerned, who felt heartbroken by some of the things that have happened,' Hornsey said. 'I have to be honest with you. There are people that have been panicked and there are people that have been anxious. If any one person feels like that, it's one person too many. My job is to turn this into a kind and compassionate and thoughtful company that puts its people first.' (As cited in O'Donovan & Anand, 2017, para. 71)

What this teaches us is that organizations can go through a traumatic life-changing event much like an individual leader and this trauma can become a catalyst to pursue new ways of thinking and acting. However, the cost to individuals and the cost to organizations can be extreme. Stress-related diseases, broken marriages, depression, and other mental health issues are a deep price to pay for any individual worker or leader. The time, energy, effort, and financial cost that Uber bears through this forced change is a huge distraction from its mission. Can leaders see the need for personal and organizational change *before* such costly consequences are experienced?

Leadership involves having a vision for change, having the courage to act toward that change, mobilizing others to join in pursing change, and then working together to see the vision become a reality. Leaders must do the deep and hard work of seeking personal and organizational health as a prerequisite for successfully pursing their mission and vision. This is a foundational commitment that wise leaders will make and it takes a radical intention that first defines organizational and leadership health and then commits to pursuing it at all cost. This requires that leaders look within, deeply within, themselves to explore their own unhealthy tendencies toward serving self that risk derailing their future leadership. Leaders must accept that they have a tendency toward self-first attitudes and commit to addressing these attitudes and actions for the health of their workers, for their organization and for themselves.

The Weakness of a Self-First Mindset

Though there is evidence that even young children have a willingness to serve and give to others, there is little doubt that people have a tendency to be preoccupied with and protective of self. On a basic level our safety depends on this natural bent. There is danger in the world and it is wise to acknowledge it and prepare proper and appropriate defenses. Our parents drill this into us, *be careful, watch out, don't go anywhere with a stranger.* These are wise warnings and we grow up learning how to manage our natural fight or flight responses. These responses are governed by our lower brain stem, the basic response system of our brains. When we haven't trained our critical thinking skills we are often at the mercy of this lower brain response system and though this can protect us from harm in threatening situations it also can cause unwise behavior in more complex situations. It is our higher brain that allows us to reason and critically consider what is really going on and what assumptions we bring to a given situation.

In August of 2017 Brian McKinney and Sam Vonderheide hiked to the top of Mount Whitney in California. When making a turn in the trail, they looked up to see a full grown mountain lion facing them from a ridge just 15 feet above them. Initially their fight or flight response kicked in providing two immediate options: challenge the mountain lion (not a great idea even though they outnumbered the lion) or run away as fast as they could. Fortunately for these two hikers, they resisted lower brain options and allowed their brains to kick into a higher, more effective gear. Their higher brain reasoned that they would be no match to fight a powerful mountain lion and that if they ran away it would trigger a natural hunting response in the mountain lion and he would likely give chase. What they decided was to stay calm and slowly back away from the big cat avoiding the conflict and serious harm. It was their higher thinking capacity that allowed them to resist a basic fight or flight response that could have proven deadly (Bittel, 2017).

When the self is our primary focus and we are in self-protective mode, our options are extremely limited. We see ourselves as the primary consideration and others as either helping us or hurting us. We limit the idea of partnership to a one-sided working relationship where I expect you to help me accomplish what I desire and need rather than seeing partnership as a way to learn from each other, give to one another, and create new possibilities out of the relationship. A self-first posture is a basic belief that I am the center of the universe, everything should revolve around me, and others are objects to be used to further my own ends.

An Outward versus an Inward Mindset

The Arbinger Institute (2016) creates a distinction between an outward mindset and an inward mindset. These mindsets, as all mindsets do, apply to both leaders and organizations. Organizations tend to take on the mindset of their leaders and the organizational culture reflects these underlying assumptions. An *inward* mindset is focused on self and views others as objects. "Those that can help me, I see as vehicles. Those that make things more difficult for me, I see as obstacles. Those whose help wouldn't matter become irrelevant to me" (p. 30). When a leader possesses an *outward* mindset they see others as valued people with unique needs, objectives, and challenges. Leaders with this mindset consider the needs of others first over their own needs. An inward mindset creates a focus based on what others can do for me and is concerned with how others impact me while an outward mindset focuses on the group's mission and those I lead.

Developing a more outward mindset even affects my ability to change my mindset.

> This capability—to change the way I see and work with others regardless of whether they change—overcomes the biggest impediment to mindset change; the natural, inward-mindset inclination to wait for others to change before doing anything different oneself. (The Arbinger Institute, 2016, p. 94)

With an outward mindset I do not wait for others to change. I recognize that as a leader I must act, put aside my own resistance and my own needs and create the change that most positively impacts others. Since "widespread mindset change happens in large measure in response to those who change first" (The Arbinger Institute, 2016, p. 101) leaders must act first rather than wait on others.

When I focus on others I open myself to new opportunities that are not limited by my focus on self. As Zander and Zander state, "a person stands in the great space of possibility in a posture of openness, with an unfettered imagination for what can be" (Zander & Zander, 2000, p. 19). These new possibilities come, in part, from focusing on others to gain their insights and then work with them to create new assumptions. Consider how two marketing people, visiting Africa for the first time many years ago, viewed the same situation very differently.

> A shoe factory sends two marketing scouts to a region of Africa to study the prospect for expanding business. One sends back a telegram saying,
> SITUATION HOPELESS STOP NO ONE WEARS SHOES
> The other writes back triumphantly,
> GLORIOUS BUSINESS OPPORTUNITY STOP THEY HAVE NO SHOES
> (Zander & Zander, 2000, p. 9)

What one person views as hopeless another views as an amazing opportunity. What is your main focus in life? Is it more on yourself or is it more on others? Certainly we all consider both, but where is our primary motivation directed? Is it to serve others first, even at our own expense, or to serve ourself first, even at the expense of others? This foundational focus serves as the beginning of our mindset pathway leading to three developmental mindset choices.

Developmental Leadership Mindsets

Three developmental mindsets are presented here as a way to build from the foundational focus of others over self. A tension exists for the leader who may desire to serve others first, but is bound by underlying assumptions that drive them toward self-protection and self-interest. These developmental mindsets can assist us to move toward a more servant-oriented mindset.

A Growth versus Fixed Mindset

A study by Heslin, VandeWalle, and Latham determined that "many managers do not believe in personal change" (as cited in Dweck, 2016, p. 139) either for themselves or for their workers. As a result, they look for people with established talent rather than people who know how to learn, grow, and change. Dweck (2016) calls this a *fixed* mindset which she defines as a belief that intelligence and abilities are fixed and cannot change in any meaningful way. This fixed way of thinking leads to protecting what you have (self-protection), a fear of failure, blaming others, and avoidance of new challenges. In contrast, a *growth* mindset is a belief that people can improve, learn, develop themselves, do better, bring more effort to improve performance, and learn something new. So, the first critical developmental mindset is to believe that you as a leader, and those who work for you, can change. You are not fixed in your level of intelligence or your competencies. You can learn new ways of thinking, acting, and behaving. You are not stuck in a limited set of leadership traits but you have rich potential with the ability and responsibility to improve and change toward that potential.

Growth mindset leaders do not claim to be the genius hero or attempt to hire geniuses. Instead, they work to build a culture of growth and development and they hire people who desire to learn and change. If you are open to new learning, then you can admit to failure and are willing to ask others for help to learn new things. You are able and willing to adopt a humble stance to allow others to lead and grow. Dweck tells us that "people who work in growth-mindset organizations have far more trust in their company and a much greater sense of empowerment, ownership and commitment" (2016, p. 143) and are therefore willing to work beyond expectations and go the extra mile. To engage servant-oriented mindsets, work to develop a growth mindset that accepts your ability to change how you view the world, how you view leadership, and how you view those you lead.

A Giver versus Taker Mindset

Grant (2013) introduces three mindsets he presents as three kinds of people: givers, takers, and matchers. He claims that "every time we interact with another person at work, we have a choice to make: do we try to claim as much value as we can, or contribute value without worrying about what we receive in return" (p. 4)? Givers are people who desire to give more than they get while takers are the opposite. Takers must get more than they give in any transaction or they have failed. Life, for the taker, is a competition, a battle where there are winners and losers and the taker never intends to lose. Givers see life as an opportunity to create value, to add something that benefits others whether it be lending a hand, providing needed resources, or making introductions and relational connections.

Matchers are those who give, but give with an expectation of reciprocity. They choose to give, but expect life to be fair and therefore reciprocal giving is expected in return. This commitment to fairness and justice drives the matcher's giving to be conditional with expectations attached. When Grant (2013) studied engineers and how often they gave to others he discovered that

> the most productive were those who gave often—and gave more than they received. These were the true givers, and they had the highest productivity and the highest status: they were revered by their peers. By giving often,

engineers built up more trust and attracted more valuable help from across their work group—not just from the people they helped. (p. 59)

Developing an attitude of giving, *true* giving with no strings attached, creates a mindset that prepares a leader to lead through a servant mindset. The leader views himself or herself as a giver, more than a taker or matcher, who is willing to give to others expecting nothing in return.

A Theory Y versus Theory X Mindset

McGregor (1960) developed the Theory X-Theory Y concept in which he defined two distinct ways managers choose to view their workers. Through a Theory X view, managers view workers as basically lazy, uncommitted to their work, avoiding responsibility and leadership. A leader with this view determines that the worker must be coerced, controlled, and directed in order to maintain a basic level of work performance. In contrast, within a Theory Y view managers choose to view workers as open to taking responsibility, able to provide creative ideas, and willing to commit to a vision and direction they believe in. Each of these two beliefs has outcomes that ultimately become a virtuous or negative cycle. If the manager sees the worker through a Theory X lens, they will treat the worker in a controlling and distrustful way. These behaviors by the manager will result in workers withdrawing relationally and lowering their commitment to the leader and to the work. This results in lower performance to which the manager responds with higher levels of coercion and control. The work relationship and worker performance spirals down. If the manager views the worker through a Theory Y lens, they treat the worker with respect, trust, and positive expectation. They give the worker a voice and seek their ideas and feedback. Instead of suspicion they treat the worker with positive regard. The worker then is drawn toward a relationship with the leader responding with increased engagement, greater job satisfaction, and higher performance. This, in turn, brings out more positive expectations and more opportunities from the leaders and the virtuous cycle continues.

The leader who desires to develop a servant leadership mindset is well served by first engaging the foundational focus on others over self and then working on each of these three developmental mindsets, setting the stage for building servant leader mindsets to produce higher leadership and organizational performance.

Summary of the Three Developmental Mindsets

Before moving on to servant leadership mindshifts, let's review the foundational focus and the developmental mindsets that set the stage for developing a new servant mindset (Table 12.1).

Table 12.1 Key mindset choices chart

	Foundational and developmental mindset choices	Preferred mindset choice leading to a servant mindset
Foundational leadership focus	1. Focus primarily on self-interest, or 2. The interest and needs of others	Focus on the interests and needs of others over self
Three developmental mindsets		
Fixed versus growth mindset	1. Your intelligence, abilities, and potential (and that of others) are essentially fixed and unchanging, or 2. We can learn, grow, and change in all areas including our mindsets, attitudes, and beliefs	Accept that mindsets can be changed, that assumptions can be challenged, and that alternate ways of thinking and acting can be developed. We each have vast, undeveloped potential that can be increasingly realized
Givers versus takers mindset	1. Give to others without expecting anything in return 2. Give expecting a fair return 3. Get as much value as you can from others. Win at all cost	See yourself increasingly as a giver who finds value in giving to others. Giving is its own reward and does not require reciprocity
Theory X versus Theory Y mindset	1. View followers as basically lazy, undisciplined, needing to be controlled, and unwilling to take initiative and leadership 2. View followers as gifted capable of motivation, creativity, and taking responsibility	Determine to view your workers through the lens of their potential. Choose to see them as creative, knowledgeable, gifted, and willing to take on a partnership of responsibility and leadership

With these developmental mindsets in process, the leader is prepared to engage the following key servant leadership mindshifts related to how we view and act toward others, particularly those we lead. First, believe that your underlying assumptions can change, that you can move beyond reciprocity to become a true giver, and that you can choose a view of your followers that provides for their best selves to emerge.

Servant Leader Mindshifts

We will now consider four mindshifts required to create an overall servant leadership mindset. It may be helpful to remember that mindsets, or underlying assumptions about leadership, can be changed by either thinking differently or acting differently. Yes, different behaviors emerge from different ways of thinking but different ways of thinking can also develop from acting differently. Consider both methods toward creating new mindsets, a change of attitude and a change of action.

Servant Leader Mindshift 1: View and Treat Your Followers as Adult Partners

Servant leaders recognize the limitations inherent within a parental or paternalistic leadership mindset that views followers as children. Servant leaders instead build a mindset that sees their workers as fellow adult partners in the work of the organization. To move to this new mindset, consider your beliefs about the following statements:

- Followers are valued for who they are (not just for what they give to the organization).
- Followers are trained and developed by investing in their professional and personal growth (not just for skills to do their current job).
- Followers are allowed to speak, as an adult, to share their ideas, critiques, and visions.

- Followers are encouraged to lead and take responsibility for the organization's success.
- Leaders and followers are boldly honest and fully accountable for their actions and performance.
- Each person serves the needs of others over their own self-interest.
- Followers are expected to move out of a dependent child role into an adult partner role and take on the responsibility of leadership.

Servant leaders expect more from their followers. Followers are expected and allowed to speak openly and honestly as an adult would speak to another adult. They are expected and allowed to take initiative to lead themselves and others. They are expected and allowed to hold themselves and others accountable for work and team performance. They function as adult partners alongside positional leaders to seek the good of the organization as well as their own incredible potential.

Servant Leader Mindshift 2: View Trust as a Gift and a Choice

Trust is something we choose to give or choose to withhold. Without it we are left with mistrust and suspicion and once these are in play, we neither serve nor lead well. Our tendency is to separate the functions of vision, planning, and implementation believing that positional leaders at the top of the organization create the vision and set the plan while workers are charged with implementation. This separation often leads to leaders and followers blaming each other when the plan does not work out. The solution is for leaders to set vision and plans *with* those who will end up implementing the plan so that leaders and followers both understand and own the vision and the process. Dan Funk, leader of a healthcare facility, decided to begin working side by side with his employees at every level, asking for their ideas and insights. Funk found himself surprised by the fact that the ideas of others "turned out to be much better than mine and by the increased energy people brought to their work when they were empowered to implement their own ideas" (as cited in The Arbinger

Institute, 2016, p. 125). Trusting others is not easy for leaders who are directly accountable for the outcomes of their organizations and this trust requires a shift in mindset to act out of a belief that good, maybe better, ideas will come from those you lead. Funk states, "at the end of the day, my leadership effectiveness is measured not by what I am able to accomplish, but by what those whom I lead are able to accomplish" (as cited in The Arbinger Institute, 2016, p. 126). Servant leaders believe in their followers such that they are able to give them the gift of trust and allow them to create vision, plans, and implement those plans as committed adult partners.

Servant Leader Mindshift 3: View Others Through the Lens of Freedom and Potential

Control is an illusion. As leaders, we think we are controlling the behavior of others because we have authority and are in a position to tell them what to do, but the truth is that people resist being controlled but respond positively to opportunities to grow and develop new skills. We give others freedom to grow by offering them new challenges and creating high expectations. The freedom the servant leader offers is not freedom for workers to do as they please, but freedom to develop themselves, to learn new skills, and to grow toward their potential as people and as workers. Resistant compliance is the lowest level of work performance but it is the best we can hope for when we opt for controlling behavior over motivating behavior. Servant leaders shoot for a much higher target, that of personal ownership and buy-in by workers at all levels. They see their followers bringing their ideas and creativity to bear on issues that they understand best and have the highest motivation to address. Servant leaders seek to provide the same level of freedom to workers that they desire from their own supervisors since they know that this freedom provides a higher level of personal motivation to perform at their best. Leaders choose how they view their workers. Leaders choose the mindset that will guide their behaviors and the choice to view others through a lens of freedom and potential creates the best foundation for others to perform at higher levels.

Servant Leader Mindshift 4: Practice Humble Inquiry Over Telling

One of the key behaviors that servant leaders can develop in relation to those they lead is asking more than telling. Under a parental mindset of leadership, we find it natural to tell others what to do with the expectation that they will comply and the job will get done. Servant leaders know that there is a unique added power that comes from asking people for their thoughts, ideas, and effort. When one asks for someone's opinion one is placed in a humble position as the one who does not know something and needs someone else to instruct them. This simple act empowers the one asked since it places them as the one with needed expertise. This is especially powerful when the one asking is the positional leader in authority and the one being asked is in a subordinate position. Schein defines humble inquiry as "the fine art of drawing someone out, of asking questions to which you do not already know the answer, of building a relationship based on curiosity and interest in the other person" (2013, p. 2). This leadership action creates an environment where workers have a voice and feel safe speaking on issues that are important to them. As leaders, we invite others to speak and we honor them through our listening. The mindset of humility that undergirds this behavior comes from an honest view of our role and contribution to the organization while respecting and honoring the contribution that others bring. Humility is not thinking poorly of ourselves. It is thinking accurately about what we know and do not know, what we are good at and not so good at, and recognizing that we, as leaders, often have more questions than answers.

On the morning of February 1, 2003, the space shuttle *Columbia* was launched sustaining what seemed to be a minor loss of insulation foam that hit and punctured a small hole in the left wing. The *Columbia* crew spent 15 days in orbit conducting scientific experiments before beginning their descent. As they reentered the earth's atmosphere the small hole expanded leading to a failure of the wing, the breakup of the shuttle, and the death of the entire crew. An investigation was conducted to determine what happened and what might have been done to avoid this catastrophe. One conclusion was that there was a lack of effective leadership by NASA's shuttle program and the Mission Management Team. NASA leaders relied on faulty assumptions, failed to ask the right questions, or connect everyone who might have had critical input into the issue. Managers who were making the decision on the ground claimed that they were not provided information needed from the engineers. The report, however, concluded that "managers' claims that they didn't hear the engineers' concerns were due in part to their not asking or listening" (Niewoehner & Steidle, 2009, p. 17). What caused this damaging lack of communication and leadership by NASA managers? The report states that "their management techniques unknowingly imposed barriers that kept at bay both engineering concerns and dissenting views, and ultimately helped create 'blind spots' that prevented them from seeing the danger the foam strike posed" (Niewoehner & Steidle, 2009, p. 17). In analyzing this tragedy through the lens of Richard Paul's critical thinking model there were several parts of the model that were not utilized. One key missing piece was what Paul calls intellectual humility. "Intellectual humility admits to ignorance, frankly sensitive to what you do and do not know. It implies being aware of your biases, prejudices, self-deceptive tendencies and the limitations of your viewpoint and experience" (Niewoehner & Steidle, 2009, p. 17). When we fail to bring humility to our leadership interactions, processes, and decision making we run the risk of creating dangerous situations for our followers and ineffective results for our organization. In this way, humility goes beyond being a nice character trait and becomes an essential requirement for effective leadership. Servant leaders, leading from a humble stance, will ask more than tell, allowing followers to speak honestly, act boldly, and develop fully as leaders.

Servant Leader Mindsets in Action

Building these four servant leader mindsets sets the stage for leaders to, out of a strong underlying belief system, act consistently with servant leadership disciplines. These actions when displayed by leaders and integrated into the organizational culture can result in key performance enhancers that will lead to higher worker productivity and performance.

The OLA Servant Leadership Model

The six disciplines of the OLA servant leadership model help to define and frame the behaviors and actions of a leader working out of a servant mindset (Fig. 12.1).

Display Authenticity. Servant leaders display honesty and transparency through their speech and actions. They are humble, open, and accountable to others including those below them in the organization. They are willing to learn from everyone and they exhibit a deep and abiding integrity that draws people toward them, their trustworthiness, and ethical behavior.

Value People. Servant leaders value people for who they are, not just for what they provide through their current work performance. They believe in and trust others and are willing to serve them ahead of their

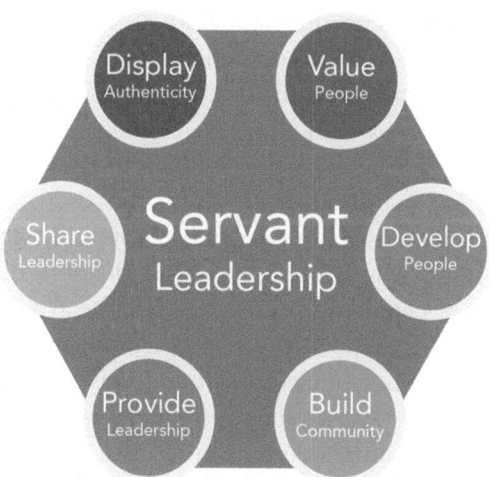

Fig. 12.1 The Organizational Leadership Assessment (OLA) servant leadership model

own self-interest. They listen in a non-judgmental and receptive manner that conveys a sense of support, caring, and commitment.

Develop People. Servant leaders refuse to use others for their own ends. They are committed to develop them to their full potential as people and professionals. To do this they provide opportunities for learning and give people what they need to be successful. They model the same appropriate behavior they expect from their workers and are consistent in providing affirmation, encouragement, and recognition.

Build Community. Servant leaders encourage the development of positive relationships. They emphasize collaborative work over competition between workers in order to create a place of belonging, sharing, and support. They value the differences of others and allow people their unique individuality while building committed teams of leaders who will serve others effectively and lead to make a difference for the group.

Provide Leadership. Servant leaders provide vision, action, mobilization, and pursue change for the good of those led and the success of the organization. Part of the vision promoted by the leader is directed toward the growth and development of each person. Our vision is to see others grow and fulfill their amazing potential. Everyone develops as a leader and all are expected and encouraged to lead.

Share Leadership. Servant leaders allow others to lead from all levels of the organization. They share the creation of vision, the use of power, and the benefits of status with all in the organization. They encourage others to live up to their responsibility as leaders to make a difference for the organization and the world.

These servant leader disciplines are in direct opposition to non-servant leadership actions that promote deceit and hiddenness, the devaluing of others, the using of people, isolation and silos, the avoidance of leadership action, and the disempowering of people. These servant actions not only produce higher worker engagement and satisfaction, but also serve to increase the use of these disciplines throughout the organization building a servant-minded culture that puts others first.

The Mindset Pathways Model

The Mindset Pathways Model provides two contrasting pathways for building either a servant or non-servant mindset and suggests that servant disciplines or behaviors are directly enabled by pre-developed mindsets. We act consistently according to our underlying assumptions and mindsets and those assumptions must be identified and challenged in order for lasting behavior change to take place (Fig. 12.2).

The OLA Model in Real Time: The Ken Rauch Story

With the development of these mindsets and the practice of these disciplines the leader is actively practicing leadership from a servant mindset and servant leadership becomes observable within the organization. These leadership behaviors lead in turn to specific performance enhancers for leaders, managers, and the workforce. Workers are provided every opportunity for high engagement, a low fear culture, high trust, and creativity and healthy communication which then leads to higher worker productivity and performance.

To illustrate these mindsets and disciplines in action, consider the Ken Rauch story where the OLA servant leadership model served as a mental model and guiding framework for Ken's decision making during a difficult organizational crisis.

Dr. Ken Rauch served as the VP of Human Resources of an aluminum smelting company based in the Midwest area of the United States that provided raw materials to the automotive parts industry. On the morning of November 29, 2007, Ken received a call from the manager of the organization's new plant, a facility built 60 miles outside of Atlanta, Georgia. There had been an explosion at the plant. On the call, the manager seemed calm and when Ken asked if everything was under control the manager stated that it was. Then the call came from the media, Bloomberg News Service, requesting a comment. Ken was the senior leader available

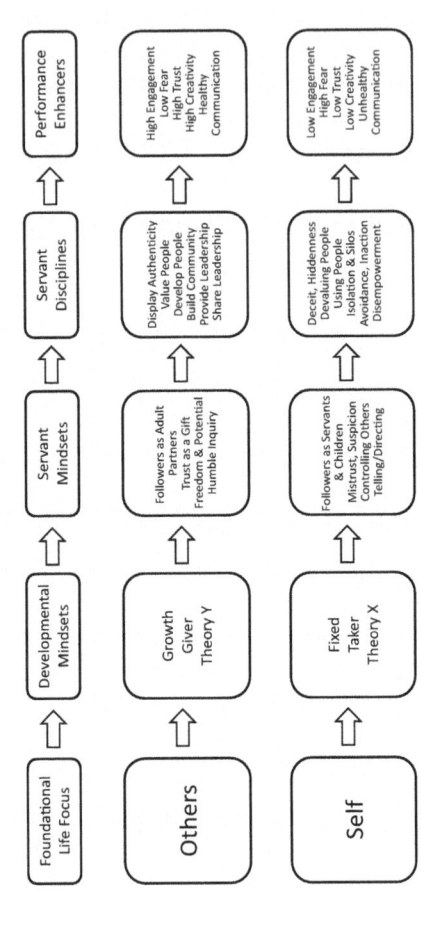

Fig. 12.2 Mindset pathways—servant versus non-servant

on site and needed to respond. Throughout the day, news continued to pour in. Three workers had been burned in the blast and were taken to the hospital. Quickly it became clear that this was a much bigger situation than Ken had realized. CNN was now showing the damaged building on national TV.

Ken moved into action and called for the company plane to take them from Indiana to Georgia and his first decision was who should make the trip with him. Instead of taking a lawyer or a senior manager who might have the most knowledge on how to avoid litigation, Ken looked for leaders who possessed the skill set to best serve the workers in Georgia. Based on their servant leadership awareness and their emotional intelligence he chose the HR Manager and the Environmental Manager. Other more senior managers were upset that they were not chosen but what was the greatest need? Loss of production? Possible litigation? Or, was it to provide what was most needed for the workers and managers on the ground in Georgia?

During the two-and-a-half-hour flight to Georgia, Ken talked and prayed with the other managers traveling with him and he asked them this question. "If you were an employee in this situation, what would you need?" He thought through the OLA servant leadership model he had learned in a doctoral course on leadership and he used it as a guide on how to effectively face the situation. The six disciplines of the model—display authenticity, value people, develop people, build community, provide leadership, and share leadership—became a grid for his thoughts and actions. He stated later that as he reflected on the model, what was complex and difficult suddenly became *easy*. He knew what he needed to focus on and he knew what he needed to do.

When they arrived at the plant, there were seven news station trucks in addition to multiple emergency vehicles in the parking lot. The explosion had been so intense that local schools were on lockdown and people were still concerned that toxic materials had been released in the blast. A huge smoke plume rose up from the building that was visible for miles. As Ken entered the building he encountered a triage situation: bags of fluid, blood, and burnt clothing. One of the men injured the worst had caught fire and starting running and before he could be stopped and was badly burned. He died a few weeks later.

The first thing Ken did was bring the employees together and work to get them connected to their families. He told them to go home and said they would have a meeting the next day at 10:00 a.m. Based on their demeanor, appearing to be in a state of shock, Ken didn't know if they would return. Other leaders in a situation like this may have isolated the employees in order to get their stories due to fear of litigation but Ken was more concerned with the employees' well-being and reuniting them with their families.

Next Ken went to face the media, asking himself, what do *they* need? He thought through how he might serve them. He asked them when the latest time was that they would need a statement. Four o'clock, he was told. He promised to pull together several people including the mayor and the plant manager to provide a statement. Ken decided not to fight the media or be suspicious of them but to be open and authentic realizing that they had real needs and a legitimate purpose to fulfill. As promised, they met with the media by 4:00. There was no grandstand-ing or stonewalling. Ken deferred to local leaders and did not try to contain or hide information. He was focused instead on displaying humility and authenticity. Due to this approach the company received positive media coverage in print and television. Ken's openness set the stage for honest reporting.

Next Ken visited the injured men in the hospital and met with their families. Over the next several days he got to know the family members well. The next morning at 10:00 he met with the workers, all of whom returned. He asked them, "What do you guys want to say? " Ken lis-tened as they shared. He let them lead and offer their suggestions as to what needed to be done to get the plant up and running. Ken and the managers had previously met to come up with a list of nine critical items to address, but the employees came up with seven of the nine items. They were becoming part of the process; they were allowed to lead. One of the most negative guys on the team came up with a timeline for devel-oping a safety response and his plan was adopted. It was a two-and-a-half-hour meeting. Ken had the patience to listen and let them share leadership to become empowered to develop their own plan and response. They took leadership, stepping up to what was expected from them. After going through some key safety principles, the employees, that same day, went back to work.

The fiancé of the man most seriously injured came up to Ken and requested to see the place where her fiancé had been injured. Remember, Ken was working from the OLA servant leadership model (i.e. authenticity, humility, valuing people) so he decided against keeping her out. He showed her the area.

Ken continued to visit the families of the injured workers. He got to know the mother of the most injured worker well. This worker appeared to be doing better but four weeks after the explosion, he died. Ken had returned to Indiana, but returned to Georgia for the funeral. The dead employee's mother invited Ken and the other company managers to come and sit with the family. Amazing, isn't it? The leaders of the organization that her son worked for and died while serving were invited to sit with the family at the funeral.

Next the Occupational Safety and Health Administration (OCEA) representative arrived from the U.S. Department of Labor to obtain a report which is always required when a workplace fatality occurs. Ken continues to think—authenticity, transparency, and humility—so instead of resisting or seeking to limit this review he calls for a wall-to-wall inspection asking that everything be looked into. This level of investigation, Ken felt, was something they owed to all of their employees. When the results came in the company was fined $5700 while a fine for a wall-to-wall inspection normally comes in at $20,000–40,000.

No one filed a lawsuit against the company after this incident. Imagine—a poor rural community and a large corporation with deep pockets and no lawsuits were filed. What allowed for this kind of outcome from a very difficult and tragic situation?

Ken shared with this author a key question. What guides our decisions in situations like this? Remember, Ken stated that it became *easy* once he was settled on his basic values and approach. He didn't have to *spin* the story or become self-protective. He didn't need to create a false positive impression. Ken decided to serve. His actions were driven by basic questions based on his values. What do my employees need? What would I want in this situation?

Ken shared "you have one chance to hit the right tone" and what you do as a leader, even in the most difficult of situations, comes out of what you believe and who you are (Rauch, personal communication September 16, 2017). We as leaders always have a choice: react to others with suspicion and mistrust or with openness and trust. With a servant mindset we have a framework to guide us, as it guided Ken, to take bold action to serve for the good of the followers and for the good of the organization.

Steps to Move into and Through a Mindset Change

When beginning or working through a mindset change, consider this seven-step process as a helpful guide.

Step 1: Develop Awareness of Your Current Mindsets

Seek to identify and understand your current mental models about leadership and organization gained from your own leaders and past experiences. Consider that there will be blind spots that need to be revealed through surveys or other ways of collecting data on how others perceive your leadership. Assume that these blind spots exist and be intentional about uncovering them and learning more about your previously unidentified leadership assumptions.

Step 2: Consider the Implications of Your Current Mindsets

Seek to understand your own leadership actions emerging from your current leadership mindsets and mental models. When reviewing these actions consider what works or what does not work to enhance your leadership practice. Are these mindsets and actions helping or hurting your leadership and how are your behaviors perceived by others?

Step 3: Identify the New Mindshift Needed

Now it is time to move toward a healthier way of thinking and acting. Senge (1990) talks about the concept of *metanoia*, a change of mind or thinking. What new and different mindset do you want to develop? Begin working your way through the *Servant Leader Mindset Pathway Model* to create new ways of thinking and acting.

Step 4: Imagine the Implications of Using This New Mindset

Imagine the change of mindset in action. Think intentionally about the potentially positive outcomes that can be realized by adopting and acting from these new mindsets. There is power in visualizing positive outcomes, much like the athlete imagining successfully meeting a goal. They play this success over and over in their minds until the possibility, even certainty, of meeting the goal overcomes resistance to pursue it. Reflect deeply on the potential available to you by implementing your new mindset.

Step 5: Act on the Belief that This New Mindset May Be True

Determine specific actions that you will take to live out the new mindset. Put these actions into practice in real-time and real situations, so you can learn how others and you react to the new behaviors. What outcomes are you seeking? What changes come from these new actions? Remember, change can come first from a change of thinking, a new attitude, but it can also come from a change of behavior. Act as if the mindset is true to begin with to see the benefits of this new way of thinking. Remain open to new learning and new possibilities.

Step 6: Evaluate the Results of Your Actions

Honestly review the feedback you are receiving, along with your own observations, to determine what is working or not working as you act on your new mindset. You are now in an action research process open to new learning and receptive to feedback from others. Utilize assessments to collect data from everyone in the organization. The Organizational Leadership Assessment (OLA) is designed to assess the OLA servant leader model within organizations (www.servantleaderperformance. com). Find out how people are experiencing your leadership and the culture of your organization. Learn from this feedback and continue to challenge previous ways of thinking and acting.

Step 7: Continue to Refine Your Mindsets

Changing mindsets is an ongoing process of learning, refining, changing, and adjusting, and it takes time. Keep a learning perspective. Allow for failure and uncertain outcomes. If you determine that your old mindsets are not working for you, give the new mindsets the time and space to grow in your thinking and your behavior. New ways of leading are possible and change is possible. Continue to work through the steps of the *Servant Leader Mindset Pathway Model* until it creates new habits and new ways of leading.

Conclusion

Change begins with a belief that we can change. Our underlying assumptions about life and leadership must be uncovered and challenged or we remain captive to their power. As we consider changing our leadership mindset to a servant orientation we must consider focusing on others over self. We must accept a growth mindset, see ourself as a giver, and view others through a Theory Y lens. This allows us to make necessary servant leader mindshifts that enable us to consistently practice servant leadership disciplines. This way of leading creates a leveraged form of power that enables us, all of us, to move the world through our leadership. Through this approach all can lead. All can make a difference in the world. All can make the choice to serve and to lead.

References

Barker, J. A. (1993). *Paradigms: The business of discovering the future.* New York, NY: HarperCollins Publishers, Inc.

Bittel, J. (2017, August 8). Watch hikers come face to face with a cougar. Retrieved from http://news.nationalgeographic.com/2017/08/cougar-encounter-caught-on-video-california-mountain-lion-spd/

Brookfield, S. D. (1987). *Developing critical thinkers: Challenging adults to explore alternative ways of thinking and acting.* San Francisco, CA: Jossey-Bass.

Dweck, C. S. (2016). *Mindset: The new psychology of success* (2nd ed.). New York, NY: Ballantine Books.

Frick, D. M. (2004). *Robert K. Greenleaf: A life of servant leadership.* San Francisco: CA: Berrett-Koehler Publishers, Inc.

Grant, A. (2013). *Give and take: A revolutionary approach to success.* New York, NY: The Penguin Group.

Greenleaf, R. K. (1970). *The servant as leader.* Indianapolis: The Robert K. Greenleaf Center.

McGregor, D. (1960). *The human side of enterprise.* New York, NY: McGraw-Hill Book Company, Inc.

Niewoehner, R. J., & Steidle, C. E. (2009). The loss of the space shuttle Columbia: Portaging leadership lessons with a critical thinking model. *Engineering Management Journal, 21*(1), 9–18.

O'Donovan, C., & Anand, P. (2017, July 17, 7:14 pm). How Uber's hard-charging corporate culture left employees drained. Retrieved from https://www.buzzfeed.com/carolineodonovan/how-ubers-hard-charging-corporate-culture-left-employees?utm_term=.jbdPVMPR2#.jsbZNbZLA

Schein, E. H. (2013). *Humble inquiry: The gentle art of asking instead of telling.* San Francisco, CA: Berret-Koehler Publishers, Inc.

Senge, P. M. (1990). *The fifth discipline: The art & practice of the learning organization.* New York, NY: Currency Doubleday.

Sire, J. W. (2009). *The universe next door* (5th ed.). Downers Grove, IL: Intervarsity Press.

The Arbinger Institute. (2016). *The outward mindset: Seeing beyond ourselves.* Oakland, CA: Berrett-Koehler Publishers, Inc.

Zander, R. S., & Zander, B. (2000). *The art of possibility: Transforming professional and personal life.* New York, NY: Penguin Books.

13

Implementing Servant Leadership to Move the World

Each person has the capacity and responsibility to lead to move the world to a better place. This concluding chapter will emphasize the call of leadership and the challenge to answer that call to make a lasting difference in the world. We begin by reviewing one of the key outcomes of effective leadership, the engaged worker. What is the state of the world's workers today and what does their level of engagement say about our current effectiveness as leaders? By moving out of an autocratic mindset and beyond a paternalistic mindset we can find a way of leading that engages our workers, maximizes our organization's health, and moves us closer to fulfilling our performance potential. We will revisit the metaphor of Archimedes lever and how it helps us understand the leveraged power of servant leadership as the most powerful way to move the world.

The State of the World's Workers

One key measurement of good leadership must be the level of engagement of the followers. It is the engaged, energized, and passionate worker who makes the difference in productivity, profitability, and creative outcomes for any organization. Organizations with a critical mass of engaged

© The Author(s) 2018
J. Laub, *Leveraging the Power of Servant Leadership*, Palgrave Studies in Workplace Spirituality and Fulfillment, https://doi.org/10.1007/978-3-319-77143-4_13

workers will find it possible to fulfill their mission, create new products and services, and ultimately move the world to a better place. This being the case, the effectiveness of our leadership should be measured, at least in part, by the engagement level of our workers. Leaders must provide more than the next great idea or the pursuit of organizational profit. Leaders must raise up workers who can both serve and lead for the good of the organization and those the organization serves. So, what is the state of the world's workers today and what might this say about the level of our leadership effectiveness?

In a groundbreaking report on the *State of the Global Workplace* (2017) Gallup presents the results of research conducted with managers and workers from 155 countries, that is, 80% of the world's countries. Gallup discovered that 32% of working-age adults worldwide are employed full-time for an organization and of these full-time workers, only 15% report as *engaged* in their work. Engaged workers are "highly involved in and enthusiastic about their work" (p. 5) and are "psychologically invested in their job and motivated to be highly productive" (p. 35). This definition of the engaged worker reveals the kind of workers we need, the kind of workers who go beyond the minimum requirements of the job to bring creativity, ideas, energy, and passion to the workplace. However, with only 15% of workers engaged, this leaves 67% (two out of three) *disengaged* and 18% as, what Gallup calls, *actively disengaged*.

Disengaged workers, the largest percentage of workers by far, are the ones who show up and fulfill the basic requirements of their job. They are not hostile or disruptive but are indifferent. Disengaged workers provide the minimal time and effort required but bring no creativity, passion, or energy to their work. This category of worker represents by itself "a stunning amount of wasted potential" (p. 5). This disengaged worker is one described by Burns (1978) as a follower within a transactional leadership model. In this arrangement, leaders and followers "have no enduring purpose that holds them together; hence they may go their separate ways. A leadership act took place, but it was not one that binds leader and follower together in a mutual and continuing pursuit of a higher purpose" (p. 20). Without this enduring purpose connecting leader and follower, the work is simply a transaction of pay for effort, time for agreed-upon compensation. Unfortunately, we have become too easily satisfied with workers that merely show up, who work without commitment, who labor just for a paycheck, and who will provide the minimum needed to fulfill their part of the leadership transaction. Out of this transactional model our organizations suffer and our workers suffer as well. Everyone should have the opportunity to provide work that really matters, work that draws on the creativity and passion of each individual. Through this reality of disengaged workers, we are losing much more than the worker's willingness to work extra hours. We are losing the worker's ideas and passion to implement those ideas that might address the huge intractable problems of our time. We need to do better, but unfortunately, the Gallup report reveals another damning statistic related to the state of our workers.

Though two-thirds of workers report as being disengaged, *actively disengaged* workers account for 18% of full-time workers throughout the world. This oddly named category refers to workers who do not just show up, but bring a negative attitude of resentfulness and bitterness resulting in actions detrimental to the work of the organization. Actively disengaged workers are working *against* the company that employs them and the leaders that seek to lead them. "They monopolize managers' time, have more on-the-job accidents, account for more quality defects, contribute to theft, miss more workdays and quit at a higher rate than engaged employees do" (p. 44). So, on a worldwide scale we find that most workers show up for work bringing little to the task while only 15% are fully engaged and 18% are actively working against the organization. It should come then as no surprise that the "global gross domestic product has puttered along at under 3% growth since 2012, well below historical norms" (p. 4). What is the cause of this dysfunction in our global workforce?

One possible cause is the type of work we offer. Unsurprisingly, professional workers are much more engaged in their work than manufacturing workers. When jobs are routinized and process is valued more than people this becomes a recipe for worker disengagement. However, the main reason we have so many disengaged workers is due to the mindset of leadership since "traditional command-and-control management models remain common throughout the world" (p. 25). Gallup (2017) states that "about 70% of the variance in engagement among workgroups can be attributed to their manager" (p. 47). This is the central issue, the mindset of leadership we bring to the workplace directly produces a level of engagement or disengagement that ultimately affects the bottom-line performance and success of our organizations. The products we produce and the services we provide are directly affected by the engagement of our workers and this engagement, or lack of it, is affected by our mindset of leadership.

Let's view this issue of worker disengagement by countries or areas of the world. The highest worker engagement in the world is found in the United States and Canada with 31% of workers engaged. Gallup suggests that the best managed companies should have 70% of their employees engaged; therefore, the best engagement levels found in the world stand at less than half of that preferred level. The lowest worker engagement level is found in East Asia (China, Hong King, Japan, Mongolia, South Korea, and Taiwan) with 6% of workers reporting as engaged. The next highest up from the bottom is Western Europe with only 10% of workers engaged. In the countries of Western Europe (Austria, Belgium, Denmark, Finland, France, Germany, Iceland, Ireland, Italy, Luxemburg, Malta, the Netherlands, Norway, Portugal, Spain, Sweden, Switzerland, the United Kingdom) 71% of workers are not engaged while a stunning 19% are actively disengaged. This means that for every worker in these Western European countries who is fully engaged there are two workers actively and negatively working against them.

There is more at stake here than mere happy or unhappy workers. Gallup (2017) states that "business units in the top quartile of our global employee engagement database are 17% more productive and 21% more profitable than those in the bottom quartile" (p. 5). These top scoring business units also have nearly double the odds of success when compared to those in the bottom quartile. Also, the engagement level of workers directly affects the success of work teams and organizations and the potential losses are staggering. Gallup estimates that "disengaged German workers cost the country's economy between 80.3 and 105.1 billion euros each year" (p. 90) due to absenteeism and negativity transferred to customers.

What will make the difference in these numbers? Gallup suggests that workers need more input and autonomy to use their best gifts and strengths on the job, but then states that this would require "a profound shift in management perspective" (p. 7). It is this profound shift of perspective, or mindset, that we are addressing in this book. We need a new mindset of leadership, one that provides the best opportunity to fully engage workers to seek higher levels of performance even in the most difficult of situations.

The Servant Leadership Mindset in Action

Imagine a worst case organizational scenario, one in which the workplace is saturated with fear, uncertainty, and doubt, a place where everyone, leaders and followers, face a future of turmoil and confusion. Could the mindset of servant leadership flourish in such circumstances or would this organizational state demand a powerful, heroic leader to bring order to the chaos? In October 2005, Delphi Automotive, the largest automotive component supplier in the world, filed for bankruptcy. In 2006, Delphi's Brake Assembly Operations plant with 1600 employees was notified that it would be closed down in two years. Everyone employed there would lose their job and the manufacturing site would close permanently on June 30, 2008.

The Challenge and a Leader's Response

Tom Green, the plant manager, faced the leadership challenge of his life. For two years, he would be required to guide a changing team of workers through chaos with little to no direction from the corporate office. The only thing offered by corporate was the expectation that they continue to meet high quotas of brake parts production while meeting all safety, quality, delivery, and cost requirements. Green had inherited the organizational culture of Delphi where the customer was always first, the needs of the corporation and its manufacturing system second, and, last of all, the needs of the employees were considered. The initial reactions to the closure announcement were as expected. Workers and managers reacted with fear and disbelief. Rumors were rampant, productivity dropped, and almost 40% of the salaried workers resigned. Green was faced with an unhappy, disconnected workforce and the need to replace and train 800 new workers.

Since the Delphi Brake Assembly Operations plant was on its own, Green had full responsibility and freedom to meet these new demands in a different way. He began with a firm belief that they must have an engaged workforce to be successful. He believed that they had "to trust that if we took care of the employees, they would take care of the business" (Green & Miller, 2012, p. 15). Green knew that his main task, and that of his fellow leaders, was to nurture employee engagement through authentic and humble leadership, ongoing communication, and creative inspiration. Leaders needed to step up and exhibit a new mindset of leading. To seek this level of engagement by both leaders and workers, Green determined that the leaders must focus on serving workers first. To capture this commitment, he identified four servant leadership principles to guide their leadership actions through the next two turbulent years.

Servant leadership Principle #1: Listen, Don't Talk

The first priority was to listen to the workers, to let them ask questions, share their fears, and express their concerns. Simply listening was very difficult for a team of leaders who were action and results oriented. It seemed like the opposite of what they should be doing. To the leaders, it didn't feel like leading when so much needed to be done. However, to engage the workers the leaders needed to create a place of trust. They needed to allow people the space to process their grief and to raise the issues that were most important to them. Workers needed to know that the leaders were on their side and would put them first. When Green and the other leaders asked people to talk, they did. The leaders learned what the workers were going through, what they were fearing most. They learned how the workers viewed their work and learned the worker's perspective on the best way forward. The leaders listened and they learned.

Servant Leadership Principle #2: Ask Employees, What Do You Need?

The essence of servant leadership is serving the needs of the followers; so a basic and essential question is to ask what they need, and then to listen fully to their response. Green believed that "the best way to help people focus on the business was to address each person's individual concerns" (Green & Miller, 2012, p. 17). This was no small task due to the ever-changing nature of the workplace with people leaving, new people being trained, and a pending deadline when everyone would walk out of a shuttered plant without a job. Green and his leaders decided they would listen to the fears expressed and seek to address the needs that they could. They determined to be truthful about what they could and could not do. They knew they shouldn't make false promises. Also, they would not tell people what they should feel or how they should react, but let them respond within a safe and caring environment. Based on what they heard from workers the leaders implemented special training programs on how to deal with change, how to prepare resumes, and how to do job interviews. Each person was provided with 40 hours of career transition training and support to help them and their families cope with the uncertainty of the future.

Servant Leadership Principle #3: Set Aside Time Every Week for Foresight and Planning

Green and his leadership team realized that one of the best ways for them to serve their workers was to anticipate, as best they could, future changes coming toward them. This action is one of the key essential elements of leadership—to envision the future, to anticipate what may be coming and prepare as best you can. The leadership team committed to a two-hour strategy session every Friday to anticipate the future, to plan effectively for emerging challenges, and then to communicate these plans effectively to the workers. This commitment to step away from the crisis of the moment to look forward and plan helped to create trust as workers were allowed to anticipate and understand the future better through the eyes of their leaders. Leaders planned and communicated; they listened and acted and this forward-thinking leadership made an uncertain future more clear and more manageable.

Servant Leadership Principle #4: Ask, "Do Those Served Grow as Persons?"

Greenleaf's main test as to how a servant leader can know if he or she is succeeding states, "the best test, and difficult to administer, is: Do those served grow as persons? Do they, *while being served*, become healthier, wiser, freer, more autonomous, more likely themselves to become servants?" (Greenleaf, 1977, pp. 13–14). Green and his team took this test to heart and determined not just to use their workers to get the job done, but to develop and help their workers grow for the future. The leaders provided needed training and skills to enhance worker's resumes and provided counseling on career development and transition. They allowed people to take on new assignments so that they could gain competencies to enhance future prospects. They actively lived out Greenleaf's creed that "the work exists for the person as much as the person exists for the work" (Greenleaf, 1977, p. 142). Everyone was expected to grow through this shared experience. Everyone was to become healthier, wiser, freer, and more autonomous regardless of the circumstances.

The Results of Servant Leadership Action

Prior to the announcement of the plant's closing, there had always been a distrust between leaders and workers at the plant, but after the announcement and the implementation of these servant leadership principles, a higher level of trust and teamwork was created. Leaders and followers were in this together and the commitment of the leaders to serve the needs of the workers created a new bond. It also created some astounding results. In the area of employee safety, in the last one million hours worked, there was no lost time due to accidents. As to the quality of their products, the plant had single digit parts per million defects meaning that out of 1 million parts assembled more than 999,990 were perfect and, this quality was measured by customer feedback. They also achieved 99.5% on-time delivery for their parts, an amazing number, and during the two-year period the plant remained open, costs were reduced by 160 million dollars and all financial targets were met. Performance was the highest it had ever been in the history of the plant.

Beyond meeting, and exceeding, these corporate standards even more was achieved. Leaders and workers established an atmosphere of trust joined with high expectations for performance. People were proud of the work they performed and the high level of successful results achieved.

Keith (2008) states that "a servant-leader is by far the best leader to take an organization through a period of change" (p. 27). Green and his leadership team created an environment that allowed leaders and workers to excel and produce beyond-expectation results. Green in reflecting on these results and the reasons for their success shared the following.

> Could it be that listening to employees, serving their individual needs, using foresight and setting aside time for people and planning, caring about employees on a daily basis, having clear goals and objectives that we all needed to achieve, recognizing and rewarding individuals and groups for performance, and building trust through open and honest communication … could it be that these were the reasons for success? (Green & Miller, 2012, p. 40)

These unexpected results came from an unexpected approach to leading, a mindset that seemed to many to be counter to what was needed. Yet, this servant leadership approach allowed people to excel in their work, to be engaged in the process right to the bitter end. As we come to the end of this amazing story, let's hear once again from Tom Green as he reflects on the experience that ended for everyone when the plant closed, on schedule, June 30, 2008.

> As leaders, we knew that our lives had become extraordinarily meaningful. We knew we were making a difference in the lives of others. We came to work energized for the challenges each day brought. As we faced those challenges, we became the best we had ever been, and did the best we had ever done. We produced the tangible results that our employees and our company needed. We found the lasting joy that comes from serving others. We cried on our last day. We cried because we all had done such a great job together. (Green & Miller, 2012, p. 43)

Servant leadership is far more than an interesting theory or concept that one hopes to be true. It is a practical and useful way of leading even in the most challenging of situations. If we are going to change the low engagement levels of our workers to create more productive and high performing organizations, we must change our mindset of leadership and unleash the unexpected power of servant leadership.

Leveraging the Power of Servant Leadership

Servant leadership is about the effective use of power. This statement will sound strange to those who view power in a negative way and see it only as a corrupting force. However, when power is viewed as a person's ability to act on the world we see that power can be used for good or evil. The servant leader uses power to empower followers allowing and expecting them to lead and serve. Servant leadership leads through a leveraged power that requires less overt force from the leader but operates through a healthy combination of relationship, influence and selflessness. When leaders choose to serve those they lead, they create a unique method of influence, one that creates in the one served the desire to reciprocate by serving the leader and others. Through this dynamic of reciprocity, gratitude, and empowerment, servant leadership creates its own form of power, a leveraged power that can move people, organizations, and the larger world around us. Let's revisit our definition and model of servant leadership to clarify what this power looks like in action.

Defining Servant Leadership

Servant leadership is a mindset through which the leader uses power to serve the needs of followers over the leader's self-interest while creating an adult partnership relationship between leaders and followers that allows everyone to lead and serve.

Through servant leadership we end up with empowered workers who view themselves as partners in the organization who can speak as adults with each other and with their leaders. This way of leading creates the best opportunity for worker engagement and performance.

The OLA Model of Servant Leadership

Servant leadership in action combines six key leadership disciplines, each with three descriptive attitudes and actions. When these disciplines, attitudes, and actions are displayed through a mindset of servant leadership, a healthy culture is created in the team or organization. This healthy organization provides the best opportunity for achieving high performance by individuals and groups.

One might ask, what should come first, the mindset or the actions of servant leadership? Actually, to develop servant leadership in our organization we, as leaders, need to approach this from both directions. We know that new attitudes can encourage new actions, but it is also true that new actions can create new ways of thinking. We need to challenge our mindset of leadership, how we view ourselves as leaders, how we view those we lead, and how we view the purpose or outcome of leadership. While challenging the assumptions we hold about leadership, we need the discipline to take healthier actions toward those that we lead. The combination of critical thinking, creating new assumptions, and experimenting with new actions is a powerful way to begin the journey of developing as a servant leader.

The OLA model of servant leadership can serve as a guide for our changing mindset and changing leadership actions. Servant leaders value and develop the people they lead, they build a strong sense of community within the group, they both provide and share leadership, and they consistently display openness and authenticity. Servant leaders:

1. Value People

   a. By trusting and believing in people
   b. By serving others' needs before their own
   c. By receptive, non-judgmental listening

2. Develop People

   a. By providing opportunities for learning and growth
   b. By modeling appropriate behavior
   c. By building up others through encouragement and affirmation

3. Build Community

   a. By building strong personal relationships
   b. By working collaboratively with others
   c. By valuing the differences of others

4. Display Authenticity

   a. By being open and accountable to others
   b. By a willingness to learn from others
   c. By maintaining integrity and trust

5. Provide Leadership

   a. By envisioning the future
   b. By taking initiative
   c. By clarifying goals

6. Share Leadership

   a. By facilitating a shared vision
   b. By sharing power and releasing control
   c. By sharing status and promoting others (Laub, 1999, p. 83).

This model creates a framework that servant leaders can use to evaluate their own mindset and actions of leadership. It can also be used as a decision-making grid to guide the decisions we are called to make day to day as leaders. The *OLA Servant Leadership Action Test* provides a set of key questions for the servant-minded leader.

OLA Servant Leadership Action Test

When considering a leadership decision or action from a servant mindset, consider its implications by addressing each of these six key questions.

1. Will this action promote openness, honesty, and authenticity?
2. Will this action bring a higher sense of value to my workers?
3. Will this action serve to develop my followers toward their potential as workers and leaders?

4. Will this action build a stronger sense of community and team commitment?
5. Will this action provide clear leadership vision, direction, and accountability for my followers?
6. Will this action enhance the empowering of my workers and encourage them also to lead and serve?

Thinking through this decision-making grid provides servant leaders an accountability that allows a proactive response within a servant leader mindset, a mindset that contains a different way of looking at leadership power and how that power is used with workers in our organizations.

Viewing Power from the Three Mindsets of Leadership

The Autocratic Leadership Mindset (Authoritarianism + Exploitation). With this leadership mindset power resides with the leader and is used in an authoritarian manner while exploiting the workers. The autocratic leadership mindset is alive and well in our world today. We see it in politics, business, non-profits, and religious organizations. We sometimes agree to sell our soul and sacrifice our values to empower a single heroic leader who will use his or her power to rescue us from the dangers we fear. This is a devil's bargain we cannot afford to make. When leaders use their power to serve their own needs first a selfish, inward focus is created and workers are viewed as a means to an end, making inevitable the ultimate abuse of these workers. We need to reject this mindset of leadership from both an ethical and a performance basis. We cannot continue to sacrifice the well-being of our workers to accomplish the short-term self-focused gains envisioned by all-powerful leaders. We need to create institutional models and leadership expectations that place the good of those led over the self-interest of the leaders.

The Paternalistic Leadership Mindset (Authoritarianism + Benevolence). Within this leadership mindset, power resides with the leader but is used in both an authoritarian and a benevolent manner—expecting compliance and deference from the followers. The paternalistic leadership mindset is the most prevalent in the world today. It is viewed as culturally appropriate and necessary in most countries that view leaders as kindly fathers who know best how to lead their children. The benevolence offered by these paternalistic (and maternalistic) leaders creates a caring and supportive environment that is encouraging to workers and allows these workers to excel at what they do. They work to comply with and please the leader and they enjoy being a part of this nurturing environment. However, with the leaders holding on to authority and offering benevolence and nurture a clear line is drawn between leaders and followers. Building a culture of leadership expectation from all in the organization is limited through this mindset by encouraging a spirit of dependence on leaders by the followers.

The Servant Leadership Mindset (Empowerment + Adult Partnership). In this leadership mindset, power is shared by leaders and followers together and is used in a partnership of shared responsibility and opportunity—expecting adult behavior and leadership from all. The servant leadership mindset takes the power invested in the leader and uses it to empower each worker to fulfill their unique potential as leaders and servants. It treats workers as adult partners rather than children and creates an expectation that each person creates vision, shares ideas, solves problems, and owns the future of the organization. To act as a servant leader one must put others first, creating an outward mindset (Arbinger Institute, 2016) that views development and growth over control and partnership over rigid hierarchy. The servant leader mindset has the best potential to create a healthy organizational environment and higher worker performance. This, of course, is easy to say, but harder to back up with solid long-term research. We need to build off of the good base of servant leadership research from the past two decades to learn more about how this mindset of leadership can help to create more engaged, healthier workers, leaders, and organizations.

Moving from Model Creation to Performance Research

Servant leadership scholarship and research, for the past decades since Greenleaf brought the term into modern awareness, has been focused on creating conceptual models and instruments to measure these models within organizations. The results from this research have brought us clearer definition, psychometrically sound measurement tools, and a broadening exposure to how servant leadership is being implemented in different types of organizations. The research results are encouraging. We know that servant leadership is correlated to many organizational health factors such as employee job satisfaction, trust, team effectiveness, organizational safety, and even student achievement scores but where does servant leadership research need to go next?

At this point we have many useful assessment tools, like the Organizational Leadership Assessment (OLA), for ongoing research, that can measure various servant leadership conceptual models and how those models are lived out in organizations. We can now determine if an organization is servant, paternalistic, or autocratically led. Now, we need to expand our research designs to focus on the following:

- How servant leadership relates to organizational performance measures like growth, profitability, sustainability, customer satisfaction, creativity, and product development, or the providing of services.
- How servant leadership relates to the ongoing and growing research conducted on paternalistic leadership. In what ways are servant leadership and paternalistic leadership similar or different? What are the effects in organizations and workers when these two different leadership mindsets are used?
- How servant leadership is being implemented in different countries and different cultures. Does servant leadership take on different forms or practices when implemented in more hierarchical, paternalistic cultures?
- What organizational structures work best to facilitate a servant-minded leadership approach? Do certain organizational structures enhance the practice of servant leadership? Do other organizational structures inhibit the practice? Do different structures tend to promote autocratic, paternalistic, or servant leadership behaviors?
- What can we learn about servant leadership and the use of legitimate power? What does servant power look like and what effect does it have on workers and the organization?
- What is the relationship between servant leader behaviors and worker engagement? Do servant organizations have higher levels of worker engagement and what might this mean to the bottom-line outcomes desired by organizations?

These and other research questions need to be considered and pursued through the use of existing servant leadership models and assessments with the goal of increasing the research base for servant leadership. To pursue the OLA instrument to address research questions like these, go to www.servantleaderperformance.com where you can view OLA research completed to date and learn how to use the OLA for your specific research design. There is a growing group of servant leadership researchers located throughout the world who are in a position to address these, and other, questions about servant leadership. It is the hope of this author that this research will continue to grow in breadth and depth to provide greater understanding and clarity about this powerful leadership mindset.

A Vision for Servant-Led Organizations: Leadership That Moves the World

There is a paradox to leading as a servant. The provocative nature of the term drives us to consider the radical nature of what we are called to do as servant-minded leaders. We are called to first serve the needs of those we lead over our own self-interest. The risk to ourselves and our own interests is clear but the risk of deciding to serve ourselves over the needs of others is even greater. Servant leadership creates a unique leveraged power that is not available any other way than through the path of service, sacrifice, and selflessness. This is what it takes to move the world and the beauty of this concept is that any of us can do this, any of us can serve from whatever role or position we are in, from whatever set of gifts or potential we possess, or from whatever situation we find ourselves in. We can always serve, and when we combine that servant-first commitment to the decision to lead we create a special kind of power, power to move the world to a better place.

When organizations are servant led, leaders use their power to empower their followers and raise them up to a status of adult partners. They value and develop people, build community, display authenticity, and provide and share leadership. This way of leading produces what Aristotle referred to as *eudaimonea* or flourishing.

The concept of *eudaimonea* gives us two umbrella questions that can be used to assess the overall ethics and effectiveness of leadership. Does a leader or a particular kind of leadership contribute to and/or allow people to flourish in terms of their lives as a whole? Does a leader of a particular kind of leadership interfere with the ability of other groups of people or other living things to flourish? (Ciulla, 2004, p. 326)

When the three mindsets of leadership—autocratic, paternalistic, and servant—are considered which of them has the best possibility of contributing to the flourishing of people? Or, which of them will interfere with the ability of people to flourish? It is clear to this author that a servant mindset that results in servant behaviors or disciplines has the best chance of moving workers to engagement but, beyond engagement, to flourishing. As Ciulla (2004) affirms, "leaders do not always have to transform people for them to flourish. Their greater responsibility is to create the social and material conditions under which people can and do flourish" (p. 326). When leaders work to create these conditions for human flourishing they open new doors for leadership impact; they create more effective ways to move the world.

Archimedes was focused more on his invention of the lever than he was on leadership when he shared his famous quote, "give me a lever long enough and a place to stand, and I will move the world," but he offers us, through this quote, a useful metaphor for thinking deeply about the leveraged power of servant leadership. Let's revisit this metaphor, central to this book, which provides us a different way of leading. Here is how we can view the various parts of Archimedes' lever and how it relates to our mindset and practice of leadership.

The Object to Be Moved: The Purpose of Leadership

The purpose of leadership is to move the world. It is to create movement toward positive change. It creates performance that provides benefit for others. For too long we have suffered under leaders who made leadership all about themselves, creating organizations to promote their personal brand and leadership prowess. Leadership should not be about the leader but about moving the world to a better place.

The Leader: Applying Power in the Most Effective Way

All leaders possess power to act in their world. Leaders also have choices to make as to how they will use the power granted to them. They can use power to benefit themselves, for the good of the organization or for the good of each worker entrusted to them. Accepting the power available to us and choosing to use it wisely to empower others is one of the necessary commitments of servant leadership.

The Fulcrum: Choosing Your Leadership Mindset

Where we place the fulcrum of our leadership lever in relation to the weight to be moved is critical to leveraging our power most effectively. The three mindsets of leadership—autocratic, paternalistic, or servant—identify three distinct ways of thinking about leadership and each requires different levels of personal power or force. The servant leader mindset optimizes the power we exert such that heroic leaders are less necessary and committed, and faithful leaders can make a major contribution. It is all in how we leverage the power available to us and position our leadership fulcrum (mindset) of leadership to create optimal affect.

A Place to Stand: The Practice of Leadership

"Give me a lever long enough, *and a place to stand.*" The leader needs a firm and solid place to stand to exercise leadership. We lead out of who we are. Therefore, leaders must have a firm set of values and beliefs that provide a solid and firm place to stand from which to exercise their leadership. The organization or group we lead also becomes an important consideration as a place to stand to practice our leadership. Does our organization provide us the best place to exercise a servant-minded leadership? Is our organization the best vehicle for the leadership vision and call we have received? If not, we may need to find a better place to stand so that our leadership can flow out of a healthy mindset and our leadership actions are free to create true places of human flourishing. When this happens our vision for a servant organization can be realized. We can lead with this outcome in mind, a vision for a better organization, for a better world.

Dangerous Leadership

Leadership is dangerous. When one person holds power and influence over another, the potential for harm and abuse is high. When the power to act is centralized in a single top leader the possibility of leading by self-interest increases. When leaders choose to abdicate their power and yield to the unexamined leadership of another, the whole group suffers and all are diminished. Leadership is both a possibility and a responsibility for all, and each person must consider and pursue their own calling and vocation to lead. Yes, each of us has the capacity and the responsibility to lead, to make a difference in the world. We also can, and should, follow and it is a high task to do so, but we dare not refuse our individual calling to lead in the unique way for which we have been gifted. Certainly, leadership can create great harm but imagine the plight of our world if we refuse our individual responsibility to lead and thereby become non-leaders, disengaged from the potential vision that only we have been shaped to see. Imagine the good that will remain undone, the people left unserved, the outcomes and visions unrealized. To refuse our call to leadership is the most dangerous option of all. The world needs leaders and it needs leaders of a particular type—leaders committed to serve others over their own self-interest, leaders who refuse to pattern their leadership after the power mavens of our business and political arenas. We need leaders who will act with courage to bring people together to create real solutions to the seemingly relentless problems of our time. We need a leadership that is dangerous to a status quo that too easily accepts that nothing will ever change, that people just cannot be trusted, and that the problems we face are too complex and beyond our creativity and commitment to address. Yes, we need a dangerous kind of leadership, a powerful leadership that will not sit by and allow the world to function as it has always done. We need a leadership that gives more than it receives, that looks outward more than it looks inward, and that serves more than it demands service from others. This way of leading is possible. It has been modeled to us down through history by courageous leaders who refused to use power over others but rather used their power to move people ahead of themselves. Servant leadership is a provocative and beautiful paradox, a way of thinking and believing about leadership that places the good of others ahead of our own privilege as leaders. Servant leadership, if unfettered by self-interest, outdated mindsets, or organizational constraints, can be unleashed to create a new reality, a new kind of power, leveraged to move the world, our organizations, and our workers to a new and better reality.

Conclusion

It is the hope of this author that our exploration together of the power of servant leadership has proven useful for you in your own leadership development. Through this book, we hope to strengthen our understanding of the concept of servant leadership and to bring clarity to it as a mindset of leading to be freely chosen and implemented. This power from serving can change the way we do leadership, the way we order our organizations, and the way we seek change in the world. It can engage workers like no other approach or mindset. Though it resonates with the best of modern thought, it comes down to us from the wisdom of antiquity. This is not a new way. It is a narrow pathway others have walked before us showing us a better more powerful way of leading.

> Here is my servant,
> whom I uphold,
> my chosen one
> in whom I delight;
> I will put my Spirit on him
> and he will bring justice to the nations.
> He will not shout or cry out,
> or raise his voice in the streets.
> A bruised reed he will not break,
> and a smoldering wick he will not snuff out.

In faithfulness he will bring forth justice;
he will not falter or be discouraged
till he establishes justice on earth.
(*Servant Song* from—Isaiah 42:1–4)

References

Arbinger Institute. (2016). *The outward mindset: Seeing beyond ourselves.* Oakland, CA: Berrett-Koehler Publishers, Inc.

Burns, J. M. (1978). *Leadership.* New York, NY: Harper & Row.

Ciulla, J. B. (2004). Ethics and leadership effectiveness. In J. Antonakis, A. T. Cianciolo, & R. J. Sternberg (Eds.), *The nature of leadership* (pp. 302–327). Thousand Oaks, CA: Sage Publications.

Gallup. (2017). *The state of the global workplace.* New York, NY: Gallup Press.

Green, T., & Miller, M. (2012). *Servant leadership in hard times: The closing of the Delphi Brake Assembly Operations.* Westfield, IN: The Greenleaf Center for Servant Leadership.

Greenleaf, R. K. (1977). *Servant leadership: A journey into the nature of legitimate power and greatness.* Mahwah, NJ: Paulist Press.

Keith, K. (2008). *The case for servant leadership.* Westfield, IN: The Greenleaf Center for Servant Leadership.

Laub, J. A. (1999). *Assessing the servant organization: Development of the servant organizational leadership (SOLA) instrument.* Unpublished doctoral dissertation, Florida Atlantic University.

Index

© The Author(s) 2018
J. Laub, *Leveraging the Power of Servant Leadership*, Palgrave Studies in Workplace
Spirituality and Fulfillment, https://doi.org/10.1007/978-3-319-77143-4

The manufacturer's authorised representative in the EU is Springer
Nature Customer Service Centre GmbH, Europaplatz 3, 69115 Heidelberg,
Germany. If you have any concerns regarding our products, please
contact ProductSafety@springernature.com

Printed and bound by CPI Group (UK) Ltd, Croydon, CR0 4YY
29/04/2026
02099514-0003